THROUGH
MY EYES

THROUGH
MY EYES

ON BECOMING A TEACHER

John Paull

To order additional copies of this book, contact:
Xlibris Corporation
1-888-795-4274
www.Xlibris.com
Orders@Xlibris.com
114047

October 1, 2010

It's October, the time when the trees, changing their leaf colors from a range of green to a bright yellow and gold, are showing that the fall season is just around the corner. It's a fitting reminder that, at the age of sixty-eight, it's my fall time too. Today, sitting on a beautiful lichen-covered rock by a mountain river after a wonderful walk on a stony riverside path, in and around mountain trees, some now turning bright yellow awaiting the advent of winter, my mind is full of thoughts about my work. It is full of thoughts about what has been and what has been my lifelong passion: understanding more and more about the processes of teaching and learning. Staring at the river running past my feet, I realize that a defining chapter of my life is coming to an end.

I've decided that this is my last year as a full-time educator.

I started as a classroom teacher. For the past forty years, I've been working with—and working for—students and teachers, in public and private schools and university classes. Helping in some small way to make a difference, directly or indirectly, in the lives of children is what, for me, makes each day special.

I want now to reflect on that passion, on my journey as a teacher.

What follows then is an account of my journey. It's a journey that begins with selected childhood experiences that contributed, for better, for worse, to my teaching persona and my teaching beliefs. It's a journey that describes the evolution of *my way* of teaching.

Volume 1 of my journey focuses on the 1960s and 1970s, a period that I think of nostalgically as my *golden age* in education, a period best described in 1968, in the book, *The Integrated Day*, written by two head teachers, Mary Brown and Norman Precious.

As I go through my journey describing what I saw through my eyes in classrooms in England and in America, what better way is there to remember and celebrate those who made such an impact on my life—as a teacher, first of young children, then of adults—and therefore, on the lives of the countless children and teachers I have had the pleasure to learn alongside.

Seven, all educators in one form or another, in particular, stand out.

First, my father, Arthur Charles Paull, who showed me the hypnotic— and teaching—power of the great storyteller who sets imaginations on fire.

Then, my mother, Hazel Monica Paull, who celebrated, dignified, honored, and heightened my sense of curiosity.

Miss Harvey and Mr. Jones, the first teachers in my childhood, who, in different ways, opened the world of education before me.

Next, the visionary, Bill Browse, Leicestershire's advisor for junior schools. Bill, willing to take a huge gamble with an enthusiastic, but very green, inexperienced teacher, hired me as an advisory teacher, a teacher of teachers, if you will, to work alongside a host of marvelous classroom teachers, to promote the use of "hands-on" science. Quiet, reflective, and thoughtful, Bill helped me establish my role as advisory teacher in Leicestershire.

Tony Kallet. Tony, originally from New York City, was my long-time colleague in the Advisory Center, my mentor, and my dearest friend. He and I worked together with David Hawkins in Boulder, Colorado, setting up the Mountain View Center for Environmental Education in 1970. Tony inspired me to be more thoughtful and more reflective when observing children and teachers at work.

Finally, the wise and profound thinker and teacher, David Hawkins, professor of philosophy, MacArthur fellow, who included me, for over thirty years, in his close friendships and interactions with such notable scientists, thinkers, and world-renowned teachers as Tony Kallet, Philip and Phyllis Morrison, Frank Oppenheimer, Elwyn Richardson, Stan Ulam, and many, many others.

Bill, Tony, and David helped me understand who I was and who, as a teacher, I could and should be. They gave me the confidence to teach children and adults *my* way. They helped me see and share the beauty, the delights, the art, the science, and the mathematics in the world around me.

Chapter 1

The Paull family—Arthur Charles and Hazel Monica; their three sons, Jimmie, John, and Charles; Grandma Paull; and Joseph, the black and white tabby cat, lived in a newly built, low-income housing area in southwest Cornwall. The house overlooked the busy fishing village of Newlyn. Just beyond Newlyn's picturesque harbor, in the far distance, was St. Michael's Mount, rising out of the beautiful Mounts Bay.

The big white stork brought me to the back garden in July 1942, the middle of the Second World War, when the cities of London, Coventry, and the naval base in nearby Plymouth were experiencing nightly bombing raids by the Nazi Luftwaffe. It was a time of fear, blackouts, oil lamps, flickering candles, and food rationing.

Dad, a born-and-bred Newlyn lad, was a bus driver for the Western National Bus Company. To supplement the family's food needs, Dad did what all our neighbors did—grew potatoes, sprouts, carrots, and sweet peas in his small back garden.

When he wasn't driving the big green double-decker buses from village to village, Dad set wire snare traps for rabbits in the nearby Bejowan Woods and the hedgerows around the manor house lived in by the famous painter, Stanhope Forbes. In the spring and summer, he'd go to Lariggan Beach, dig in the sand for the brown and red sand lugs, then set and bait a long spiller, a fishing line holding perhaps twenty or more hooks, tied to tins that were buried in the sand, hoping to catch flounder or bass.

Dad also kept a few chickens in a nearby farmer's field, selling the eggs to neighbors in our street.

To celebrate the birth of his sons, first for Jimmie in 1938, then me, in 1942, and finally, Charles, in 1947, Dad planted three gooseberry bushes near the back garden fence behind the few rows of vegetables.

When we were in the garden, picking sweet peas, eating *goosegogs*, or more likely, looking for worms and other small creatures, Dad would always say, with a smile and a twinkle in his eye, *"That's where the big white stork left the three of you, just there, right under those three gooseberry bushes."*

I had no idea what a stork looked like, but as it had carried me, I sensed it was much bigger than the herring gulls that perched on our roof.

I remember the day Charles was due to be born, I wanted so badly to see the stork and waited patiently in the garden, next to the two gooseberry bushes, with next-door neighbor, Johnny Hoskins, hoping to see the big white stork swoop down to the garden with Mum's new baby. When it was time for bed, ten-year-old Jimmie wasn't surprised when I told him the stork didn't arrive with our new baby.

"See," he said, as we got into bed. *"Told you. Ain't true. It's just a story."*

The next morning, over breakfast, a very tired-looking Dad told us that the big white stork had indeed brought baby Charles during the night and left him under the new gooseberry bush he'd planted. Aunty Stella, the neighborhood midwife, brought him upstairs to our mum's bed.

So it was true. I was so thrilled that, yes, we were left under the gooseberry bushes by the big white stork. Dad said so, didn't he?

In the daytime, I played with neighborhood kids outside in the street, down the Bowjey, or when the weather was nice, we'd kick a ball around in one of the nearby farm fields.

After clearing away the teatime dishes, Mum, a Lancashire girl, usually sat in the kitchen with my Grandma, close to baby Charles lying comfortably in an old wooden drawer. Sometimes she listened to the latest news about the war on the crackly yellow Ferguson wireless as she worked on her weaving, making fishing nets to sell to the fishermen.

My brother Jimmie and I sat on the small worn carpet in front of the open fireplace. He'd read aloud *The Beano* and *Dandy* comics before we played with my long-gone granddad's clay marbles. Sometimes, we played a game of cards, tiddlywinks, ludo, or snakes and ladders.

If Dad wasn't on the late night shift, he always sat on the soft green chair under the front room gas lamp, with Joseph stretched out on his knees, reading the boxing and rugby reports in *The Cornishman Newspaper* sports pages. He'd set aside Sunday afternoons, when he wasn't driving his bus, to take the family on walks to the beach or to the nearby lanes.

It was Dad's chance to show off what he knew about the hawks, owls, ducks, rabbits, badgers, and foxes that lived in the old granite hedgerows, and the jellyfish, sharks, seals, and dolphins that swam in the warm currents of Mounts Bay.

Lariggan Beach was the best place to go though. I loved going there most of all because you never knew what you might find lying on the pebbly sand, especially after a stormy night.

After the Sunday midday meat and potato pasty dinner, washed down with a cup of hot, steaming tea, if the sun was shining, Mum would pick up her old, scratched black leather bag. She'd drop in a big Farley's Rusks tin filled with a sliced apple, cheese sandwiches with the thick crusts cut off, two empty OXO tins, and two of Dad's empty Old Holborn tobacco tins.

We knew then it was time to put on our thick socks and rubber wellies. Then, with Mum pushing Charles's pram, we'd make our way down the winding lanes, across the harbor, to the pebbly beach.

If the tide was out, we'd see what had been washed up on the beach, and we'd collect beautiful, eye-catching black and gray and white pebbles that had been worn smooth by the constant rolling motion of the sea. We'd then hunt for small green and red crabs or brown bullcods in the rock pools. If we were lucky, we'd find a stranded jellyfish that we could return safely to the sea.

Pebble collecting was, for me, the most fun. I'd search for heart-shaped pebbles, or even better, black pebbles with a vein of white quartz running through the middle.

These pebbles with the line of quartz were special. Mum and Dad called them *wishing rocks*.

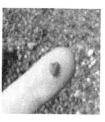

Finding a *wishing rock* that rested comfortably in the palm of your hand made you feel good. You'd pick it up, slowly wrap your fingers around it, and squeeze it really tight. When your fingers warmed the pebble, you closed your eyes and thought about someone you wanted to send a special wish to. Then slowly, you uncurled your fingers, knowing that somebody, somewhere, suddenly felt a warm shiver down the spine, just as that lucky person got your wish.

I always sent my very best wishes to Mum and Dad.

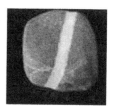

When the wish had been sent, you put your *wishing rock* into what Mum called your *treasure tin*, a small red OXO meat-cube tin. Mum and Dad put theirs into the bigger yellow Old Holborn tobacco tins she'd carried in her bag.

When we filled our tins with our best finds of the day, ate our snack, we made our way home. If we were really lucky, we'd first visit the corner shop at the bottom of Old Paul Hill, and Dad would buy everyone a three-penny crispy cone filled with Daniel's delicious homemade ice cream.

When we got back home, we'd take off our wellies, sit on the carpet in the front room, and empty our *treasure tins* on to a sheet of *The Cornishman* newspaper. Mum usually boiled the kettle on the gas stove, made a pot of tea, and cut up a couple of scones and a fresh  saffron cake. As we drank tea and munched slices of currant-filled saffron cake, sweetened with thick yellow margarine, Dad, with Joseph the cat curled up on his knees, would choose what he thought was the *best* wishing rock. He'd hold it in his hand, look at us all, and always ask the same question:

"Who found this one? Was it you, Jimmie? You, Hazel?"
"You, Johnny? Is it yours? OK, then you, Johnny, you can make a wish for us all."
"Then, you make a wish, Jimmie, all right?"
"Oh, then me and Mum, OK?"
"First, though, we'll all make a wish for baby Charles."

After Jimmie and I closed our eyes and everyone made their wishes, Dad put the best, most beautiful *wishing rock* in the old chipped green-glass jar on the small wooden table near the window in the front room. Most of the rest were put into Mum's bag to return to the beach another day, so, as Mum would say, someone else could find and enjoy them. Then, lighting his hand-rolled cigarette, Dad would take his first deep puff, slowly blow out a circle of white and blue smoke, and say,

"Ready, now? Ready for a story?"

Collecting *wishing rocks* was great, but this was always the best moment of the day.

We were always ready for one of Dad's stories because he told the best tales about badgers, foxes, stoats, weasels, rabbits, sharks, and whales.

When you listened to his soft voice, it was as if you could see everything as he had seen it.

"Yes, Dad. We're ready."
"'Onest, we are."
"Tell us the one about the day you and Mum collected wishing rocks," said Jimmie, *you know, when you found the dead seal. You know, when the crabs and stuff that were chompin' on it."*

"No," I said, *"tell us about the man who had his thumb bit off by a conger eel."*
"That's the best 'un."
"It's brill."

"Go on, Dad, tell us both stories."

"OK," he said, shifting Joseph from one knee to another. *"Here's the one about the conger eel, then, the one about the poor seal eaten by—well, first I'll show you what I found today."*

Leaning back in his chair, Dad stubbed out his cigarette, slowly closed and rubbed his eyes, opened his tobacco tin very slowly, cleared his throat, and showed us what he'd found that day on the beach.

Dad's *best* find always surprised me. It was always something different and was always something that he'd link with a story.

"Look at this," he said, after a walk on the beach, showing us a small bleached jawbone.
"Found it on the big rocks."
"You know, where you were bullcoding."
"Look at the sharp teeth"
"Think it's a weasel's skull."
"Couldn't find any other bones. Just this part of its head."

"Wonder why it ended up on the beach?"
"They live up in the woods."

He put his jawbone treasure inside his Old Holborn tin and rested it on the side of his chair. Then, with the quietest voice, Dad told us how, when he was out in the woods very early, one bitterly cold morning, he'd seen a family of stoats surround a wounded weasel, waiting to pounce, kill, and eat it.

As his story unfolded, I closed my eyes like my dad closed his, really tight. It helped me see the stoats and the weasel and hear the wild sounds that his words drew in my imagination.

"I waved my arms," he said. *"I shouted really loudly, and the stoats ran off. I saved the injured weasel's life. When the stoats had gone, the little weasel stood up, shook its head, and hobbled off to the bushes."*

Transfixed, I sat at his feet and stared up at him, sucking in every word.

When I went to bed, under which was my growing collection of pebbles and shells in an old cardboard box, my head was filled with bright images of pebbles, animals, birds, and fish—and filled with hope, hope that the little weasel was alive and well.

I wondered, *was the weasel OK?*
Was it badly hurt?
Did it get home safely?
Did its mum and dad look after it?

Chapter 2

The second week of September 1946, when I was four, I started going to school.

Newlyn Infant School for Boys, a small Cornish granite building, surrounded by high iron railings, tucked away at the bottom of Trewarveth Street, overlooked the beautiful Newlyn Harbor. After gulping down my boiled egg, I put on my woolen jumper, my hardwearing short pants, woolen socks, and my hard leather shoes. Grandma Paull took me down Jack Lane to school and handed me a small paper bag.

"'Ere. It's yer school dinner."
"I'll be 'ere, waitin' for thee. End of the day."
She looked me in the eye.
"Behave yerself," she said, and off she went.

The school's headmistress was Miss Elaine Harvey. I was in her class, joining a room full of boys most of whom were five. Miss Harvey was gray-haired and bespectacled.

"Ah," she said, as I entered the room, *"so you're Jimmie Paull's brother, Johnny. Welcome to school."*
"Your ma tells me you can read."
"That true, Johnny Paull?"

"Yes, Miss," I replied. Indeed I could. Well, I could read some of the words in *The Beano* and *Dandy* comics. Miss Harvey picked up her chalk and wrote a word on the board.

"Can you read this?"

I blinked. How did Miss Harvey know that it was the same word I had seen in *The Beano* comic the night before, the one that Jimmie had read to me? Crikey. Dad was right. Miss Harvey knew everything.

Slowly, I read out the word the way Mum showed me*: "Ch . . . er . . . ch . . . church!"*
"Good, good." Miss Harvey beamed at me. *"You can read."*

"That's the ch sound everyone."
"Good boy, Johnny Paull. Now go and sit over there, next to Alan."

As I sat down, even though I felt nine feet tall, my feet hardly touched the floor. Miss Harvey turned to the class and introduced me.

"This is Johnny Paull. His brother, Jimmie, was in this class a long time ago. I hope you, Johnny, behave better than he did."

Everyone laughed.

"That's enough," said Miss Harvey. *"Quiet down."*
"That's enough!"

Miss Harvey had a sharp, high-pitched voice, and I knew right away she was strict. For my benefit as a new boy, she said, Miss Harvey began the day by going over the class rules. If anyone got into trouble for talking too much, fiddling with something under the desk, spitting out the midmorning's dose of cod liver oil, eating his OXO cubes in class, or leaving his desk without permission, then, she said, they were in for it.

As Miss Harvey talked, she kept touching the thick blue wooden stick that lay conspicuously in the middle of her desk. She picked up a storybook and began to read aloud, reminding everyone to listen carefully. Just when she'd finished the first paragraph, she stopped and snapped loudly,

"Stephens. Billy Stephens! You're not listening to me."
"Again!"
"Come out here! Now.*"*

Billy got out of his chair and walked towards Miss Harvey's desk.
"Hold out your hand."
"Turn your hand upside down. I want to see the back *of your hand.* Now.*"*

Miss Harvey picked up the blue stick, gripped it tightly, stared hard at the boy's knuckles, and said,

"If you talk out loud again, that's where I'll hit you next time."
"Now, go and sit down."

Ouch! Everyone in class winced as Billy grimaced, bit his lips, and wiped away a tear on his shirtsleeve. No one, especially Billy Stephens, misbehaved for the rest of the day as we focused on learning to read and write and add and take away. Well, not so Miss Harvey could see anyway.

Just before playtime, I stood at the back of the line, as everyone took turns to swallow a spoonful of thick cod liver oil. I nearly choked when it was my turn.

"Hold your head back. Let it slide down, Johnny Paull. That's it—slide down."
"This'll keep the sickness away, you know."

"Here, now drink this." She gave me a swig of orange juice, which cleared my mouth of the stickiness of the cod liver oil.

At midday, I opened the paper bag that Grandma had given me. Inside was a new OXO tin, filled with four small meat cubes that I quickly sucked and swallowed before going out into the yard to play. Everyone, it seemed, except me, had hobnailed boots and scraped their feet on the granite-covered yard to see who could make the best sparks.

Reminding Billy to sit up straight, Miss Harvey started afternoon school with a story about a fisherman. I closed my eyes as she read, just like I did when Dad told us a bedtime story.

At half past three, Grandma was waiting for me near the school gates, and I told her right away about Billy Stephens getting into trouble with Miss Harvey.

"Well," she said sharply, *"Billy must have deserved it. You go to school to listen and to learn, so let that be a warning to you."*
"Got yer OXO tin? Need that for tomorrow's dinner."

"Yes, Grandma," I replied, deciding then that I wouldn't tell Mum and Dad about poor Billy Stephens in case they said the same thing to me. I did ask, though, if I could have a pair of hobnailed boots but was sternly told, no, those kinds of boots were for *poor kids.*
"We're not poor," said Dad. *"We don't rely on the social."*

The next day was a repeat of the first day and was repeated the following days and weeks. In an atmosphere of almost total silence, Miss Harvey told us to sit up straight, be quiet, and taught us how to read, how to write, and how to add. She also taught those who didn't have stories read or told to them at home how to listen and see pictures in their heads.

I soon learned the routines and the expectations.

I soon got used to the taste of the cod liver oil and the OXO cubes and the high squeaky sounds of hobnailed boots rubbing against the granite slabs in the yard.

Ill with pneumonia, in January 1947, I missed nearly four months of school and, on my return, found that little of the routine had changed.

There was one day, though, before the start of the summer holiday, that was different, very different.

Chapter 3

On the day of my fifth birthday, Monday, July 14, two weeks before we broke up for the long summer holiday, I was really surprised when my dad, not my grandma, met me at the end of the school day. Dad had never picked me up from school before.

He was in his driver's uniform so I knew he'd come straight from work. My stomach turned over. Was something wrong? Was Grandma ill? Or Mum? Was she OK?

Standing by the rusty iron fence, Dad smiled when he saw some of the children rush out of the school yard, up to the street corner, and turn and slide down back toward school, skidding on the cobble road, sending up a stream of yellow sparks from their hobnailed boots. Then he took my hand, and we walked together in the afternoon sun toward the harbor. Dad said we were going pebbling, pebbling on Lariggan Beach.

Just Dad and me. Pebbling. On Lariggan Beach. After school. Could it get any better than that?

I felt so special and knew in my bones that something magical was about to happen. It was, after all, my birthday treat.

And what a memorable and lifetime treat it turned out to be.

We walked hand in hand on the cobbled street to the Fradgan, past Uncle Steve and Aunty Flo's white cottage, past the tall icehouse towering over the small inner harbor, and crossed over to the open fish market. We reached the small stone bridge by the Fisherman's Institute at the end of Newlyn pier, where the Coombe River ran into the sea. Dad lifted me up so I could see the swans and the seagulls dipping their heads into the refreshing, bubbling blend of fresh and salt water.

We walked around the corner by the Austin and Morris garage onto the seafront, then down the smooth, worn granite steps onto the beach. The sky was bright blue, and the sun, a shimmering yellow. St. Michael's Mount, way off in the distance, looked very majestic, its fairy-tale castle catching the late afternoon sun that was setting behind the Mousehole granite cliffs.

The tide was out, and the large smooth rocks, black and gray and white, were wet and shining in the late afternoon sun. As the greeny blue water lapped back and forth, herring gulls squabbled as they looked for food scraps.

We stepped over the pebbles, making sure we didn't step on the strands of slimy brown and yellow seaweed. Dad reached in his pocket and brought out two of his Old Holborn tobacco tins.

"Here," he said, giving me one, *"take this and fill it. Just wishing rocks, mind you."*
I was thrilled. I'd never had an Old Holborn tin before. With a broad smile and a knowing twinkle in his eye, he said, *"Bet I'll fill mine first."*

The competition was on. We walked slowly along the seashore, and we looked and we touched and we talked and we collected. The beach pebbles were so endearing, small, round, smooth, and warm to the touch. Soon my tin was full of tiny *wishing rocks* and heart-shaped pebbles that I wanted to take home to show my mum. I so wanted to tell her and Jimmie that I filled my Old Holborn tin before Dad filled his.

Just as we were walking toward the granite steps, I spotted something different. There, lying with all the pebbles, was a bright yellow object. It didn't look like any of the other stones. It was so different from all the others, more like the picture I'd seen at school of a small slice of pineapple. What was it?

It stared up at me, wanting, I felt, badly to be picked up, wanting to be touched and admired. By me, Johnny Paull.

And that's what I did. I bent over, picked it up, held it in the palm of my hand, and touched it. It was a magical moment. It was lighter than a pebble. Wide-eyed, I showed my dad. Because I knew he knew everything, I asked,

"What's this, Dad?" He looked down at it, smiled, and then, half-closing his eyes, frowned.

Dad had no idea what I'd found. *"Dunno. Never seen anything like that before."*
"Good, though, isn't it?"

Funny, because I thought he had seen everything there was to see. I couldn't believe that he had never ever seen anything like the yellow *thingy* before, and he'd been to the beach over a thousand, thousand times in his life.

But Dad did know it was different, and, therefore, very, very special.

"Take it home and show your ma. She might know."

I stared at my orangey-yellow, rock-like, *magical* find. It looked soft. Not wanting to scratch it, I wrapped it up in my white hanky and put it in my right-hand pocket. It didn't seem right to mix such a special *thingy* in the Old Holborn tin with the other pebbles I'd found. My dad took my hand, and we made our way back home. As I walked up the very steep hill, I kept feeling the Old Holborn *treasure tin* in one pocket and checking the lumpy hanky in the other.

I knew I'd found something very special. *I knew* it was lying on the beach waiting for me to come along and find it. *I knew* it was a special day. I was excited. My discovery made my head glow. It was something that *I knew* belonged just to me—and would, forever.

When we reached Treveneth Crescent, I quickly skipped up the back garden path, past the three gooseberry bushes (one for Jimmie, one for Charles, and one for me), pushed open the glass door, and ran straight into the kitchen. Mum and Grandma were standing by the white enameled cooker, waiting for the kettle to boil. Charles was sleeping in Mum's arms.

"Mum, Mum, Grandma, see what I found."

"It's brilliant."

I took out my Old Holborn tin and showed them what I'd found on the beach. I knew then by the look on my mum and my grandma's faces that the yellow rock I had found was something very special. And I found it on my birthday too.

"Where'd you find that?" asked Grandma.

"Dad, where'd he find that? Did you give it to him for a birthday surprise?"

Mum said softly, "That *beautiful yellow rock was waiting for you. Just for you."*

"It's a treasure. A real treasure. Put it in one of your OXO treasure tins, Johnny, and keep it there, forever."

"Forever. You hear me? It's treasure."

"Forever and a day."

I squeezed my *treasure* tightly in my hand and took it into the kitchen. I had never held *treasure* before. I put it under the hot water tap and washed off the grainy sand with hand soap, dried it with newspaper, stroked it, and looked at it again. I put it on the dinner table, next to my birthday tea treats—the big blue-and-white plate covered with splits, homemade blackberry jam, Cornish cream, sticky treacle, sausage rolls, and yellow saffron buns.

"What's that?" asked my brother, Jimmie, his mouth full of bread and treacle, looking at Mum and Dad. Mum and Dad shook their heads and said they didn't know, but as Mum explained, the yellow discovery was something very special.

Jimmie picked it up and stroked the yellow *treasure.*

"T'ain't heavy. Ain't a pebble, is it, Mum? I ain't never found one."

"Don't say 'ain't,' Jimmie, please," said Mum. *"You'll find one next time we go pebbling Just have to keep looking."*

Dad's story after my birthday tea was about his dad working in the tin mine in St. Just, digging in dark and wet tunnels under the rolling sea.

"Bet he never found a yellow rock like yours, Johnny," he said. *"If he did, he never showed us kids."*

He looked at Grandma.

"No," she said, *"yer grandpop ne'er found nowt like that."*

When I went upstairs to bed, I put the Old Holborn *treasure tin* containing my special find under my pillow, curled my fingers around it, and fell asleep with a broad smile on my face.

As I dressed in the morning, I put the treasure inside a small OXO tin in my left trouser pocket, next to my favorite small seashell, to take to school so I could show my teacher, Miss Harvey.

Dad reminded me as I went out the door with Grandma. *"Got your yellow treasure for your teacher, Johnny? Don't forget it. You know what your Ma said."*

"Got your OXO cubes too?"

Running ahead of Grandma as we approached school, I couldn't wait to show Miss Harvey my treasure. The bell went, and I ran into school.

Even before all the boys sat in their seats, I was standing by Miss Harvey's tall desk, the OXO *treasure tin* in my hand, spluttering, *"Miss Harvey, Miss Harvey, see what I found. I found it on the beach after school yesterday. You know, next to the harbor wall. I found it on Lariggan. Went there with my dad. You know, when the tide was out, when you can see what the tide brought in."*

Every word came out in a rush.

As Miss Harvey looked inside my scratched OXO tin, her eyes widened. It wasn't, apparently, a rock at all. It was ancient fossilized tree resin, and she said, it was called *amber*. Miss Harvey knew amber was millions of years old and came from the inside of trees.

Resin? Fossilized? Amber? Ancient? What beautiful words, I thought. I rolled the words around in my head. *Resin. Fossilized. Amber, amber . . .*

She held my beautiful amber in her hand, smiled, looked down at me through her glasses that balanced on the end of her sharp nose, and said loudly, so everyone in class could hear, that it had come from a far-off country and probably had been washed ashore after a long, long trip in the sea.

She wrote the word *amber* on the board.
"And Johnny Paull was lucky enough to find it."

I could tell Miss Harvey was thrilled. I don't think I had ever seen her wide smile before.

What a great teaching moment it must have been for her—and what a great learning moment it surely was for me. Her words made me realize that I had found something very, very special.

"Show it to everyone," Miss Harvey said. I proudly turned to face everyone in the room. As I held out my hand and showed the class, everyone stopped chattering. They really wanted to see what I had found.

Johnny Hoskins put up his hand and asked, *"Where'd you find that, Johnny Paull?"*

I looked at him and told him. *"Down at Lariggan, Johnny, you know, when the tide's out,"* I answered. *"You've been, ain't you?"*

"Course I have. Been every day. Ain't never seen one of those yellow things though," said Johnny. *"I'm going there this afternoon. I'm goin' to get one of them."*
"Was it close to the harbor wall, Johnny?"

He looked around. *"After school. Les go. Anyone goin' wiv me?"*

Four boys quickly put up their hands. *"We'll come."*
Miss Harvey sternly told the class to be quiet.

"OK. Fun's over. Back to work."

She turned to me.

*"Johnny Paull, why don't you draw a picture of your amber? Here, here's
some white paper. Use this! Don't just draw the amber, draw the other beach
pebbles too. Just as you remember. Can you see them in your head?"*

I couldn't wait to grab some yellow, black, and brown crayons from the
big biscuit tin. Closing my eyes, I tried to remember just how the amber
looked when I saw it lying with all the other pebbles.
    When I'd finished my drawing and showed it to Miss Harvey, I could
tell from her eyes that she liked it.

"Good drawing. Good color, Johnny Paull."

Quickly, she glued the picture onto some black paper, then taped it
to the wall close to my desk, and told me to write my name and the date
underneath.

Wow! It felt so good to see my picture on display so that everyone in
class could see it—a teaching lesson I was to remember time and time again
much later when I worked as a teacher with young children.

As I was drawing another picture of one of my *wishing rocks,* Miss
Harvey came next to me and, with a broad smile, said very emphatically so
that everyone could hear,

*"Keep it, Johnny Paull. The amber. And that wishing rock. They're
wonderful. Keep them. Keep the amber. Keep it in your OXO tin—your
treasure tin, sorry—and save it."*
    "Save it forever."

*"And you, Johnny Hoskins, go and find your own. Go and find your own
amber on the beach the next time you're there."*

When playtime came, everyone wanted to see and touch the beautiful yellow amber. Roger Symons said loudly, and with a note of frustration, that he'd been down to Lariggan and to the beach off Penlee Quarry, a million times.

"Wow! Amber. S'great. Ain't never found anything like that. Let me touch it, go on, let me touch it."
"Wish I found it."

I told him and Johnny Hoskins, in a secretive whisper, that I was going to save the amber forever, safely, in a *treasure tin,* just as Miss Harvey told me. Just like pirates did when they had treasure.
"Wassat?" asked Johnny. *"Wos a treshure tin?"*
"Come over 'ere," I said. *"I'll show you."*
I took my OXO tin out of my pocket, held it in my stretched-out hand, and told him my mum said if you keep things in a tin, they're safe, just the same way as pirates kept their treasure.

At first, he wasn't impressed. *"That ain't no treshure tin. It's an old OXO tin. Got plenty of them at my 'ouse. But I can make 'em into treshure tins, right?"* He giggled. *"That's funny."*
"Makin' treshure tins. Pirates bury theirs, don't they?"
"And I can use my dad's ciggy tins, and his baccy tins, right? Don't matter which, right?"
"When they're empty, you can fill 'em, with treshure."

That evening, that's what Johnny did, after his tea, when his parents were reading the newspaper, showing me the very next day his own *treasure tin*, filled with golden-yellow banded snail shells.

"I'm gonna find some amber—these shells are just keepin' my tin warm 'til I do."
"Good, though, ain't they? Found them ages ago in the garden."
"'Olidays in a couple of weeks. Tide's out in the afternoon too. Stacks of time to find amber."
"Bet I'll find a bagful."

He didn't. Johnny searched and searched Lariggan Beach but never found a piece of amber.

Neither did I. And I searched and searched and searched too.

In September, when school reopened after the summer holidays, I took my amber to school again and told Miss Harvey in front of the class that I hadn't lost it.

Johnny Hoskins put up his hand.

"I ain't found no amber, Miss Harvey."
"And I've searched the beach a million times."
"Johnny Paull's dead lucky."
"Sure you found that amber thingy down there, Johnny?"
"Weren't on the other beaches, was it?" he asked.

For well over sixty years, from my very special fifth birthday, the smooth yellow treasure, my special amber, resides in the OXO tin.

Sometimes, the precious, magical amber's in my right trouser pocket, sometimes in the left.

I touch it a million times a day, just to make sure that it's still there, just to make me feel good.

As I touch it, I remind myself of that magical birthday all those years ago.

It's a big part of my life. Especially my teaching life.

Chapter 4

Granddad Wilkes, Mum's dad, was a gambler. He loved to bet on the horses. When Pearl Diver won the Epsom Derby in 1947, ridden by Granddad's favorite jockey, George Bridgland, he made a bundle of money. With his winnings, he bought the Globe Inn at the top of Queen Street. Then, following another big win on the horses a couple of years later, he bought adjoining houses in Gwavas Street, Penzance, for his two daughters, Aunty Joan and Hazel, my mum.

In the middle of the school summer holiday, our cat, Joseph, died. Grandma Paull became gravely ill and quietly passed away in West Cornwall Hospital.

I was seven; Jimmie, twelve; and baby Charles, now just two. I didn't want to leave our Treveneth Crescent home in Newlyn. Neither did Jimmie. Like me, we were happy and comfortable at school, even when my teacher Miss Harvey was grumpy. I was happy at home and even happier when I was scouring the pebbles on Lariggan Beach with my mum and dad, and my friends—Roger Simons, Johnny Hoskins, and Dick Jenkins. Now we probably wouldn't be taking family walks to Lariggan anymore.

I became very upset the day before we were due to leave our Newlyn home. To stop me from crying, Mum took my hand to reassure me and said it would be a really good idea if we each buried a memory in the garden. Although it sounded as if that was something special, I wasn't sure what she meant. How do you bury a memory? A memory is something in your head, isn't it?

Mum, using her quietest voice, explained that if we buried something important in the garden, we would never completely leave the house. There would always be something there of each of us.

"That, Johnny, is what a memory is."

She said we should put something special in a *treasure tin*, something that we'd found on one of our walks at the beach. *Oh*, I thought. What a great idea. I liked the idea that I could leave part of me behind, buried in the ground, in just the same way that pirates buried their treasure chests.

That evening, after a teatime of sliced white bread, margarine, treacle, and a cup of tea, we filled our *OXO treasure tins*. It took me awhile to decide what to put in mine. Should I, I wondered, put my Lariggan amber in the Old Holborn tin Dad had given me, or in an OXO tin, and bury it in the back garden in Newlyn, forever?

No. I knew I couldn't part with my yellow amber. If I buried it, how would I ever see and touch it again?
I decided that I would miss it too much; I didn't want it to become a memory.

I chose, instead, one of my favorite *wishing rocks,* a limpet with a hole in its shell, a small smooth white pebble, part of one of my grandfather's grayish white clay pipes, and one of his small clay marbles he'd had as a child.
When we'd filled our *treasure tins,* Jimmie and I went downstairs, jumping two steps at a time.

"OK. Ready? Let's go and bury our special memory tins."
"Oh, here, put these in your tins," Mum said, giving us each a special coin from her brown leather purse.

Each coin was minted the year we were born.

She handed me a farthing, dated 1942, with a picture of a robin on one side. It was my favorite coin, as she well knew. Jimmie's favorite was a 1938 halfpenny, and baby Charles had a 1947 penny.

We wrapped our little but very sentimental treasures in a small piece of yellow silk, cut from Uncle Donald's torn parachute that he brought back from the war. Then we shut and taped our tins so that the earthworms and maggots couldn't get inside.

As we went through the kitchen door to the back garden, no one spoke. Even baby Charles was quiet. The atmosphere was emotionally charged. Jimmie fetched his small garden spade and, staring at the earth, dug a really deep hole near the gooseberry bushes in the back of the garden. It was just the right place, as Mum always said that's where she found us.

Without a word, Mum held our hands tightly as the tears ran down our faces, and we buried the *OXO memory treasure tins* deep in the garden and then covered them over with earth, beach pebbles, twigs, and dead leaves.

We went quietly inside to gather all our belongings and began to say *good-bye* to our Newlyn home.

Mum gave me a large empty cardboard box, just big enough to hold my growing collection of OXO tins, *Woodbine* cigarette cards, my *Beano* and *Dandy* comics, three birds' nests, blown seagull eggs, seashells, a box full of conkers, and some oak apples I found in Penlee Park. When I went to fetch the old glass jar on the windowsill filled with *wishing rocks*, I saw that it had already gone into one of Mum's cardboard boxes.

Early the next morning, Dick and Bill Simons helped Dad and Mum load our furniture and cardboard boxes filled with clothes—and the big glass jar filled with *wishing rocks*—on the back of Dick Jenkins's lorry. Waving good-bye to the neighbors in Gwavas Estate, Dad began to drive slowly down Paul Hill, to begin a new life in 23 Gwavas Street in Penzance.

And so it was that Jimmie, Charles, and I left our *treasure tins* filled with our memories of family life, of walks down country lanes and across the Lariggan seashore, deep down in the soft brown earth in the back garden of 16 Treveneth Crescent, Gwavas Estate, Newlyn.

Chapter 5

I didn't like our new house in Penzance. It looked very small.

"Where's the garden, Mum?" I asked.
"Johnny, there isn't a garden at the front or at the back."
"Just a back lane," she replied.

Jimmie grimaced.
"No inside lav, either, I bet."
"'Ow do we go lav at night?"
"Scabby!"

With so much unloading to do, Mum was in no mood to talk about what the house did and didn't have.

"Hey, go inside, don't unpack your stuff, OK? until I tell you where you're sleeping, and I'll make us all a good cup of tea."
"And, Jimmie, you can fetch fish and chips when we're done."

We soon discovered that Jimmie was right: the house didn't have an inside lavatory or a bath. It did have three bedrooms though, and Jimmie and I rushed downstairs to tell our parents that we chose the middle room, leaving the one at the top of the stairs for our baby brother, Charles, and the big room at the front, for them.

I needed to know where the jar with the *wishing rocks* was going to be placed, so Mum quickly found a home for it on the mantelpiece in the small front room. I put my cardboard box of my treasures under the bed.

After a restless first night, the next day, out in the street, I met and made instant friends with a couple of boys who lived in St. Mary's Street when I showed them my amber and my best *wishing rock.*

Roger and Dudley told me, no, they didn't wear hobnailed boots and that my new school, St. Paul's Junior School for Boys, was up at the top of Adelaid Street, past Nigh's corner shop. Mr. Nigh, they said giggling, sold the *best* soft licorice stick for a penny. Oh, and Harvey's was the best place for fish and chips.

Roger made a face when he told me about the teachers at St. Paul's.
"*Some are good. Some ain't.*"
"*Some get mad if you can't add.*"

Both boys said Mr. Miller shouted, made you sit up straight all day, hit you on the legs with a ruler if you slumped, and took away everyone's milk when the class was too noisy.

"*His nickname's Ginger.*"
"*He's got red 'air, you know!*"
"*Shouts a lot.*"

I soon learned that the two boys and every boy in the neighborhood liked Mr. Tonkin and Mr. Jones best. Dudley and Roger said that were going to be in Mr. Jones's class.

They told me about Mr. Jones and his tall green glass-fronted bookcase that stood next to the brass fireplace in the corner of his classroom. All kinds of rocks, they said, and seashells, fossils, bones, birds' eggs and colorful feathers were crammed in the top three shelves. I could see the images in my brain as they talked.

Sometimes, Roger said, if you were good, Mr. Jones would reach inside the bookcase and take out a fossil or a seashell, show it to the class, and then tell them everything he knew and everything we wanted to know about it. *Wow!*

I wondered whose class I would be in. Mr. Miller's? Crikey—I hoped not. I looked through my collection of *wishing rocks*, found a really good one with the white line of quartz running right down the middle, and closed my eyes, sending Mr. Jones a very special wish.

"Please, Mr. Jones, let me be in your class. If you do, I'll show you my treasure tin and my Lariggan amber."

It was all that I could think about. I kept my fingers crossed and every day sent a million or so more best wishes to Mr. Jones from one of my Lariggan *wishing rocks*.

Would the wishes work? Would I be in Mr. Jones's class?

One teatime, a few days later, after playing footy with Roger and Dudley, Mum told me she had met Mr. Curnow, the headmaster, at school.

"We talked about you starting there."
"And I filled out all of the forms."
"You, you, Johnny Paull, are going to be in Mr. Jones's class."
"I knew you'd like that."

"Thanks, Mum," I said, *"can I have some more bread and treacle?"*
"Please? Go on—one more piece?"

As I ate, my mind went into overdrive. I was in Mr. Jones's class. Perhaps, perhaps, I could show Mr. Jones my wonderful golden amber. Would he like it? Would he like it as much as Miss Harvey did? And what about my *wishing rock*? Would he like that?

"And," Mum said, *"that's not all. We're having a new cat."*
"Bill Young, Dad's conductor, his cat's had kittens."
"Dad's bringing it home after work."

"What's the new pussy like," I asked, *"What's its name?"*
"Can it sleep on our bed?"

The *wishing rock* brought me good luck—and without asking, a new cat. Phew! That, I thought, was great, knowing how much Mum and Dad missed Joseph. Thank you, *wishing rock.* Sending wishes worked. It really worked. *Wishing rock* wishes do come true.

Well, not always, because I had stroked my favorite rock and my amber, closed my eyes, and wished that I would wake up and find that we really did have a garden. We needed a garden. I missed the gooseberry bushes and wondered what would happen if we had a new brother or sister.

Where would the stork leave the baby?

The next day, Dad brought home the newest member of the family. The dearest little male cat was quickly named Spotty because of the big black circle of fur on his back. Spotty had no trouble settling in and did, thankfully, choose the bed in which Jimmie and I slept.

Chapter 6

On my very first morning in St. Paul's School, after morning assembly in the small school hall, at twenty past nine precisely, Mr. Jones welcomed me to his class. Then he adjusted his tie, buttoned the middle button of his green corduroy sports jacket, and selected an unused piece of white chalk from the cardboard box sitting on the rim of the blackboard. He looked up at the top left of the board and slowly, squeakily, wrote the day and the month, followed by the *work of the day*—sums, writing and reading—and with extravagant gesture wiped the powdery chalk from his fingers.

Then, he smiled, sat on his polished high chair, watched us dip our pens into the black inkwells, carefully copy his words in our books, and reminded us as we did our schoolwork about the need to "do things right."

All morning, seated in five rows, one behind another, we followed the  same routine. By midafternoon, when we had added, subtracted, multiplied, and divided, recited the alphabet, and written sentences with capital letters, all to his satisfaction, we went in the yard and had our class photograph taken. We came back in, sat up straight, and behaved ourselves. Mr. Jones stood up in front of us. Clearing his throat, he began to read a chapter from one of Enid Blyton's great children's adventure books, *The Famous Five.*

His storytelling voice was soft, like my dad's.
I was hooked. I loved the story.
I loved the characters. I loved the way Mr. Jones used his voice.
I told Mum and Dad that night that I thought my new school was really good, and I said, *"No one wears hobnailed boots."*
"Mr. Jones read a dead good story, all about kids having a real good adventure."

The same thing happened in school on Tuesday. We worked and worked and worked, and then sat and listened. And the same thing happened again on Wednesday morning. All work and no play and no *big spark* competitions at playtime. But I did love hearing about the adventures of the *Famous Five* during the afternoons.

After the Wednesday dinner break, as soon as we had sat down at our desks, Mr. Jones checked to see what Graham, not, it seemed, the fastest or the best writer in class—Charles was the best—had written during the last part of the morning.

"Finished, Paul? Show me what you wrote."

Mr. Jones sniffed loudly. Satisfied, it seems, with Graham's efforts, he told us we'd worked really hard. Mr. Jones was, he said, really pleased with all of us.

As he spoke, Mr. Jones walked slowly over to his green cupboard, leaned over and opened the door. It creaked as he pulled it completely open. We craned our necks, and we could see it was filled with all sorts of wonderful things. Mr. Jones looked inside, chose something that took his fancy, and placed it, with great care, on his old wooden desk, just to the side of the chipped ceramic pot of Stephenson's ink.

Sitting up as straight as I could, I could see it was a yellowy white limpet shell, just like the shells stuck to the rocks on Lariggan Beach. There were little blue marks near the top.

When every eye in the room was fixed on his, Mr. Jones slowly, very deliberately, picked up the shell and gently ran his fingers over it. He held it up against the sunlight coming through the window, looked at us, and quietly asked if we knew what it was. No one said a word. We'd all seen limpets every time we'd gone to the beach. But I was to discover, I, for one, knew nothing about them.

Using magical, enchanting words, he set fire to our imaginations. Mr. Jones told us he was holding *treasure*, treasure from the sea, then told us what it was, where he'd found it, and how long he'd had it.

His story about his *treasure* was as spellbinding as *The Famous Five* and the best of Dad's tales. Mr. Jones described the life of a limpet, why it stuck so firmly to the smooth granite rocks when the tide was out, how it fed on tiny algae when the tide came in, and why blue barnacles lived on its shell. I was entranced. I closed my eyes. I could see the limpet shell sluggishly sliding over the seaweed-covered rock, rasping and feeding as it crawled. I could see it sticking tight to the rock face when the sea receded. I felt I knew why barnacles loved to spend their lives on the backs of limpet shells.

It was then, for me, that the classroom—and the learning—came alive. The atmosphere in the room sparkled, making my hair on the back of my neck stand up, my fingers and my brain tingle. I had no idea that limpets that clung to granite rocks were so interesting. I wondered how they chewed their food.

Did they have sharp teeth?

"*So,*" Mr. Jones said.

"*I've shown you the common but very beautiful and very interesting limpet.*"

"*A fascinating creature, yes?*"

Gilbert looked across the room at everyone and smiled. He knew what was going to happen next.

Mr. Jones asked loudly, with his eyes widening,

"*OK, who's got something in their pockets?*"

"*Anyone got anything good to show us all?*"

"*Empty your pockets, boys, on top of your desks so that everyone can see what you've got.*"

"*Move your desks closer. Show each other what you've got.*"

"*Who's got something* really *good?*"

A chorus of *"I 'av, sir, Look!"* filled the air. We all did. We all had something special to show off to our friends.

In a second, the desks were covered with all sorts of bits and pieces that, for whatever reason, had caught the eye and the curiosity of young boys.

During afternoon playtime, everyone in Mr. Jones's class talked about the limpet shell and the special things they'd brought to school in their pockets. Three of us made plans to go and find our own limpet shells down on the beach near the promenade as soon as school finished.

Just after four o'clock, I ran down Adelaide Street, with Dudley and Roger, onto the promenade, down the steps to Battery Rocks. We couldn't get there fast enough, wanting so much to find limpets like Mr. Jones's, with barnacles on their shells.

We weren't fast enough. Barry, Roger, and Gilbert had beaten us there. There they were, hands full of shells, standing by the best rock pool. *"Hey, you boy, what you lot doin' 'ere?"* they asked.
"Same as you, twerps!" we shouted back.
"Finding dead good limpets."

Laughing, we climbed over the rocks and explored more of the shallow rock pools, gently moving the strands of brown-and-green weed and shouting loudly when we saw a shrimp or tiny jellyfish and, even more loudly, if we saw a limpet actually slithering slowly across a rock.

When we found as many empty shells as we could handle, we sat on a flat rock, putting our finds in front of us. Barry had found the best limpet shell, one covered with barnacles.

As soon as we each had a good close look, Barry took it back to the rock pool where he'd found it, anxious not to hurt the barnacles.
"They're great, ain't they though?" he exclaimed.

We tried to outdo each other about what we had learned about limpets and tiny barnacles from Mr. Jones, and as we each knew something the others didn't know, we agreed it was a draw.

When I got home, I showed my mum the empty limpet shells I'd found and told her about Barry's shell that was covered with tiny blue barnacles, adding proudly what I had learned about them.

I washed the shells and put them in an OXO tin to later show Dad what I had found.

Dad was very impressed with how much I'd learned in school.

The next day, we lined up by Mr. Jones's desk and showed him what we had found.
He smiled.
"Hey, good for you. Save them, ok?"
"Now, go and sit and get on with your schoolwork."
"When it's writing time, you know what to write about, yes?"
"Everything you now know about limpets."

I went to my desk, neatly copied what was written on the board, used my fingers and thumbs to do the multiplication sums, and, during writing time, made up a short story about the life of a limpet.

Chapter 7

On the second Wednesday, I knew everything was in place for *amber* time, the right time to bring and show Mr. Jones *my* treasure. I knew by then he must have felt my wish from my *wishing rock.*

Over the boiled egg and bread *soldiers'* (finger-sized pieces of bread) breakfast, I told my mum I was going to show Mr. Jones my amber that I'd found on the beach with dad on my fifth birthday.

She smiled. *"He'll like it,"* she said. *"I bet he knows what it is."*
"He's a teacher, don't forget. Teachers know everything. Bring it back home though."
"Don't leave it there."

 Sure enough, during the afternoon, when everything and everyone was quiet and the work of the day completed to Mr. Jones's satisfaction, he went to his cupboard. As he opened the door, Barry and Gilbert glanced at me and winked. Mr. Jones looked inside and took out one of his treasures. He held it up and told us where he'd found it. He asked if anyone in class knew what it was.

No one said a word. They hadn't seen anything like it before.

I had! My heart missed eighty-seven beats! I felt my hands go hot and clammy. I knew what it was. It was amber! He *had* felt my *wishing rock* wish. My moment had arrived. *This* was the time.

"That's amber, sir, amber!" I blurted. *"I know 'cos I found some amber."*

Telling Mr. Jones I knew he held amber in his hand made me feel really important. All the class stared at me. What an incredible experience for me. I was the only boy in class who had seen amber before.

Mr. Jones looked at me. *"What?"* he asked. *"Paull! You know amber? You* found *some amber? Where? Are you sure it's amber? What color is it? Can you see through it? Is it heavy?"*

"You got it with you?"

You bet, I thought. It's always with me.

I put my hand in my pocket, quickly took out my amber and, spreading out my white hanky, put it out in front of me on the desk.

"Look, Mr. Jones, look!"

He put his amber back in the cupboard and came toward my desk. His eyes lit up.

*"*Wow! *Wherever did you find that amber, Paull? You* found *it?"*

"Sure someone didn't give it to you as a prezzie?"

Mr. Jones held it in his hand and looked at my amber lovingly, in the same way that Miss Harvey, my infant school teacher, did. I knew right away that the amber, to him, was very, very special. As I told him about finding it lying with the thousands of pebbles on Lariggan Beach, Mr. Jones stared at the amber, his eyes aglow. Even though Mr. Jones didn't live in Penzance, he knew the beach well. I'm sure he knew every tide pool, every rock, every pebble.

Mr. Jones's eyes—and his smile—widened.

"Speak louder, Paull, tell everyone in class."

"Tell them about your amber."

I faced the class and showed them my amber, telling them where and when I'd found it. It was a magical, sparkling moment.

My day, my year, my life, especially in school, was made. Thank you, thank you, *wishing rock.*

That evening, during the hot tea, white bread, and sticky yellow treacle teatime, I couldn't stop talking about what happened in school.

"Mum, Mum, Mr. Jones goes to Lariggan."
"He's never found amber though, like I did."
"He told everyone in class I was dead lucky."
"He's never found anything like it, either at Lariggan, Battery Rocks, or the beach at Eastern Green."
"He lives near Praah Sands. He said he's never found amber there either."

"There you go, Johnny," Mum said.
"Didn't I tell you what you found was extra special?"
"Now finish your treacle sandwich, please."
"Oh, and thank your wishing rock too, OK?"

"Worked, didn't it?"

"Sure will mum," I said.

The following Wednesday, some of the other boys brought in rocks and pebbles they'd found, either in the country lanes or at the beach. It was really exciting seeing everyone's treasure, during the afternoon, when we'd finished our work. Everyone went very quiet when Adrian, a new boy to school that day, raised his hand and told Mr. Jones he had something very special to show us that his grandmother had given him.

We all turned in our seats and stared at him.

"Listen, everyone," said Mr. Jones. *"Listen to Adrian."*

His grandmother, Adrian said, in a voice that sounded different from everyone else, sailed on the big liner, the RMS *Titanic*, on its doomed voyage to New York on April 15, 1912.

To a wide-eyed class who had never heard of the *Titanic*, Adrian told us about his life in London and about his grandma, who was returning to her home in America, when the liner hit an iceberg and slowly began to sink. She, Adrian said, jumped fully clothed off the ship's deck into the icy sea

With huge tears in his eyes, he told us how some of her friends drowned.

Adrian reached into his brown duffel bag and passed around part of the lifebelt that, he said, had saved his grandma's life.

Everyone, including Mr. Jones, wanted to touch it, and we all wanted to hear more about the ill-fated *Titanic*.

Adrian, on his first day at his new school, became the shining star of the playground during the afternoon playtime. When we returned to our room and settled in our desks, Mr. Jones asked Adrian to draw a picture of the *Titanic* to tape it to the classroom wall.

"Can you write the story too, Adrian?" he asked.

Adrian was a really good writer and quickly filled a page, gave it to Mr. Jones, and then started his drawing on a big sheet of white paper.

That night, I told my mum and dad about what had happened to Adrian's grandmother on the *Titanic*, asking them if they had heard of the sad ending of the liner's first trip to sea.

Dad said he had had read about Adrian's grandmother in *The Cornishman*, our weekly newspaper, and told me more about the *Titanic*'s sad voyage.

The next day, I badgered Adrian with more and more questions about the doomed ship. I needed to know how many people were saved. I need to know how they stayed afloat. I couldn't get the sad story out of my head and stared at the piece of lifebelt on Mr. Jones's desk throughout the day, the lifebelt that had saved Adrian's grandma.

I so enjoyed my Wednesdays with Mr. Jones so much, especially those special Wednesday times when, by opening his cupboard of treasure, he opened children's minds, especially mine. This was the only time in the week when Mr. Jones was prepared for the unforeseen, for the lovely things that happened when the boys shared and talked about the *treasures* in their pockets or about some fascinating small creature they'd seen or of some family trauma, sparked by Adrian's story.

The impact was always so magical: shifting from the day-to-day drudgery of rote learning, once a week, the classroom throbbed briefly with energy and excitement and rich learning. In that short space of time, we looked really closely and touched everything that was shared on all the desktops. We talked, counted and measured, weighed and recorded, drew pictures and wrote.

We laughed and enjoyed each other's company.

I felt I had a special *amber* relationship with Mr. Jones. When he walked toward his green cupboard, Mr. Jones would always turn to me, smile, and ask,

"Well, Paull, found anything great at Lariggan? Did you go there again?"

Walks with Mum and Dad now, though, were around the lanes and fields closer to our home. Hunting for wishing rocks was replaced with searching for birds' nests and, best of all, for banded snails that lived in the gaps between the rectangular slabs of granite.

I did go again with my friends though. I loved looking under flat rocks, always surprised by what I saw, and loved searching among the millions of pebbles for those that were special to me. I filled tins and jars of all sizes with some wonderful heart-shaped pebbles and plenty of wishing *rocks,* but it wasn't the same without my mum and dad.

And I never found another piece of amber.

Chapter 8

In September, after the long summer holidays full of fishing and rock hunting, school, for me and for my learning, changed again.

I went into Mr. Miller's class. I learned quickly that, first of all, not all teachers were like Miss Harvey and Mr. Jones. I quickly learned how to read and learn from a teacher's angry body language, get on with my schoolwork, keep out of trouble, and not get hit.

I raised my hand but once in the school year. In the first week, when I asked my question about a sum I couldn't understand, he didn't answer my question. Instead, Mr. Miller shouted sarcastically at me, *"Hey, Paull, are you the Paull with two Ls or the Paul with one L? Your family got a problem with their name?"*

I was embarrassed when everyone laughed. *"Two Ls Paull, two Ls Paull . . ."* someone chanted.

That evening, when Dad got home from work, I asked him why our name had two *l*s.

"The other Paul's, they only have one L," I said. *"Why do we have two?"*

"'Cos we're posh, stupid," said Jimmie with a chuckle.

"Well," said Dad. *"Your grandfather, my dad, couldn't read or write very well. He was called John, like you, Johnny. John Paul the Younger.*

Two other baby boys had died before he was born, you see. They were called John too."

"My dad was born a long time ago, November 1873. He left school early. He was twelve, I think, and went to work down the mine, up at St. Just. Dug for tin underground, way out under the sea. I'll take you there. The spot is called Botallack."

"Beautiful area, but damned hard work. Digging tin in granite. Damned hard."

"No pension for miners, you know. Just like us bus drivers."

"Your granddad walked from Newlyn Coombe each day . . . Don't think he had a bike."

"Then he worked on the trawlers, fishing and helping out in the harbor when they landed the fish.

"He died at the start of the war."

"Anyway, on his wedding day, he scribbled his name on the wedding papers as best he could, and he left a blob of black ink on the paper. And the recorder, the man who writes down the details, read the blob as part of his name, and wrote it in the record book as P-A-U-L-L."

"So from that day on, me and my brothers and sisters had two Ls in their name."

"My cousins all got one L."

I didn't tell Mr. Miller why my name had two *L*s.

I never showed Mr. Miller my special amber either. I knew it wouldn't interest him and probably would tell me rock collecting was for sissies.

I never raised my hand again and never asked Mr. Miller another question.

I did well to go through the whole school year without getting whacked around the head like Philip did almost every day for biting his nails or picking his nose or just for, well, being Philip. Mr. Miller didn't like Philip at all.

Philip got hit really hard one afternoon. Mr. Miller, hearing a loud snore during quiet reading time, caught him sleeping at the back of the class. He swiped Philip on the back of the neck, jolting his head onto the desk, bruising his forehead, and making him cry. Mr. Miller's behavior changed as he quickly tried to make it up to Philip. For the first time, he called Philip by his first name, using a softer-than-usual voice.

"Hey, Philip, you OK? That was an accident! Didn't mean to hurt you, laddie. You OK?"
"Philip?"

Philip, for a while, became Mr. Miller's pet. I think I—and everyone in class—figured out why.

We all knew Mr. Miller was being extra nice because he didn't want Philip to tell the headmaster or tell his parents what had happened.

Days for me, and for Mr. Miller too, I think—at school were excruciatingly boring and exceedingly long. Mr. Miller never showed my class of bored boys anything of interest that I can remember. Classwork was tedious work, repetitive work, and always *copy from the board in silence* work.

Every morning, I dipped my long pen into my grubby inkwell and copied pages and pages of writing and sums from the blackboard. To keep myself from falling asleep, I fiddled with my amber under my desk, squeezed, and I sent wishes from my *wishing rock,* dreamed dreams of Dad's stories about wild animals, birds, and interesting rocks and kept very quiet and out of trouble.

Roger, one of my best friends, said he was OK with learning from the board.
"I just read it a few times in my head, and it sticks there," he said. Well, I tried that, and it didn't work for me. I always remembered the details from good stories, especially about nature.

I needed to see and touch things.

John said it didn't matter to him. He knew everything he needed to know because he had a copy of the *Rinso Book of Knowledge.*

Who needed to go to school if you had that? It contained everything about everything anyone needed to know.

The following September, I moved into the top class, and Mr. Hitchens was my new teacher.

I was now ten years old, one of forty-five boys in Mr. Hitchens's classroom, the one room in the school that always smelled of pipe tobacco and the only one that overlooked the street.

Mr. Hitchens's job each day, he said on the first day of school, after he put out his pipe and laid it, still smoking, on his desk,

"My job is to prepare you for the scholarship—the test you have to pass to go to the grammar school. So work hard. If you work hard, you learn. If you learn, mark my words, you'll pass the scholarship."

"And that's good," he told us. *"Your future depends upon it."*

That meant a great deal to me as Dad had already told me many times that I had to pass the scholarship if I wanted to become a teacher.

"You want to be a teacher? Yes? Better than driving a bus, you know. Better than being a fisherman or digging tin underground under the sea. Well, you gotta work hard at school. You have to pass the scholarship, go to the grammar school, and then you can do what you like."

"I never had chance."

"You can be a teacher."

"Anyone can drive a bus . . ." His voice trailed off.

"When you're a teacher, people call you sir."

"They don't call me sir. That's 'cos I'm a bus driver."

"Teaching, it's a posh job, and people look up to you."

"And you get a pension when you finish. That's important."

"The only pension I'll get will be my old age pension, if I live that long."

Chapter 9

The thought of going to the grammar school filled three quarters of my mind up until something really bad happened at home.

On Saturdays, Mum shopped at Bailey's the Butchers for our Sunday roast, then she went to the Home and Colonial Grocery Shop for general household needs, and finally, Boase's for fruit and vegetables. Food was cheaper, though not as fresh, at the Cooperative Society, a small but busy shop at the bottom end of Market Jew Street. If money was short and she couldn't wait until Dad got his Friday pay packet, she'd shop at the Co-op.

Sometimes, after school, Mum would ask me to go and pick up groceries from the Home and Colonial. I liked going there because sometimes the shopkeeper would give me a free Penguin chocolate bar. Going shopping on my own was an adventure too, and I would run as fast as I could across Morrab Terrace, down the Arcade steps, and onto Market Jew Street. The Home and Colonial was a beautiful shop. Its big brass-plated window was set in a wall of green-and-black tiles. Mr. Wakfer, the manager, a small man with thinning hair, black mustache, and long white apron tied at the back, would take my mum's shopping list, gather what she wanted from the shelves, lick his yellow pencil, then cross off each item one by one as he placed everything in my big leather shopping bag.

"Mum'll pay you Friday, OK?"

With a knowing smile, he would always pack in an extra Penguin biscuit. *"You're a good boy, Johnny Paull. Eat this Penguin on the way home."*

"Oh, and say hello to your mum for me. All right, is she?' 'Ow's Arthur doin'? Still driving buses?"

After giving Mr. Wakfer a kid's shy smile back, I'd say, *"Thank you, Mr. Wakfer. Mum and Dad are fine, really fine."*

Then, holding the bag under my arm, I'd run up the thirty-two granite arcade steps at the side of Simpson's the Tailors, two, sometimes stretching my legs to three, steps at a time, to Bread Street, up to Morrab Place, and back home to Gwavas Street. I'd empty the shopping bag, then share my chocolate Penguin bar with Charles. Well, sometimes.

We didn't buy bread from the Home and Colonial though. It was too expensive. Bread came either from the Co-op down by the station or from Gendall's, the bread man. But there was a difference, not only in the price, but also in the quality. The Co-op sold Wonderloaf Bread. Wonderloaf Bread came in a plastic wrapping. It was white, sliced, thin, and tasteless. It wasn't good for making a sandwich or for spreading with marge and strawberry jam. Wonderloaf Bread was at its best when fried in bacon grease and added to the bacon and egg breakfast we had at the weekends.

Really good tasty bread was baked and sold by Mr. Gendall. His bread was always fresh, warm, and crusty. It was a teatime treat, especially when Mum cut a thick slice and covered it with yellow butter, not the tasteless yellowy white margarine, and topped it with a spoonful of thick yellow treacle. Yummy! Washing down a mouthful of bread, butter, and treacle with a hot cup of Brooke Bond tea, sitting in front of the fireplace, listening to the wireless, holding a *wishing rock*, was really special.

Even more special though were Saturdays when we had strawberry jam and Cornish cream on our Gendall's bread.

Mr. Gendall delivered his freshly baked bread in our street three times a week—Monday, Wednesday, and Saturday. As his black-and-yellow bread van would pull up in the middle of Gwavas Street, he'd toot his horn, and the front doors would fly open as the mothers came out of their houses to buy a loaf or two. And, perhaps, to buy half a dozen saffron buns.

One particular Saturday. when I was playing cricket in the street with Brian and Titch Thomas and Scocher Rowe, I saw Mr. Gendall's striped van turn at the top of the road. Knowing he'd soon park by the street lamppost outside Ma Smith's house, we ran indoors to tell our mums that the bread man was in the street.

My mum came out right away. She went over to the back of the van where Mr. Gendall, wearing his long brown dust jacket over his white shirt and tie, hair slicked with Brylcreem, was wrapping a couple of loaves for Mrs. Donnisthorne, our neighbor across the street.

When he'd finished serving Mrs. Donnisthorne, Mr. Gendall turned and looked at my mum.

His face tightened, and his smile disappeared. *"Hazel,"* he said grouchily, *"you owe me from last time—and the time before. Pay that off, please, now, otherwise no bread. Sorry. I have a business to run."*

Mum turned away, upset and embarrassed. The neighbors stared at her. They'd heard what Mr. Gendall had said. I could see her lips trembling. Starting to cry, she sobbed. *"Johnny, go in.* Now!*"*

I followed my mum inside the house, and as she slumped down on the kitchen chair, she wiped her eyes with her sleeve. I asked her what was wrong.

"Your dad's going to be mad," she said. *"There's only Co-op bread for tea. Can't have any Gendall's bread."*

She was right. At teatime that night, you could cut the atmosphere with a knife. Dad pushed his white plate to one side, refusing to eat his bread, jam, and Cornish cream.

"It's Co-op bread!" he said. *"You know I don't like Co-op bread. It's like cardboard. It ruins the cream. You know that."*
"Didn't Gendall come today?"

My mum looked at the floor and didn't answer. She was ashamed, and her eyes were full of guilt. She didn't want to tell him why we didn't have fresh bread for tea. We all knew how much Dad liked Gendall's bread.

Without another word, he left the table and sat on his chair, opening his Western library book. Mum quickly cleared away the table.

Mum and Dad didn't speak or look at each other all evening. I couldn't sleep when I went to bed and kept my brother awake, telling him about Mum crying in the street.

"Shut up, Johnny," I was told, *"and go to sleep. There's nothing we can do about it."*

I couldn't help it though. I couldn't get my mother's eyes full of tears out of my head. I lay awake for ages, holding my *wishing rock*, thinking about what I could do to raise the money my mum owed the baker. What could I do?

The next day, Sunday, after a silent, edgy breakfast (*Co-op* bread fried in bacon grease and topped with a fried egg), Dad stood up, put on his thick overcoat, and then took his double-barrel shotgun from the cupboard under the stairs. We knew what that meant. It was his day off from work, and even though it was a bitter-cold day, he was going hunting mallard duck in Bejowan Woods. He didn't, though, say what he usually said, *"See you, soon, Hazel. I'm off to check the traps, get a rabbit or two. Might even get a duck."*

Picking up a sack from the backyard shelf, Dad opened the back door, mounted his green Raleigh pushbike, and pedaled up the back lane.

He didn't wave. He didn't look behind him as he usually did.
I knew what that meant. It meant trouble. *Big* trouble. It meant Dad wanted to be out of the house, alone, in the woods, with his double-barrel shotgun.

As Dad cycled around the corner, Titch and Fatty came to the door. As soon as they saw my face, they knew something was wrong.

"Wos wrong with thee?" asked Fatty.
"Nothing. And I ain't playing out."

The next day at school, I kept thinking about my mum and the money she owed the bread man.

I couldn't concentrate on what Mr. Hitchens was teaching the class, and he became really angry with me when I did my sums wrong. *"Wassup, Paull? You're not listening to me. You on the moon?"*

"What's going on?"

Adding pounds, shillings, and pence didn't seem that important to me. All I could think about was the incident with the bread man, the tension between my mum and dad. I didn't want Mr. Hitchens to know what was really bothering me.

What could I do?

Then, an idea came to me. I knew what I could do.

I often ran errands after school for the old lady next door up. She was in a wheelchair and banged on the wall when she needed something. Every day I fetched what she needed from the corner shops. She always gave me a three-penny bit to buy a bag of Smith's crisps. I could, I thought, ask some of the other old people who lived in our street if they needed anything doing.

Perhaps, I thought, as I rubbed my amber and my favorite *wishing rock*, they'd give me a penny or two. Or even sixpence, if I was really lucky.

As soon as school finished, I went down to the end of Gwavas Street into Penlee Street and knocked on Mrs. Johns's bright blue door. I knew Mrs. Johns lived on her own and hadn't been well lately. I was sure she needed someone to fetch some shopping.

Mrs. Johns opened the door. A long tattered gray shawl covered her shoulders. She looked surprised when she saw me.

"What do you want, Johnny Paull?"

Hands in pockets, squeezing my amber, I looked up at her.

"Anything you want doing, Mrs. Johns?" I asked. *"Anything you want from Stone's corner shop?"*

Well, my timing was good.

"*What? You go fer me?*"

"*Get my stuff?*"

"*I really need some ciggies. Oh, and some Smith's crisps. One packet?*"

"*Get 'em for me, will you?*" "*There's a good boy! Five woodies is all I need. One of 'em small packs. I can't get out. I'm sick, you know.*"

She gave me a shiny half-crown. I ran up to the shop, bought Mrs. Johns's ciggies, a bag of crisps, and ran back to the blue door.

"*That was quick. Thank you, Johnny.*" Mrs. Johns gave me the change. Two pence. Hey! I'd started. How many more errands did I need to buy a loaf of bread and how many to pay off the money Mum owed?

Mmmm . . . I thought. I'd have to run to the corner shop a lot of times.

I was determined though, so I knocked on a few more doors.

By teatime, I'd been to the corner shop about five times, the Co-op twice, and Rowe's the Carriers once, and raised over two shillings—enough to go to Mr. Gendall's shop to buy a loaf today and another for tomorrow. As Mr. Gendall wrapped the bread, he told me to tell my mum that she needed to pay him what she owed by the end of the week. If she did, he would start delivering our bread again.

As I was giving my mum the loaf and telling her what I'd done, we heard Dad opening the back door.

His eyes widened when he saw the bread on the dining table. Mum looked at me and put her fingers to her lips.

"*Ah, good, Gendall's been then, today, hey?*"

Having a couple of slices of Gendall's bread and three slices of fried bacon put him in a much better mood.

After school, the following day, I went down to the Co-op and fetched a really heavy bag of potatoes for Mrs. Sloggett.

"*Oh, thank you, Johnny. Needed them spuds. Couldn't get them today—them knees,*" she said, pointing at her legs—"*them that knees are bad.*"

"Bring 'em inside, can you?"
"Just drop 'em in the kitchen."

Her house was just like ours and I knew exactly where to leave the
bag.

On my way out, Mrs. Sloggett gave me a bob. Helping her felt good,
and with a skip and a jump, I knocked on more doors and ran more and
more errands.

By Friday, Dad's payday, I'd raised over eight shillings. That evening,
Dad gave Mum the house money for the week. When he had gone upstairs
to change out of his uniform, Mum looked at me and, putting her fingers
to her lips, quietly said we'd go to Gendall's first thing in the morning and
pay off the debt. Mum looked at me for a long time and then gave me a
kiss.

Later that night, after I'd gone to bed, she told Dad what had happened
and what I'd done. Over breakfast the next day, he smiled at me, and a
tear dropped on his cheek as he gave me one of his special big, wide-eyed,
ear-to-ear grins.

"Here," he said, as he handed me an empty Old Holborn tin, *"this is
for you."*
"Stack some of your rocks in there."

I don't know why my mother owed so much.

I don't know why we couldn't afford to buy bread that particular
week.

It was never mentioned again, at least not in front of us three boys.
But the three of us did experience how much stress was created in a family
when money was short—and how the atmosphere in the house changed
drastically when there was tension between our mum and dad. It filled my
head at school, and I couldn't concentrate on the things I had to do.

However, it was great clearing my mum's debt with the bread man. With that big worry out of my head, I began to pay more attention again to what was going on in class.

Scholarship day, after all, was fast approaching, and I knew how important that was.

I knew because Dad kept telling me.

Chapter 10

On a particularly cold, windy, and wet January day, we took off our sopping wet wellies and left them on the thick brown mat outside the classroom door. The warm smell of tobacco gave way to the damp smell of sweaty and dirty socks. It was scholarship day.

"Put them boots, wellies, whatever you're wearing, in pairs," ordered Mr. Hitchens. *"Then come and move these desks. Come on."*
"No assembly for us today."

"Why we movin' us desks, sir?" asked one of the kids.
"So we couldn't see each other's work and cheat, twerp," said another. *"It's scholarship, 'member?"*

"That's right," said Mr. Hitchens. *"I'll rip up your paper if I see you as much look at anyone else's test."*
"Gotta be all your own work."

"And you, Stephens," he said, looking directly and smiling at John Stephens, *"put away your Rinso Book. If I see you open it and cheat, you're in trouble."*
"Big trouble."

John laughed, waved his *Rinso Book of Knowledge* in the air, then put it in his desk.

As we shuffled our desks, our nerves added to the tension. Even though the coal fire was lit, the room felt cold.

Mr. Hitchens, holding out a wooden tray, gave us our instructions.

"It's your big day. Scholarship day. This is important. No cheating. No copying."
"Turn out your pockets. Empty everything into this tray."

He passed the tray around the classroom. I deliberately disobeyed the instructions. I was not going to be parted from my precious Lariggan amber and my *wishing rock*.

Mr. Hitchens collected the tray and put it on one of the shelves and said,
"We're using pens. Not pencils."
"Everybody needs a blotter, so get some from my table. Quick."

"Good. Done that, everyone?"
"OK. Take the paper, put your names at the top, read the questions. Read them carefully." He looked at the big wall clock.
"OK. Start!"
"Oh, writing first. That'll take the longest. Then do the sums, OK?"
"Best of luck. C'mon. Do your best."

Martin, with a pained look on his face, put up his hand, closed three fingers, and immediately got Mr. Hitchens's attention.

"No, you can't go to the lav, Martin, you should have gone before."
"You'll have to wait."

"Can't, sir," said Martin. *"It's a number two. Gotta go bad."*
"Can't wait. It's coming out."
"OK, quick, quick. Take the lav paper, quick. Here. Two sheets. Take 'em."
"Martin, don't forget to put your wellies on. It's still wet outside."

When Martin came back from the outside lavatory, Mr. Hitchens checked the clock again.

"OK, Martin's back."
"No more questions."

As Mr. Hitchens handed out the papers, everything went deathly quiet. Everyone knew this was *the* day.

"OK . . . Start."

We opened the paper and read the instructions and started the test.

Forty-five pens dipped into forty-five inkwells and scratched the surfaces of the white sheets of paper.

Knowing for sure it was going to help me if I sent a big wish on this very important day, I touched the *treasure tin* of amber and a small *wishing rock* in my pocket.

I disobeyed instructions again and did the maths first.

I wanted to get the sums out of the way so I could really concentrate on the writing part of the exam.
The multiplication and division sums were easy.

Chewing the end of my wooden pen for a bit, I read that I had to write a story and underline the nouns, adjectives, verbs, and adverbs.

I wanted to write what was bursting inside my head. I wrote the title, *Feeling Happy and Feeling Sad.*

The first part of the story focused on my special birthday walk on the beach, searching for *wishing rocks* with my dad, the day I found my precious amber. I drew a picture of my face, smiling from ear to ear, and described how I felt when I first saw my amber.

Then, dipping my pen into the clay inkwell, I wrote about the day Mum couldn't pay our bread bill. Describing my emotions with adjectives and adverbs that really meant something to me helped clear much of the bad memory out of my head.

Then I underlined all the nouns, the adjectives, the verbs, and the adverbs.

After drying the ink with my blotting paper, I drew another picture of my face, sopping wet with tears.

Exactly an hour after we had started, we were told to put down our pens and hand in our papers, drink our milk, and go out to play.

Playtime was filled with raucous top-class boys shouting loudly, getting rid of their pent-up emotions.

"*That was dead 'ard,*" said one boy. "*Don't wanna go grammar, anyways.*"

"*Weren't,*" said Charles. "*Dead easy. My dad wants me to go to the grammar.*"

"*I bet I pass.*"

Mr. Hitchens filled up the rest of the morning with singing time and let us draw in the afternoon, saying,

"*Too late now to teach you anything new.*"
"*Scholarship's done and dusted.*"
"*Here, use the crayons, draw what you like.*"
"*Just be quiet.*"

The weeks went by painfully slowly as we waited for the scholarship results.

I *so* wanted to go to the grammar school because Dad said, again and again, that going to the grammar school was the first step on becoming a teacher.

If I passed the scholarship, I'd be the first one ever in my family. That, said Dad, would make him very, very proud.

I kept urging my amber and my very best *wishing rocks* to bring me luck.

"*C'mon, amber, c'mon wishing rock, you can do it.*"

One cold and cloudy day in February, the new headmaster, Mr. Paltridge, who had recently replaced Mr. Curnow when he retired, came into Mr. Hitchens's classroom just before playtime. Telling us to be quiet, he loudly called out four names.

"Rowe."
"Murley."
"Hawkins."

He paused.
"Paull. Paull with two Ls."

"You," Mr. Paltridge said.
"You lot passed. You passed the scholarship. You can go and tell your mothers. Now."
"The rest of you didn't."
Mr. Paltridge's voice trailed off.
He turned and left the room.
Thank you, thank you, *wishing rock.*

Dudley gasped with surprise.
"Me? Not me. Never. I don't want to go to the grammar."
"Mum can't afford the uniform. Won't have no blazer."

The other boys looked at the four of us. Some of them cheered. John Stevens threw down his *Rinso Book of Knowledge.* It didn't work for him.

"Anyone want this? For threepence?"

Stephen Palk, sitting near the front, started to cry, and then clasped his hands over his head. Stephen had wanted so much to pass the scholarship. It was all he talked about for weeks in the yard.
Poor Stephen.

The four of us cleared away our books, fetched our coats from the coat pegs in the corridor outside the classroom, and ran home to tell our mothers. Racing through the front door, I heard Mum upstairs, making the beds.

"Mum!" I shouted. *"I passed. I passed!"*
"And Dudley . . . Dudley passed too. And funny, he doesn't want to go to the grammar."

Mum knew right away what I meant and, her face beaming, came downstairs. *"You passed, Johnny?"* You passed? *Your Dad'll be pleased. Now you* will *be a teacher."*
"Who else passed? Did Stephen Palk pass?"
"Dudley passed? Roger, Roger Roach, did he pass?"

She put on her coat, and holding my hand, we flew across Alma Terrace, into Bread Street, down the Arcade steps, and into Grandfather's pub at the top of Queen Street.

Granddad was really pleased.
"Here," he said, handing me one of his Parker pens and a ten-shilling note.
"Spend this in Woolworths."

Within the hour, Grandmother Wilkes marched me up to Simpson's the Tailors, proudly told Mr. Simpson that I had passed the scholarship, and bought me a new school uniform. I then had my photograph taken at White's the Photographers.

"Right. Now let's go to Woolies, and you can spend the ten bob."

I bought two balsa wood model planes in Woolworths, something I had wanted ever since a boy at school brought one to school and played with it at playtime. One plane was for me and the other for Charles.

As we left Woolworths, a huge black thundercloud had moved across the sky, revealing the big and bright yellow sun. Life was so great, I thought. I'm going to the grammar, and in one hour's time, I was going to be flying my balsa wood plane.

In seven months' time, I was going to be attending Penzance Grammar School.

In seven months' time, I was going to be taking my first step on the right path to become a teacher.

Dad was tickled pink with the news.

"Proper job, Johnny, proper job."
"Now, Johnny, you can *be a teacher."*
"The first in the family."

The next day, the four of us who passed the scholarship were separated from the rest of the class and taken by Mr. Hitchens into the small staff room.

There was a small gas ring on the table that the teachers used for boiling the kettle when making tea. Mr. Hitchens told us to sit on the floor as he lit the gas. He carefully placed a pan half full of water on the top and told us to watch. We sat in silence and waited . . . Soon the water bubbled and boiled.

"That," said Mr. Hitchens, *"is science. You'll do science in the grammar school. Science is about watching and thinking and writing notes. Here, use these sheets of paper. Draw this experiment."*

In awed silence, we drew and recorded everything we saw. Because it was such a change from writing stories, putting in capital letters, underlining nouns and verbs, writing and drawing like a scientist was exciting, even though I couldn't quite understand why boiling a pan of water was science.
"Go on. Draw and write about the science experiment."
"We'll do this again next week, OK?"
So I thought, this was *science.*

When we finished, Mr. Hitchens turned off the gas, and we trooped smugly back to our classroom, ready to face the barrage of questions from the rest of the class during the morning break.

I couldn't wait to get home and tell Mum and Dad over tea about the science lesson.

"It's great. We did science. It's dead good. Really, really special."
"I'm going to do science in the grammar school."

Mum and Dad looked quizzically at each other.

"Mmmm," said Dad. *"That sounds great. Doesn't it, Mum? Boiling water. Great."*

"Here, Johnny," he said handing me a small cardboard box. *"This is for you."*

I opened the box and peeked inside.

I couldn't believe what I saw. I was staring at my very first wristwatch.

Lying at the bottom of the box was something I had wanted so much, a *Hopalong Cassidy* watch.

"That's for passing the scholarship. We're so proud of you."

Chapter 11

On the Friday before Coronation Week in June 1953, when Princess Elizabeth was to be crowned Queen Elizabeth II of England, Graham nicknamed Scotcher, Dudley's brother, asked me if I wanted to go potato picking. Farmer Matthews was looking for more kids to gather his early crop of potatoes in Gulval, a small village about two miles from my home. The pay was one shilling an hour. My brain went in to top gear: eight hours a day, for six days, the whole week. That, I worked out, would be two pounds, eight shillings for the week. Wow! Yes, please. That was a lot of dosh. Imagine, I thought, clutching my amber, what I'd do with all that money.

"You have to wear your wellies, Johnny. You got a proper pair, ain't you? We're working in the muddy field all day."
"I've been before. Spud picking's 'ard. 'urts your back. You'll see."
"Good dosh though."
"Oh, bring a sarney for grub, OK?"
"And some pop."

Mum and Dad agreed that I could try it out and see what I thought of spending all day bending and picking potatoes.
"Can't wear your Hopalong watch though," said Dad.
"Get earth in it, and it won't work."
"Leave it home, please."

As we had to be in Gulval by eight o'clock, Graham and Dudley, wearing their black wellies, knocked on my front door really early on Saturday morning.
"Ready? Got your sarney?"

"Great. Les go."

Whistling, we skipped down the back lane and turned on the main road toward Gulval. When we reached the farm, Graham took me to Farmer Matthews who was sitting and smoking a woodbine on his red tractor at the gate of the potato field. Mr. Matthews asked me my name.
"You Arthur's middle 'un?"
He knew my dad.
"Watch what Graham and Dudley do, OK?"
"Stay with them, all right, my cock?"
You do the same thing, Johnny, all right?"
"Today, Monday and Coronation Day, right?"
"School's closed for the week, then, isn't it?"
"Go over with the other kids and fetch yerself a few bags."
"Put your spuds in them. Put your snap in the barn."

The three of us picked up some sacks. At eight o'clock, the farmer started his tractor and started plowing, followed by about a dozen boys, all clutching their brown sacks. I quickly learned what to do—you see the potato, you bend over, pick it up, and throw it in your sack. And then you pick up another and another. When your sack is filled, you tie it at the top with some string and leave it in the field.

I soon learned that potato picking was not much fun. In fact, following the noisy, smelly tractor as it turned over the soft deep brown earth, bending over picking up potatoes, shaking off the coating of damp soil, not having time to look closely at the stones, the fat brown earthworms, bagging and leaving them for the farmer to collect later, was, as Graham said, backbreaking work.

At twelve noon, after four hours of work, we were more than ready for some rest and for something to eat. We sat in the sun on the top of a hayrick, ate our sandwiches, and washed them down with some pop. Work started again around one o'clock.

The day finished at four o'clock in the afternoon.
I arrived home at five o'clock, aching from head to toe, dirty, and absolutely exhausted. I wasn't sure if I could last all week.

When the three of us left for the farm on Tuesday morning, June 2, we saw Mrs. Donnisthorne hanging Union Jack flags outside her two front bedroom windows.

"Don't forget the party, Johnny," she shouted. *"It's in the street, St. Michael's. Your mum coming?"*

"Hey, Mrs. Donnisthorne," I replied. *"Yes, I think she's coming, not sure though, Granddad isn't very well. I'll be back in time though, I hope."*

"Hey, you two," I said, *"let's get back for the street party, OK?"*
"You bet, Johnny. Ain't missin' that," answered Graham.

As we bent our backs, filled our sacks with more and more potatoes, we so looked forward to the Coronation Party. We loved our new queen and wanted to be part of the street celebrations.

We left the farm just after four o'clock, anxious to get home, get washed, and join the fun. Walking as fast as our aching bodies allowed, we turned the corner into St. Michael's Street in record time.

We had missed the fun. The mums were taking down the tables and stacking the chairs. We'd missed the balloons, flags, the free pop, the singing, and the hot sausage rolls. Scotcher swore.

"Bloody 'ell!"

Ivan James, the young kid with glasses from three doors up, stared at us and shouted,

"You've missed it, Johnny. Where you been?"
"Been pickin' spuds, Johnny? You too, Scotcher?"
"Missed a great party. We've been singing and eating crisps, drinkin' Corona and stuff."
"And waving flags. Dead good fun."

"Never mind," said Mum. *"Here. Have these."*

Mum had saved me two sausage rolls that Mrs. Donnisthorne had made and a bottle of Mrs. Monkton's homemade ginger beer.

"Better have this first though."
"It's melting."
She handed me a Wall's chocolate ice cream bar.
Although the ice cream was melting and ran between my fingers, I wolfed it down.

It was some compensation for missing the street party.

After eight days of picking potatoes, my muscles were so tired. I felt very proud though, when I handed my pay packet to my mum. She counted out my earnings and, smiling, gave me back eight shillings.

"That enough?" she asked. *"You can have more, you know. And, Johnny, thank you."*

My potato-picking job lasted two more weekends, and I wasn't too unhappy when the last potato was picked and bagged.

Usually, when school closed for the summer holidays, July and August were the time for fishing on the pier, shell collecting around Battery Rocks, hunting for *wishing rocks* on Lariggan Beach, and chasing to Trevaillor Woods to hunt for spiders before playing Robin Hood games.

This year was different though. It was the most important year in my life.

In July, I was eleven, and I was soon going to the grammar school.

Even though I had my new school very much on my mind, I thought more and more about what I could do so the family wouldn't be shamed again. My brain was overloaded with worrying about money. Running errands for our neighbors was OK, but it took forever to raise the money my mum owed the bread man. Now that the early potatoes had all been picked, almost breaking my back in the process, I needed to do something else to raise some money.

It was time to grow up. No time anymore for kids' games. It *really* was time to grow up.

I needed a weekend job with regular pay. What else could I do? What exactly?

One early August Saturday, not so long after the bread man incident—which kept stinging my brain—an opportunity presented itself. My *wishing rock* had worked again.

The preadolescent phase of my life was about to change.

Chapter 12

It all started when I heard Doris, the tall milk lady with the very loud, shrilly voice, talking in the kitchen with Mum.

Doris was very well known in the neighborhood. She drove a noisy big dark-blue Morris J-Type van with an open back filled with crates full of milk bottles. Doris delivered milk, cream, eggs, and butter in the neighborhood. She came to Gwavas Street every morning, dropping off a one-pint bottle of fresh dairy milk on our granite doorstep. When Mum paid Doris her weekly milk bill on Saturdays, she made a pot of tea, then she and Doris swapped gossip before Doris drove down to Wherry Town.

I heard Doris tell Mum that Stewart, her boss, had added more deliveries on her milk round.

"I now gotta to go to Long Rock village," she said crossly, *"and deliver eight new streets."*
"I have enough to do as it is—don't want no more."
"Ain't gitting no younger."
"I need some help, 'Azul, don't you think?

My ears pricked up. There it was, the opportunity I was looking for. My *wishing rock* had worked again. Of course, I could be a milk lad.
I went into the kitchen.

"Doris," I asked appealingly, using my eyes as well as my voice, *"can I help you on the milk round?"*
"Please?"
"I have to get a job. I'm a good worker."

"Ain't I, Mum?"

Surprised, she looked at me and then at Mum. *"Course you can. Can 'e, 'Azul?"*
Doris smiled.

"Have to get up early though, you know, Johnny. About five o'clock in the morning is when I load up and then start delivering. I can pick you up, around six o'clock, I think, when I get to Gwavas Street."

"Could get you home again at around eight o'clock."
"I need help every day though. Not just weekends. Fancy being a milk lad before school?"
"Up early? Every day?"
"Can you do that? Your old man be OK with that?"

Doris looked at my mum.
"Will Arthur let him, 'Azul?"

Doris laughed out loud, and I knew then that she wasn't taking me seriously.

"Hey, I can do it. I can, you know."
"Mum, tell her, I can, you know."

"We'll see," said Mum, somewhat thrown by the conversation.
"Better ask your dad when he gets home tonight."

Squeezing my *wishing rock* and my amber in my pocket throughout the day, I asked Dad over teatime, just as he was lighting his cigarette. He exhaled the perfect smoke ring, licked his lips, thought for a bit, and then, with a serious look in his eye, looked at me.

"If you think you can do it, do it. A milk lad. Mmmmmmm."
"Try it for a week, and let's see how it goes."
"School starts soon though, and you will have plenty to do then."
"Homework, school, come first, don't forget."
"Try it, delivering milk, for the week."
"See what you think then."

And so, with no counterargument at all from either Mum or Dad, at eleven years of age, I became a milk lad, working with Doris, the milk lady.

Thank you, *wishing rock*. You've done it again, I thought.

I went to bed early on Sunday, telling Jimmie not to wake me up when he came to bed.
Mum switched on my bedroom light around five in the morning, and I quickly put on my clothes, had some tea, and waited for Doris to arrive. I was ready and as nervous as three kittens.

In the pitch dark, we delivered half and full-pint bottles around the streets of Penzance, and around seven o'clock, we sat and watched the sunrise beyond Penzance harbor as Doris sucked on her first Player's cigarette of the day.

We finished delivering milk around eleven o'clock, cleaned out the van, and I got home just in time for a midday feast of bread, marge, and treacle.

Over the next four days, I soon learned how much milk and what extras (cream, butter, eggs) our customers around the town wanted—a half pint there, two pints here, a pound of butter for the Donnisthornes on Wednesday, six eggs on Thursday for the Rowes, a quart of Cornish cream on a Friday for Mrs. Johns.

Friday, I learned, was payday for those who worked. Saturday, predictably then, was *pay-yer-milk* bill day. That meant an entirely different routine. After delivering the milk first thing in the morning, we went back to those houses that didn't leave their money out on the doorstep.

I didn't like this routine as much as weekdays because I didn't want to be seen by anyone I knew.
When that happened, I felt uncomfortable, even a touch ashamed, to be seen delivering milk, thinking I'd get teased.

Even though I had no reason to think that people lived so differently from the Paull family in 23 Gwavas Street or any of our neighbors, I discovered on my first milk-lad Saturday, they did. People lived very differently—a lesson about life that would later have bearing on my teaching.

I was fascinated and in awe of the opulence and grandeur my eleven-year-old eyes saw in some homes, especially the big three-story houses on Clarence Street and Morrab Road.

Equally, I was taken aback when I saw the inside of some of the overcrowded and dingy little houses near the harbor at the bottom of Queen Street.

Doris, I think on purpose, sent me into one small cottage in particular to collect the week's milk money.

"You can go in that 'ouse. I don't like it. You go in, Johnny."
"Half a pint every other day. 'Cept Sundays. That's all she has."
"Just knock, then go in."
"She'll be there, and she'll give you the right money."
"No change."
"Pick up the empties."
"They're sticky and greasy, mind you."
"She doesn't wash out her bottles."

I knocked on the door and, following Doris's advice, pushed it wide open. I stumbled in the dark and almost fell over the bags and boxes of rubbish inside the hallway. The front room was dark and smelly. Threadbare sacking covered the windows.

A lighted candle flickered on a small table, giving just enough light for me to see an old lady, half covered in a blanket, sitting in the corner by the fireplace. Her straggly gray hair and deeply lined face were covered with a thin veil. There were white-and-gray cobwebs hanging above her head.

She was wearing long white gloves. Her long nails were poking through the fingertips.

Without looking up, she held out one of her hands and growled.

"Where's Doris? Who are you?"
I was speechless.
"Milkman," she said, *"you the milkman? 'ere's the money. Teck it. Just teck it."*

"Then go."
"Don't you look at me."
"You hear me?"
"Stay away, don't get close, you hear?"

Without a word and not looking her in the eye, I took the money out of her hand.

Her voice crackled. *"Teck yer money. Go!"*

I forgot to pick up the three dirty milk bottles that were lying near her feet.

Doris, cigarette dangling from her mouth, was waiting for me in the van.

"Well?" she asked with a knowing smile.
"You OK? Got 'er money? And the bottles?"
"See 'er? Was she by the window? In 'er chair?"
"Faces the sea front, you know."
"See all the spiders dangling in their webs?"
"Big buggers, ain't they?"

Doris continued. *"That old lady lost her 'usband at sea, off the Lizard. She ain't moved a thing in that 'ouse since!"*
"Put on her wedding dress and she ain't moved since!"
"Told me she's waitin' for 'er 'usband to come out of the sea."

I had never seen or heard of anything like that before. Who looks after the scary old lady? I wondered.
Who gives her tea and dinner? How long is she going to wait for her husband?

"OK, Johnny Paull, now go to that 'ouse over there," said Doris, pointing to a creamy white door.
"They owe quite a bit. See if there's any money on the kitchen table."
"Empties. This time, don't forget the empties."

The door was half-open, and not knowing now what to expect, I shouted, *"Milkman!"*

I went straight in, intending to drop the milk bottle on the kitchen table where Doris said I should find our money.

Four little boys, two of them naked, were screaming loudly, in front of the open fire. A boy about my age was standing in the kitchen, trying to put food on some plates. He turned and shouted at me.
"Money's there, milkman."

Then,
"Hey, Johnny, that you? Johnny Paull? You OK?"
"Din't know you were a milk lad."

I couldn't believe my eyes. It was Philip, Philip Washer, from St. Paul's school.

"These are my brothers," said Philip.
"Keith, here, he's the oldest. He's five. Five and a bit."
"Jack's four. Tom and Pete are twins."
"They're buggers when they want to eat."
"You brought their milk?"

I handed over the bottles.

"Good, Let's 'av 'em 'ere."
"Then they'll have their cornflakes."
"Ma's out."
"She'll pay you next time."

When I told Doris I knew Philip, she told me that his dad went to look for a job over a year ago, and no one had seen him since.

"Mum's on the social, you know."
"Goes out early in the mornin' see wot she can find."
"Philip's bringin' up those kids."
"Her," she said, *"Go and leave him some free cream."*
"Kids'll like it."
"I allus," Doris said, *"leave a bit extra if his ma's not in."*
"Philip's a dead good kid."

It was no wonder, I thought, that Philip fell asleep that day in Mr. Miller's class. He must have been exhausted with so much to do at home.

I knew now why some boys at St. Paul's Junior School were so badly clothed, some without socks, and often hungry when they got to school. They, like Philip, were poor.

I knew now why Dad worked so hard every hour so he could give his family what they needed.

When we finished the morning rounds, we unloaded our empties. Doris filled a bucket with hot soapy water and scrubbed the inside of the van and left it ready for the following day. After we counted and checked the money, Doris gave me three one-pound notes and one ten shillings note, my first pay. Ten bob a day.

When I got home, around half past one, I was so excited. *"Hey, look, see how much I got."*

I gave it all to Mum then told her about the poor old lady, sitting all alone in the dirty house.

"And I saw a kid I know from school. Philip Washer. He looks after all the kids."

Mum listened as I told her about all the different houses I had seen. Then she smiled.

"Don't worry. Here, take this," she said and gave me back the ten-shilling note.

The kettle began to boil.

"Here. Drink your tea and eat up." She handed me my plate covered with baked beans sitting on top of a slice of Gendall's bread, covered with margarine.

I finished my beans and gulped down my second cup of hot tea quickly. As Mum cleared away my plate, I ran to Stone's corner shop to buy two bags of Smith's crisps—one for me and one for Philip—and a bottle of Corona. I then ran up the street to see John Stevens and bought his *Rinso Book of Knowledge. Can use that in the grammar*, I thought.

Finally, I went to the newsagents and bought my first ever copy of *The Eagle*, a weekly comic that described the adventures of Dan Dare and his rocket trip to Mars and other planets.

I ate the crisps on my bed, looking through *The Eagle*, then my *Rinso Book of Knowledge*. It had everything in it that I wanted to know. It even had colored pictures of different kinds of spiders. I wondered if any of them were the same as I saw in that old lady's house.

I put five shillings in an old battered OXO tin that I hid under the bed and put the remaining three shillings and sixpence in my pocket, next to my amber.

Sunday, I learned, was a different milk delivery routine again. Dads didn't go to work on Sundays, and families had breakfast together. I could smell the fried bread, bacon, and eggs as I collected empties and put down milk, butter, and clotted cream on the granite doorsteps around Penzance and Treneere Estate.

When we reached the old lady's cottage, I took in the half pint and put it next to her.

"Milk boy? That you?"
"Put it there."
"Teck empties. You left 'em yesday."

"Hello," I said. *"I know. Sorry."*
"Forgot."
I looked at her, and asked,

"You OK today?"

I handed her a *wishing rock* and a note I'd written that said, *"Let me know if there's anything I can get for you."*

Before she could say a word, I left.
The next stop was Philip's house. I left the milk and the bag of crisps I'd bought for him on his doorstep.

The following Saturday, the old lady gave me two letters.

"'Ere. Post these, will yer?"

This was the start of another Saturday routine until the day she was taken to hospital, never to return.

Chapter 13

After seven long months of waiting, it was time, at last, to start wearing my new school uniform and attend my new school. It was time to learn what I needed to learn.

I got home early from the milk round, had a fried bacon sandwich, put on my new gray shirt, my new gray short trousers, brown braces, black-and-red striped tie, and red blazer. I checked my Hopalong Cassidy watch, slipped my leather satchel over my shoulder, adjusted my school cap, and pocketed my precious amber and a *wishing rock*. I picked up my Parker pen, my *Rinso Book of Knowledge*, and skipped toward Dudley Rowe's front door.

Mum had told me that Dudley's father was now bedbound with a terminal illness, so I looked through the front bay window to see if I could spot Dudley.

Dudley came to the door holding a folded paper shopping bag under his arm. He wasn't wearing a new uniform like me and didn't have a satchel. I could see the worn patch on the elbow of his oversized red blazer.

Dudley looked at me. *"You got a satchel, Johnny? I ain't."*

"Got me Dad's old school coat. Like it?"

"Fits OK, doesn't it?"

"He went to the grammar, you know."

"Ain't got a fountain pen either, though my aunt said she'd get me one soon."

"Think I'll get into trouble?"

Then, he asked,

"You delivered milk this morning? What time you get up? Ain't you tired?"

"Nope," I said. *"I'm great. Got up, you know, usual time."*

We walked up the hill to the recreation ground, across Tolver Road, and joined the other new boys waiting quietly in the school yard next to the big sign which read,

NEW BOYS HERE

Pulling and stretching their throats to make funny, squeaky voices, two boys pointed at Dudley and me.

"You our milk boy? Don't you deliver our milk?" Then, with a mocking posh voice, *"Did I not see you yesterday?"*

"You with the paper bag. You broke or something? No satchel?"

"Don't you wear socks? Ha-ha. You gotta hole in your blazer! Got no money, spastic?"

"Dun't yer ol' man work?"

Well, my dad did work. He worked hard every hour he could, driving double-decker buses for two shillings an hour. Dudley's mother scrubbed granite doorsteps at sixpence a time. Dudley's father was dying. I delivered milk every day before most kids got out of bed.

We did our best to not show the other kids that their words hurt. The words did get under my skin though, and I wished and wished that my dad wasn't a bus driver. Dudley wished he didn't have to go to school. Dudley wished he had socks and a school cap and a satchel. I wished I didn't have to go to the grammar school. It didn't feel as if I belonged there.

The antagonism stopped when Mr. Wightman, one of the senior masters, blew his whistle and called out the names of the boys in Class 1A, then 1B, and finally, 1C. Our names were in the last list to be called. We were in the bottom class of the three-form entry. 1A and 1B, of course, were for the boys from the preparatory schools.

1C was told to go in first, led by the teacher, Mr. Hogg, and I began my very first day at the grammar school. Because the taunting words rang loud in my head, I couldn't concentrate throughout the morning classes.

When Dad, home because he was on the late shift, asked me over lunch how my first morning went, I couldn't stop myself. I told him and Mum what had happened and how everyone teased Dudley and me before school started. He wasn't very pleased.

"What class are you in?"

I told him that we were in 1C.
"It's the bottom class, Dad."
"I'm not smart enough to be in the top class."
"St. Paul's kids go into the C class."
"'Cos we didn't do French and stuff at school."
"At least I won't be with them kids that teased us."

Looking first at me and then at Mum, Dad said sternly,

"Bottom class?"
"Then you'll have to work damn hard and get to the top class."
"Wanna be a teacher, don't you?"
"You show 'em. Show 'em St. Paul's was a school for smart kids too, you know."
"Now, get off. Don't be late."

Dudley didn't go back to school in the afternoon because his dad had taken a turn for the worse.

I went to bed right after tea. I was tired and worn out from worrying the aggravating behavior of some boys. Would it be like this every day, I thought?

Doris was very inquisitive the next morning when she picked me up in her milk van.
"Ow'd it go? Like it, you know, your new school?"

"Yes, Doris, it's great," I lied. *"Really, fab. Brill,"* I replied.

We delivered milk around Penzance until Doris dropped me off at home.

"Enjoy school today, Johnny."

I changed my clothes, wolfed down my breakfast, and got ready for school.

Life took on a new routine. I was awakened each morning very early by my mum, had a bacon sandwich, went on the milk round, came home, had a cup of tea, changed, and went to school with Dudley. I walked home with Dudley for lunch every day and walked back to school every afternoon.

Each school day started with Mr. Hogg, nicknamed Boris by all the class, ticking our names in the morning register, collecting the dinner money, then telling us to walk like young gentlemen up the stairs for mathematics with Mr. Guard. That was followed by English language and English literature, with Mr. Batten, then history with Mr. Pascoe, and French with Mr. Tregenza.

Twice a week we had science lessons with Mr. Waller, geography with Pop Wightman, and worst of all, I thought, Latin. I couldn't figure out why I had to learn Latin. Speaking French was hard enough, but Latin was all Greek to me. As far as I could work out, no one in the whole world spoke Latin.

I took my precious amber—and my favorite *wishing rock*—in an OXO tin in my pocket to the grammar school the first week, thinking I might show it to my form teacher or my science teacher. I rubbed my *wishing rock* and wished big wishes about being successful. It didn't have much effect though, because the classwork, mainly reading and writing, was boring. Not one teacher read or told us a story.

Homework, set every Monday, Tuesday, Wednesday, and Thursday, was even more boring as it was, more often than not, copying out in my best handwriting what I'd already copied from the board. My *Rinso Book of Knowledge* helped though and often gave me the information I needed to answer some of the homework questions in geography, science, and English history. Doing homework each night became an issue for me—not always the content, although I needed to know more than the *Rinso* book could help me with, but more on finding space to study quietly at home. Our house was small, and I had nowhere except the bed to spread out my books, where six-year-old Charles came to play when it was cold or wet outside.

The only way to do my homework was to go to the library at the top of Morrab Road after school, and when I had a lot to do, I'd finish it upstairs in bed, right after tea, before Charles came upstairs. Going to the library though turned out to be a good idea because, not only was it quiet, but I could use the books to help me answer my homework questions.

They were bigger and had more detail than my *Rinso Book of Knowledge.*

On Friday afternoon, when I got home from school, Mum gave me a big brown paper bag that was taped at the top.

"Here," she said, *"before you start your tea. Go and give this to Dudley. It's his birthday tomorrow, isn't it?"*
"It's a satchel."
"Your dad got it from someone at work. His kid doesn't need it anymore."

Smiling, I ran over to Dudley's house, knocked on the door, and gave the bag to Dudley.

"Look inside, Dudley. It's a prezzie from my mum and dad."

Dudley hugged the leather satchel close to his chest.
"They ain't got no reason to tease me now, 'av they, Johnny? Wait 'til I show my ma."
"Hey, my Dad's bad though. Getting worse."
"Dr. Young's coming again soon."
"He might have to go to hospital."
"Gotta go and help my ma."
"Tell your mum thanks."

Dudley's father passed away that evening.

Chapter 14

Even though I stroked my *wishing rock* during break time and wished and wished that something special would happen at school, for the first time, the *wishing rock* didn't work.

In my fourth week at school, Mr. Behenna, the music teacher, caught me fiddling with my OXO tin under my desk when I should have been listening to him. I wasn't listening to him because I was bored.

"What's going on, Paull? What are you playing with?"
I was caught, fair and square. And I told a whopping big lie.
"Nothing, sir, just an old button," I replied.

"Show me," he asked.

I showed him my OXO tin, but he didn't ask to see what was inside, assuming, I suppose, that it contained a button. *Phew*, I thought, *that could have been bad*. Mr. Behenna told me that if he ever saw me playing with anything again, he would take it away from me. I took that threat very seriously and kept my OXO tin in my satchel and never stroked my amber or my favorite *wishing rock* in his class.

At the end of the first year, after all the class tests were marked, I was placed sixth in class. I moved from 1C to 2B at the beginning of my second year, just as Jimmie was leaving school, having secured a job as farm laborer at Tredavo Farm.

At the end of my second year in the grammar school, I was second in class and moved at the start of my third year, from 2B to 3A, and now worked alongside the high-flyers and the *posh* kids.

In the first week of October in my third year at the grammar school, Russia launched the first satellite, *Sputnik.* Sitting and listening to the crackling wireless and hearing the *beep, beep, beep* from *Sputnik* was electrifying. Dad couldn't believe what was happening.

"It's up there somewhere," he said, pointing to the night sky. *"That's amazing. Just see what science can do. Great. Bet someday Dan Dare will come true . . . you know, that Eagle comic stuff you read."*

Before I went to bed, I drew a picture of what I thought *Sputnik* looked like.

Doris too talked about nothing else the following morning as we drove around the dark streets.

"Ruskies are going to make a rocket, you know, and fly a man up there," she said, looking up at the starlit sky.

I was disappointed though, when it wasn't mentioned at school during the science lesson. I wanted to know more and did raise my hand to ask about *Sputnik* but was told curtly to get on with my work.

From 3A, I moved to 4A, taking the Oxford Board of Education Ordinary Level Examinations a year early and passing English language, human biology, and art. In 5A, I passed English literature, mathematics, biology, chemistry, physics, and history. I failed miserably at French and Latin. There was a consequence to that—it meant I wouldn't be able to apply to university for an academic degree.

My resolve to be a teacher was strengthened, though, one particular day when I was not paying attention in Mr. Rising's Latin class.

"Paull, wake up," he shouted across the classroom.
"Pay attention. Are you playing with that silly rock again?"

"You need Latin, you know."

When I told him I was hoping to go to a teacher's college, Mr. Rising looked at me and snapped.

"Heaven help us if the next generation of kids have teachers like you."

Everyone jeered.

It was then, at the age of fifteen, the age one could leave school and go to work, that Dudley, and many other of my friends, left school to find full-time employment so they could help pay the family bills. Because I was going to be a teacher (and therefore earn a really good retirement pension), Dad said that if I continued working and earning money on the milk round, I could stay on at school.

As important to me though was that I was given my first pair of long trousers and my own snake belt, which meant no more short pants, no more black braces. Soon, I thought, I'll be shaving.

I entered the sixth form, studying advanced level physics, chemistry, and biology.

Two years later, just after my seventeenth birthday, the careers master, knowing I so wanted to be a teacher, recommended that I apply to the City of Leicester University College of Education.

"No one's been there from our school before, Paull. It's a brand new college."
"Go and show them what a Cornish lad can do."

Following the family expectation that I was going to be a teacher and taking the teacher's advice, I applied to the college, was eventually interviewed in Leicester, and offered a college place.

It was a sad fact that, in the seven years I attended the grammar school, I had never met another Mr. Jones. I never had another shared precious *amber* moment. I know now I should have raised my hand more often, I should have asked more questions, and I should have concentrated more and been a better student.

However, I had done enough, it appeared, to be on my way to becoming a teacher.

Chapter 15

In September 1960, I began my three-year-long college career in Leicester, an industrial city way up in the Midlands, far, far away from Penzance.

I looked forward to this new phase of my life, now stepping out on my own, with my amber and *wishing rock* in an OXO tin in my pocket, ready to live for the first time away from the family.

Of course, I had no idea then how fortunate I was, not knowing that Leicester was becoming the focal point of *progressive* education and that I was lucky enough to be going there at the beginning of my teaching career.

Most important of all though, after years of sharing a small bed and delivering milk every morning before going to school, I would be catching up with my sleep.

When the bank check with my first installment of my college grant came in the morning post, I went with Mum to open a bank account in Lloyds Bank. This was a very special moment. I felt very proud to be the first one ever in the immediate family to have money deposited in a bank.

Breakfast, three days later, was a somber and emotional time. As I tucked into fried bread, eggs, and bacon, Charles, Mum, and Dad hardly said a word.

"It's going to be funny here without you," said Charles. *"You'll write though, and tell us what it's like, won't you?"*
"Bet college will be great. You're dead lucky."
"I'm going to go, you know, now that I'm at the grammar school."
"You see if I don't."

When Mum began to clear away the table, I went upstairs to put on my new charcoal suit, white shirt, and tie. I made sure my best OXO tin, containing my amber and my favorite *wishing rock*, was tucked away in my pocket. As I was getting ready, Jimmie, on his way to work, came by to wish me well, saying loud enough for Dad to hear,

"Don't get posh and come home with big ideas, OK?"
"Plenty of them around. Don't want anymore, OK?"
"Leavin' all them tins here? Under the bed?"

"Sure, Jick," I said. *"Not all of them. Don't worry."*
"Hey, hands off my tins though. Leave them be. They're not for you."

Dad helped me carry my big suitcase, full of winter clothes, and of course, a bag of empty OXO tins, down to the railway station. Charles helped me find an empty compartment. I put the suitcase and sandwiches in the overhead luggage rack and looked through the window. I could see tears running down my mum's face as she and Charles waved me good-bye. My father looked down at his shoes, put up his hand over his head, and then waved before striding across the yard to the bus station. For a moment, I wanted to get out of the train and go back home.

Later that evening, after a long nine-hour journey, changing trains at Birmingham Central Station, I arrived at Leicester Railway Station.

I eventually made it to the Coppice Hall of Residence, rang the front doorbell, and was met by the warden, Mr. Sharp, and his wife.
Mrs. Sharp showed me to my room. *"You're sharing with two other students, OK? They came this afternoon."*

As I unpacked, exhausted and feeling very nervous, I discovered an envelope, full of postage stamps and a note: *Don't forget to write. Be good. Mum.*

When everything was packed away, I joined the other new students for dinner and was officially welcomed to the college.

I sat with Doug Ellis and Graham Garner, who were sharing a room with me. Doug was from Peterborough, and Graham was from Stoke-on-Trent. They both had odd accents, and I was surprised when they said I talked too fast and *"spoke funny."*

Huh! It was they who *"spoke funny—well, posh."*

Doug's father, I learned, owned a large garage and had given Doug a sports car as a gift for getting into college. Graham's dad was a hairdresser, and he, said Graham with a giggle, had given him a shorter than usual haircut the day before he came to Leicester! I told them my dad smoked a lot and had given me an empty tobacco tin and then showed them what I kept in my collection of tins. They were both curious about the amber and wanted to know where and when I'd found it.

Doug was looking forward to studying English language and English literature and wanted to be a secondary school teacher. Graham was all set to become a history and geography teacher.

I was intent on becoming a science teacher.

 I was wide-awake at four o'clock the next morning, thanks to my years working on the milk round. I dressed and made my way out of the room to the kitchen area at the bottom of the corridor. I opened the fridge and took the milk, found the tea and three cups, quickly boiled the kettle, made a pot of tea, and carried it to the bedroom.

As I opened the door, it creaked loudly and woke Graham.

Rather grumpily, he asked, *"For Christ's sake. What you doing up at this bloody time?"*

Doug turned over in his bed, opened his eyes, looked at me, and asked what was going on.

I made each of them a cup of tea, and as they rubbed their eyes and checked their watches, I told them about my job as a milk boy. When I finished, we agreed that it would be a good idea if I moved my bed very close to the door, as far away from their beds as possible. *"Then,"* said Doug, *"you can go for a walk and leave us in peace."*

We began classes on the main campus the following Monday. My schedule was straightforward: three days a week, I studied physical science and biology and the history of education for the other two.

Chapter 16

The education classes were really interesting, far more, to my surprise, so than the physics and the biology classes that were based on reading from textbooks, group discussion, then regurgitating the notes in a science journal.

Talking objectively about education, a process I had been a subjective part of for years, was fascinating. I learned, for example, that significant education reform was under way in some parts of England. Some education authorities, led by Leicestershire, Oxfordshire, and the West Riding, had, at last, abolished the insidious testing system, the "scholarship," which as I well knew, all pupils (except those in private schools) in England took at the age of eleven as they completed their primary school education. A small percentage (including me and Charles) went to a grammar school that prepared them for higher education (colleges of education, universities), and the vast majority (including Jimmie) went to a secondary modern school that, it was said, prepared them for nothing.

Some British educators were now agreeing that the *11 plus* was not an appropriate prediction of a young child's future and thus a dreadful waste of talent.

School authorities, such as Leicestershire, created comprehensive high schools, a move supported by Prime Minister Harold Wilson for all children when they left primary schools, whatever their academic ability.

Miss Whitworth, the vice principal and my college education instructor, described what was taking place in some Leicestershire schools that college used as bases for student teaching.

"The Leicestershire method," "the integrated day," and "vertical grouping," were phrases, she said that *"referred to an innovative approach to junior school teaching."*

"The restructuring of the curriculum and the teaching-learning setting was first worked out by a number of infant schools."

"Many teachers," said Miss Whitworth, *"are attracted to the ideas of educational thinkers like Montessori, Isaacs, Dewey, and Piaget. Jean Piaget's work was proving particular practical in the area of school mathematics and was shaping the direction of educational innovation. Some of Piaget's assumptions included the notion that primary school children can't just be told things, that they learn basic concepts in mathematics slowly. They learn mathematics best through a variety of rich practical activity."*

Mmmm . . . that made sense to me, I thought.

Miss Whitworth told us that changing the classroom-teaching model appealed to head teachers, she said. Pupils appeared to be more motivated about learning and appeared to learn more. Parents, Miss Whitworth said with a twinkle in her eye, liked that very much.

Discussions about the inflexible primary school curriculum and undesirable social side effects among those who failed brought back memories for many of the college students. As we shared our experiences, I remembered the day in Mr. Hitchens's class when I took the *11 plus*.

I told the class how upset many of my classmates—especially Stephen Palk—were when they failed the test, knowing they were virtually excluded from a secondary education that would qualify them for eventual college or university entrance. I also told them about Dudley who didn't want to go because of the snobbery element. Getting rid of that system seemed a good idea to me.

On Thursdays, we visited a variety of schools. I enjoyed the opportunities to see what was going on in real classrooms and then coming back to college for class discussion. When I could match experience with texts and discussions, I could make better sense of it all.

The first primary school I went to visit was so different from what I remembered about St. Paul's Junior School. I sat in the back of the classroom for the whole morning. The children sat in groups around circular tables, not in rows of desks. There was a table standing square in the middle of the room. Resting on a sheet of back paper was a bird's egg, some tree leaves and two rocks.

Written on a large white card were these words:

OUR NATURE TABLE

CAN YOU FIND OUT WHAT THESE ARE?

USE OUR BOOKS OF KNOWLEDGE ON THE BOOKSHELF.

The teacher talked about the bird's egg and the tree leaves, reminding me of Mr. Jones and those wonderful Wednesday afternoons at St. Paul's Junior School.

"Right," he said, *"this morning, there's maths, writing, and science on the nature table."*
"Off you go."

The children fetched their resources, sat in groups of four, and began working—writing, doing their maths, drawing, and researching the objects in books.
The teacher moved around the room, sitting and helping individual children.

I couldn't wait to get back to college to tell everyone what I had seen.

Like me, some of the student teachers were quite surprised by actually observing firsthand the fundamental changes in the teaching style that encouraged children to work together in small groups to learn basic mathematics, for example, using mathematical resources. Kids, it appeared to all of us, seemed really content and enjoying what they were doing.

The tone of the lively discussion was best summed up when someone said loudly,

"This new way works."
"Kids behaved themselves even when not sitting up straight in their chairs, in rows—it was great."
"Liked the idea of group work and sitting around tables."
"The kids I saw were really doing some really difficult maths problems."
"Working together, with plenty of equipment, it seemed to work."

"Helped them understand mathematical stuff."

Chapter 17

When college closed for Christmas holidays, I took the train back to Penzance, excited to be able to share my college experiences with my family. Over a Cornish pasty tea, I used my new posh, *teacher* voice, of course, just to tease and aggravate Jimmie.

As I talked, I realized how lucky I was to be away, becoming familiar with city life, expanding my somewhat narrow life experiences.

Dad asked,

"So do you like it? Is it good being a teacher?"

"Well," I replied, *"I haven't actually done any real teaching yet. Just talked about it, really. Sounds good though. And I've visited a few schools, and that was fun."*
"I like being at college, though, and meeting lads from other parts of England."
"They all think my accent is, well, quaint, one person called it."

I returned to college in early January.
Halfway through the second term, I experienced my first teaching practice in Great Glen Primary School.

The teaching practice lasted three weeks. I loved every minute of it. From my first day, I was fascinated by how easy the teacher, Mr. Turner, made it look. I was intrigued by the way he set up his classroom and organized the children into small groups. I felt honored when he included me as a co-teacher when he felt it appropriate.

One playtime, Mr. Turner asked me if I knew anything about fossils. This was my moment. I took my OXO tin from my pocket, opened it, and held my amber in my hand. I was taken aback at his reaction.
"Show the kids. They'll love it."

Really? I thought. *What do I tell them?*

When playtime ended, I stood as tall as I could in front of the class and nervously showed the children my OXO tin. Slowly opening it, I talked about my fifth birthday when I combed the beach with my father. The story appeared to fascinate the children. When I'd finished speaking, their questions came thick and fast.

"You found that?"
"What's the tin?"
"What is it?"
"Where did you find it?"
"How much is amber worth?"
"Did your mum and dad take you walking every weekend?"

When I ran out of steam, Mr. Turner stepped in, winked at me, and showed an ammonite to the class, told everyone where he'd found it, and then placed it on the nature table.

"OK," he said, as he began to write on the blackboard.
"Take out your writing books. I want you to draw and write about Mr. Paull's amber—and my ammonite. See what you can find out about them from our reference books."
As I sat and helped some of the children with the assignment, I couldn't help thinking that teaching was a wonderful job. And so easy—especially if you told the kids a story.

Well, perhaps not every minute, because one episode turned out to be far from easy and really embarrassed me, although it was an episode that did teach me a valuable lesson about teaching.

Knowing that Mr. Kitson, one of my college instructors, was coming to observe me in the classroom setting, Mr. Turner suggested I showed the kids how tea is grown and harvested.

"Use the projector," he said. *"Show the kids a film loop. I've got a good one about tea."*
"That'll impress the college fella."
"Take the kids to the church hall," he said.
"They've got chairs and stuff there, and you can black out the windows."
"It's not far from here."

What a great idea, I thought. Mr. Kitson will be so impressed. I'll take the whole class, on my own, and use black-and-white pictures projected onto a white wall. *That's being pretty progressive,* I thought.

When Mr. Kitson arrived at school, I had already packed the loop projector in a bag and told the pupils to choose a partner. We walked on the pavement down the village main street to the church hall. The children sat patiently in the hall as I set up the equipment, telling them—and my supervisor—that they were in for a real treat.

Before I pulled down the window shades and switched off the lights, I took a packet of Brook Bond Tea from my pocket, saying,

"This is what we are learning about today. How the tea got inside this bag."
Then, with great ceremony, I put the tea down, reached over, and switched on the projector.

There was a loud bang and a blue flash of light as the projector bulb exploded, showering fragments of glass over the floor. Blue smoke wafted up from the projector.
The children stared wide-eyed at me and at the projector.

"What happened, Mr. Paull?"
"You OK?"

One or two began to laugh. Catching my breath, I calmly looked at my class, saying,
"Hey, it's OK. No big deal. OK, everybody stand, please."
"Find your partner. We're going back to school."

One boy, looking very upset, shouted,

"What about the pictures you promised us?"
"Oh, that's not fair. We ain't seen how tea's made yet."

"Later, later," I said, as I began to lead them out of the door, leaving the broken projector behind me.

Mr. Turner was surprised to see us all back from the church earlier than he'd expected. I told him what had happened. He looked across the room at Mr. Kitson and laughed.

"Hey, in teaching, that's what happens much of the time."
"True, true, true," said Mr. Kitson.

"Hey, no big deal," said Mr. Turner and joined me in telling the children a story about growing tea in a plantation way across the ocean, pointing to a globe as we talked.

Mr. Kitson shared the experience with all my college friends during the next class, reminding them, and me, "Always, *always, plan for the unexpected and, Mr. Paull, always, always carry a spare bulb when using a loop projector! Oh, and a few teabags for the children to look at to take their minds off any unforeseen disaster."*

He did though, with a wry, knowing smile, compliment me on not panicking.

Not panicking? Huh. If he'd seen inside my brain that morning, he'd have realized how bad I felt. Teaching, I realized, wasn't all plain sailing.

In my second year, with my amber and my *wishing rock* locked in my pocket, I taught for three weeks in a secondary school. Teaching in the secondary school meant, I soon discovered, standing tall at the front of the class and reading through a science textbook—well, at least that was what was modeled for me. And I found it very boring, as I'm sure, did the kids.

I chose not to use a projector when my college instructor came to observe my teaching.

Then, in my last year, for my formal and final teaching assessment, I spent six weeks in another secondary school and, to my surprise, was awarded an overall credit for my teaching. I was surprised because I wasn't convinced that I had taught my pupils anything about science.

What a pity, I thought, that my education courses were preparing me to teach older children.

However, now it was time to start looking for my first teaching appointment in a secondary school as the science teacher.

I had no idea about the job hunt process and had no idea where I wanted to teach.

As was to become a pattern in my life, I had no need to worry.

I like to think my *wishing rock* helped things work out for me.

Chapter 18

Trying to put the anxiety about getting a job deep in the back of my mind, I bought a return ticket to Penzance at the start of the Easter holidays. As the train pulled into the station, I opened the nearest carriage door.

"Paull, Paull, is that you?"
Someone was calling my name. Who should be sitting there in the eight-seater compartment but Mr. Elvet Thomas, one of the Latin teachers I remembered in my time at Penzance Grammar School. What was he doing on this train, I thought?

Catching my breath, I said, *"Hello, sir, what you doin' here?"*

We were both surprised to see each other, and by the look in their eyes, Mr. Thomas and his wife seemed pleased to see me. *Mmmmmm. I must have been a good pupil in his class,* I thought to myself. But no, that can't be right. I knew I wasn't a good Latin pupil at all. I spent much of my time each day dreaming, squeezing my amber, and as a consequence, miserably failed the examination.

It didn't seem to matter. We talked. Well, really, I listened as they talked.

I learned why Mr. and Mrs. Thomas were in such a good mood. After many years teaching classics, Mr. Thomas had just the day before been appointed headmaster of Trinity Fields Secondary Modern School in Stafford, a small market town in the middle of England. Mr. Thomas told me about his new school and about his big plans to *"make Trinity Fields*

Secondary Modern School as good as Penzance Grammar School—even though the pupils had failed the scholarship."

I told him I was in my last term in college.

"How are you doing?" he asked.
Self-consciously, I added, I had been awarded a credit in my teaching practice, and now, I was hunting for my first teaching job.

Mr. Thomas smiled and said, *"There's a science job going at my new school. Fancy teaching science there?"*

You bet, I thought. *"Yes, sir, of course. I'd like that very much."*
I smiled, not fully realizing he was serious, and asked half-jokingly,
"When shall I come for an interview? Do I need to come to Stafford for an interview?"
"Would I have to drive all the way up to Stafford during the spring break?"

He smiled. *"No, Paull—oh, can I call you John? Let's say this is the interview."*
"Here, now, on this train."

Mrs. Thomas nodded and smiled. I could see that Mr. Thomas was serious.

And that, indeed, was the interview, sitting and sharing tales of our old school in a packed and noisy train on the long journey home to Penzance.

By the time the train reached my destination, I was now a full-fledged science teacher. I was 5' 9" when I boarded the train. I felt I was 6' 5" when I arrived I Penzance.

Mum and Dad, of course, were thrilled with the news that I had my first teaching job.
"Hey, worries over." Said Mum. *"You already have a job. That's great. A science teacher—the first ever in our family to be a teacher."*

After the short break in Penzance, I returned to Leicester and told everyone I knew of my news. It turned out that I was the first in my class to get a teaching job.

Everyone laughed when Mr. Kitson asked me in class, *"Did you tell the headmaster the story of the growing tea lesson? You remember—the explosion?"*

In August 1963, after college graduation and a summer job as a waiter, I filled a small suitcase with clothes, put my amber and a *wishing rock* in an OXO tin in my pocket, packed most of my tins in a box, and moved to Stafford.

I began the new phase of my life sharing a small flat with two teachers, in Jail Square, named because it was directly opposite the town jail.

Chapter 19

The day before school officially opened for pupils, I put on my charcoal suit, white shirt, and tie and met my new teacher colleagues at the first staff meeting of the new academic year. After brief introductions, the meeting focused on administrative details, especially the new school rule about giving a lavatory pass to pupils going to the lavatory. I was told that I was the form teacher for a class of first years. The staff then broke up into team meetings.

During the science team's short get-together, I heard that I would be teaching general science to the bottom classes of the first, second, and third year pupils. John Matthews, the head of the science department, handed me the school science syllabus and a thick, well-used textbook.

"Here's what you have to teach, John," he said.

"First years, start with famous scientists, second years, gases, third, mosquitoes."

"Oh, they'll also be doing sex ed., OK?"

"Just follow the text, John Paull. It's a good book. Got everything in it you'll need."

"Just make sure you follow the text."

"I'm here to help."

"Just tell me what you need, you know, what equipment, science stuff, and I'll get it for you."

"Get to know the text as soon as you can, and bring me your questions, OK?"

He turned to the group. *"He'll like his kids, won't he? Especially Tiger, yes?"* Everyone laughed loudly.

After the meeting, John took me to my science classroom.

"There's nothing in the cupboards yet. Tell me what you need, and I'll get it stocked, OK?"
"Get any trouble with Tiger, send him to me, OK?"
"All yours. Get it organized the way you want it."

It was a big and empty room. I set out the stools next to the workbenches, sharpened the pencils, opened a pack of science journals, wrote my name and the date on the blackboard, and went home. I was ready.

In the evening, sitting at the kitchen table with a cup of tea, I opened my science textbook.

The chapter on *famous scientists* was straightforward. By an odd coincidence, Humphry Davy, the first scientist in the text, was from my hometown. I could tell the kids that his statue was in the town's main street. I knew that I'd have to do some homework on gases and mosquitoes. But sex education? Now, *what* was that, I wondered, with a smirk on my face? I couldn't remember being in a class that focused on sex education at college. Did I miss it somehow? And Tiger? Which class was Tiger in? What did he do that made everyone at the meeting laugh?

As I flicked through the other papers given to me at the staff meeting, I read through the Teacher Union papers. My starting pay was £620 per year.

If it stayed at the same level—a general science teacher—my pay, at the age of thirty (in nine years' time), would just break £1,000. And of course, as I would contribute 6 percent of my salary toward my retirement, I would get a good pension when I was sixty-five. Dad would be pleased about that, I thought.

"So I should get about a tenner a week. That's OK. I'll manage," I said to myself and picked up my science textbook again and read the two chapters on sex education.

With my OXO tin, amber and *wishing rock* in my pocket, I started the next day in my small *homeroom* classroom on the second floor. I introduced myself, telling the class that I was a new kid too. I filled in the attendance and dinner registers, handed out the timetable, and escorted them to their first lesson. Then I made my way down to the science lab.

The class of thirty-two boys and girls were waiting for me. I opened the door and stood by as everyone rushed in, put down their bags, sat on the stools, and stared at me. My throat felt dry. My heart was pumping faster than it should. Quickly, I took the register, told them my name, and handed out the science textbooks.

"OK, open your books to page 29," I said.
"Follow the text as I read out loud the life story of the scientist, Humphry Davy."
"And you'll never guess, Davy comes from the same town as me, Penzance."

Saying that was the first mistake.

"You know him, sir?"
"Penzance? Where's that then?"
"That place in England?"

"OK. OK," I said. *"Calm down."*
"OK, open your science books and copy this down," I said as I read out the text, stopping occasionally to write a key word or phrase on the blackboard.

I wrote more and more science information about Davy on the board. There was little conversation, and I kept the class writing until the bell went for the end of my first science lesson.

As the class trooped out, I wiped the board clean and wrote *mosquito* in large letters. The next class came in.

"Where do we sit, sir?" asked a girl.
"Oh, anywhere you like," I replied. *"Open your books and copy this down."*
I scribbled as many facts about the mosquito as I could on the board. As they began to write, one tousle-haired boy put up his hand.

"Hey . . . What's yer name? Mr. what?"

Oh, damn it, I thought. I hadn't called out the class names in my register at the beginning of the lesson.

"Can I go lav, sir?"

"Yes, of course you can," I said. *"And my name's Mr. Paull."*

"What's yours?"

"Kenny, sir, Kenny. But everyone calls me Tiger."

"You can call me Tiger if you want to. What shall I call you? Ain't Paul yer first name? Want me to call you by your first name?"

"You," I said with a sniff, *"can call me sir."*

Aha . . . Tiger, I thought, *first round to me.* He looked scruffy but harmless. Forcing a smile, I gave Tiger his pass, told him to hurry, and he left the room, slamming the door behind him.

"OK, everyone, before we get started, let's do the register."

"Put up your hand when I call your name."

I called out everyone's name, added up the total, closed my register, and turned to the class.

"OK, don't forget to put the date at the top of your page."

"Copy everything down in your best handwriting."

After about ten minutes, another hand went up.

"Where's Tiger, Mr. Paull?"

Where, indeed, was Tiger? I thought, just realizing he hadn't returned from the lavatory.

I opened the classroom door and looked down the corridor. There was no sign of Tiger.

I kept watching the clock, wishing that time would go faster, wishing I knew where Tiger was.

Just before the bell went for the end of the lesson, Tiger came through the door.

"Kenny," I shouted, *"where have you been?"*

"Lav, sir. Remember? You gave me a pass."

"Yes," I said, *"that was at the beginning of the lesson."*

"Had stomachache, sir, it wouldn't come. Better now."

Not wanting to hear any graphic detail, I had no idea what to say other than, *"Lesson's nearly ended. Get these blackboard notes down. Quick."*

At the sound of the bell, everyone, including Tiger, handed in the notebooks, all filled, I assumed, with exactly what I'd written on the board. The boys and girls picked up their pencils and books, pushed their stools under the benches, and walked noisily out the door.

As I was waiting for the next class, I noticed Tiger's notebook lying on top of the pile. I opened it. Underneath the word *mosquito,* he'd drawn a naked girl with a big mosquito on her shoulder.

My heart sank. Now what am I supposed to do? My question was soon answered as my next class walked in.

After they had settled in their seats and tucked their satchels under their chairs, I introduced myself and took the register. The pupils smiled, looked at the board, took out their pencils and notebooks, and quietly began to copy what I'd written under the heading, *Gases.* The ensuing science lesson was merely a reading and writing activity. Because of my experience with Tiger, no one was allowed to visit the lavatory.

That was it—my version of three science lessons, my version of teaching on my first day ever as a full-time science teacher.

John Matthews popped his head around the door at the end of the day.
"How'd it go?"
"OK was it?"
"Tiger behave himself?"

"Dead good," I lied. *"Dead good."*

"Good, keep it up then," he said.

The next day, after I called the class register and got them started on their writing, I took Tiger to the corridor.

"Kenny, Tiger, whatever your name is . . . you drew a naked girl in your science notebook."

"Sorry, Mr. Paull. Yeah, I know. Didn't know what to write. Couldn't make sense of what you wrote on the board. Boring. 'Member? I went to the lav? Had stomachache."

He looked me squarely in the eye and smirked. *"Did you like my mosquito, Mr. Paull?"*

I didn't know what to say other than,

"No lavatory pass again for you, Kenny."
"Now go and sit and get on with your work."
"And, no, I didn't like your mosquito."
"And no more naked girls, OK?"

"OK, sir, Mr. Paull. Won't do no more naked girls."

By Friday, my confidence truly burned. I knew that relying entirely on presenting the facts from my science textbook wasn't going to be effective.

But that's how it was. It was me talking *at* the class, me writing bits of irrelevant textbook scientific information on the blackboard, word for word from the book, the pupils then reading their science textbook, and the pupils (well, some of them) filling in their science journals.

Just as my science lessons bored my classes, they bored me.

I didn't know how to make science grip the attention of my pupils.

I was learning the hard way that college teaching credit award notwithstanding, I had no idea how to impart information about mosquitoes, gases, and famous scientists, in a manner that engaged my classes.

I had no idea about the kind of science that interested the adolescent brain.

I was very unsettled, and that feeling was compounded when I received my first pay stub—a check for thirty-nine pounds and ten shillings.

Did I deserve that?

Chapter 20

Thirteen-year-old Tiger always sat alone at the back of the science lab. Sometimes he smiled benignly at the thirty-two other boys and girls, six of whom had recently emigrated from India and could speak but two words of English (*"lav, sir?"*). Tiger always was looking for trouble.

My science lessons on *mosquitoes and other insects* didn't interest Tiger. He did not sit politely through each lesson. Sometimes, to prevent himself from falling asleep, he'd run his fingers through his greasy hair, scratch his head, and interfere with anyone sitting close to him working diligently through the science textbook.

Occasionally, Tiger shouted that he was fed up with school and very fed up with *boring* science.

School didn't interest him, and science didn't engage him. His dad told him that he'd have a job with him as a bricklayer on the building sites when he was fifteen, so why should he *"do his best"* in school? What was the point of it all? Nothing I did in my science lessons made any connection to Tiger's life experience or appealed to his sense of curiosity. The science I read from the textbook was irrelevant to his world—especially the way I presented it.

My science lessons didn't involve my non-English speaking Indian pupils either. They did, though, sit politely through each lesson. They spent their time scribbling and drawing in their science writing books, often whispering to each other. They always looked poorly dressed, out-of-sorts, tired, and hungry. I wondered what was going through their heads.

In the first week of October, my luck changed. The miracle of miracles happened—a big change for the better came over my teaching. Tiger, of all people, and a small garden spider, were my divine inspirations.

Walking back from shopping for the weekend food, I spotted the most beautiful orb-web spider sitting in her intricate silky web in the black currant bush outside the steps leading to my flat. Surprised to see one so late in the year, I fetched a jar, popped her inside, and took her upstairs.

 She reminded me of when my dad and I had found some garden spiders in the back of our house on Gwavas Estate. I kept them safe in a jar tucked under the bed, quickly learning that you don't keep spiders together as they eat each other. Looking after the survivor was really fascinating. Keeping her safe and well fed with flies and moths made me feel good, especially when she deposited an egg sac on her silky web.

I took the spider to school the following Monday, put her in a large bell jar with a little soil, greenery, and a branch and set the new home on a small table at the back of the science laboratory.

I never showed the spider to any of my science classes. After all, why should I? We were studying the quirks of the six-legged mosquito from the textbook, not an eight-legged garden spider. Well, to be precise, we were reading about the mosquito that spread malaria in some far-off country and then perfecting our handwriting and spelling skills.

The following day, I noticed a silk egg sac was dangling from near the center of the spider's orb web. Sensing the spider was hungry, I found a small silverfish darting around the base of my desk, unscrewed the top of the spider home, and put the small creature on the web. Immediately, the spider came running toward her prey. I sat and watched, fascinated by the process, until Tiger's class came through the door, breaking the atmosphere by noisily throwing their satchels under their stools.

They were ready for yet another particularly dull science lesson (all *chalk and talk*, then reading and writing, and no hands-on science investigation). They looked bored before I even started. I got up quickly, pushing the spider home to one side.

Then Tiger came through the door late. He looked upset. When I asked him where he'd been, he stared at the floor and mumbled he'd been sent to Mr. Thomas's office because,

"I was caught looking through a dirty book, sir, 'fore school started."

"Who caught you?" I asked. I wanted to know more about what had happened. His tone changed, and he looked across the room at me and shouted loudly,

"Mr. Jelbert, you know, Mr. Paull, he looks at us lads through his telescope from the class upstairs. He saw me. Looking at pictures. You know. Dirty pictures. Weren't my book though, Mr. Paull. It's Fatty White's. Now Mr. Thomas has it. Fatty'll murder me. I've got to go back to the boss's office after school. And I'll get caned. I'll get six, I know I will."

I calmed him down as best I could. Tiger turned and went to his usual spot at the back of the classroom. He looked sulky and angry.

As I was writing on the blackboard, asking the children to open up their journals and copy my notes, there was a loud shout of *"Christ!"* from the back of the room. Startled, I looked up. Everyone in class turned their heads to see what was going on. Tiger was standing up and pointing his index finger and thumb at the bell jar. His eyes now were wide open.

"F—'ell! Look! Mr. Paull, Mr. Paull, there's a spider 'ere! It's killing a creepy-crawly! It's f—killing it! Look!"

I raised my hand. *"Tiger, watch your language!"*

"Mr. Paull, Mr. Paull, I can't f—ing believe it. Look at that! The spider, f—great!"

I told him to sit down, leave the spider alone, and get out his science journal. I turned to the class, some standing near their seats, wanting to know what was going on.

"Wassup wiv Tiger, Mr.Paull?" asked Michael. *"'e sick or summat?"*

I tried to settle everyone down. *"C'mon. Everybody! Never mind Tiger. He's just having one of his moments."*
"Get on with your writing."
"C'mon everybody, no big deal."

The spider eating her lunch, of course, was, for Tiger, far more interesting than my science-reading lesson. Tiger swearing loudly was much more captivating than my science-reading lesson for the class. I gave in.
"Go on, then, everyone, take a look. Go and see what's in the jar—then get back to your seats."

The class didn't need telling twice. Everyone rushed to join Tiger at the back of the room, seeing and then chattering excitedly about the spider—*excited chatter* was something I had never heard in one of my science lessons.

"Ain't never seen a spider like that!" What is it? Wos it doin'?" asked one pupil.

One of the girls, Dianne, said the spider was so beautiful.

"Can I look at it, sir? Please? Can I get a maggy glass from the drawer?" she asked.
I thought for a moment. Why not?

Dianne fetched a magnifying glass and peered through it.
"It's great. Can I draw it, sir? The spider? Please?"

"Of course. Use your pencil, not your pen."
"Oh, don't though, draw it in your science book."
"That's for science. Here, there's a piece of scrap paper on my desk you can use!"

Dianne looked at me and asked dryly, *"Aren't spiders science, Mr. Paull?"*

"Course, Dianne. Sorry. Do it, drawing, oh, go on, put it in your science journal."

The idea caught on, and a few more girls also wanted to draw the spider, sitting in her web, clasping the poor silverfish.

Tiger did not draw the spider in his journal. He sat very still, ignoring me and everyone else, watching the jar, mesmerized.

Not all the pupils liked the spider. One or two said they killed spiders when they saw them at home, reminding me of the conflicting long-ago conversations about small creatures in Mr. Jones's class. Children, I remembered, generally liked and protected what they liked and ignored or killed what they didn't like.

We spent the rest of the lesson drawing and talking about spiders.

Tiger stayed behind after class and, with a warm grin and an impish twinkle in his eye, asked me where I'd found the spider. When I told him, he said,

"The spider's great, sir, ain't it great? You like 'em? Spiders? They're brill!"

He looked up at me.

"Sorry I swore, sir, sorry. Won't do it again. 'Onest!"
"Can't draw, you know. Scabby drawer."

"Well," I said, *"I think you can draw, but your pictures are rude, you know."*

Tiger smiled and then said he was going to get some spiders of his own as soon as he got home.
"Good, but now get off to your next class. Don't be late," I said.

"Oh, and don't forget to see Mr. Thomas . . . and be sure to give the book back to your friend."

Chapter 21

The next day, there was Tiger waiting for me before school started, with that impish smile on his face.

"Found 'em, Mr. Paull, found 'em." Tiger had a jar in his satchel. *"There were stacks of 'em. Tiny 'uns. Babs, I think, ain't they? I got three or four. Can I keep them in the lab, Mr. Paull?"*
"Go on! Can I? Next to yours?"

Then, he added. *"Found out about 'em too, Mr. Paull. My dad knows what they are—they're garden spiders, and they eat flies and stuff!"*

"You know what? You're OK, Mr. Paull. Sorry, sorry, I swore."

"Thank you, Tiger, thank you. I appreciate that," I said. *"I'm sorry you swore too."*

I gave him four jars, telling him that spiders can't live together without paralyzing and eating each other. *"Make a home for each one, OK? Quick, school's starting soon. Oh, and you can tell your class what you know about spiders, OK?"*

When his class came for science, Tiger stood sheepishly at the front of the room, by the blackboard, and told a very respectful, quiet, surprised, and very attentive audience what he had learned about spiders. I was fascinated to see how Tiger caught everyone's attention with his excited, twitchy body movements. Tiger had at last discovered something in my science period that made him feel that wonderful, *inside-your-head* glow when the brain is alive and alert. His classmates felt it too.

"Spiders," he said, *"are dead good. Look at this one. It's a beaut."* He held up one of the jars.

"Guess what I found out . . . Spiders suck their food after they've crushed and made it watery. Ain't only the gals that make silk. The fella spiders make silk too, but only when they're young. Then they stop and go looking for a spider girlfriend. They mate on the web. Sometimes the gals kill and eat the fellas."
"They don't spin silk, you know. Some spiders chase after stuff they want to eat."

I was taken aback by how much he knew, thinking, *"Where did he learn that from, then? All from his dad?"* *"It weren't from me in science lessons."*

He'd really done his homework. This was Tiger's *amber* moment. As I listened and watched Tiger's nervous twitches as he spoke to his classmates, he reminded me of the sharing time on Wednesday afternoons with Mr. Jones. It also reminded me of Mr. Kitson's advice at college, *"When you're teaching, always plan for the unexpected."*
Tiger told his audience that, if anyone wanted to watch, he was going to release the spiders and their eggs in the school garden at lunchtime.

"They're goin' to die soon, y'know, and the eggs will 'atch next year, spring, right, Mr. Paull?"

When he'd finished, everyone clapped. *"Any questions for Tiger?"* I asked. The hands went up, and Tiger was asked a million questions, some of which he could answer.

Almost everyone turned up at lunchtime to see Tiger release the spiders.

That night, I checked my spider's identity in a spider book, learning that it was *Meta segmentata*, a common garden species related to the garden spider. Its courtship routine was different though. The male, I read, drives off other male suitors, but doesn't advance toward the female until an insect is caught on the female's web. Both spiders then move toward the struggling insect. The male's front legs are larger than the female, and he uses them to push the female away from the insect.

He then gift-wraps the prey. As the female tucks into her dinner, the male wraps silk around her legs and then mates with her.

The following day, I went to school early in the morning, an hour or so before the official start of the day, and went to the science storeroom. I gathered a box full of microscopes, racks of test tubes, flasks, and other scientific equipment. I set them out in the science lab. And I rearranged the stools.

When Tiger's class came through the door, the boys and girls noticed what I had done and looked at my displays of science equipment.

"Hey," said one, *"look . . . look at all this science stuff . . . and hey, look, we ain't sitting alone. He's put us in groups. Mornin', sir, this stuff looks great. Can we touch it?"*

Tiger showed me a picture he'd drawn at home of the beautiful orb-web spider. *"Hey, you did it. You drew your spider. You can draw, see?"* I said.

"Can I glue it on the cover of my science journal, Mr. Paull?"

"OK," I said, *"but first let me rip out those inappropriate doodles, OK?"*

Seeing Tiger operating *like a young scientist* was a first-time experience in my classroom. I had learned, by sheer luck, what motivated and engaged my most challenging pupil: observing and studying a small spider.

I started off by sharing the spider snippet with everyone. They were enthralled.

I was very struck with the ensuing class conversations and how the class listened when Tiger had something to say. When talking and learning about the spider, the pupils were very animated, commenting appropriately and asking good questions.

When I told the class it was time to open their books and begin the science lesson, the atmosphere changed. When I opened the science textbook and read aloud everything one needed to know about insects, they were quiet and withdrawn and didn't ask me a single question. There was a disconnect between the two. Without the class's engagement, my science lesson went nowhere beyond formal handwriting exercises, similar to the ones I experienced as a pupil when in Mr. Miller's and Mr. Hitchens's classrooms. With the class's engagement, I could, in part, reproduce something of what happened on those far-off Wednesdays in Mr. Jones's classroom.

It was, in fact, an incredible teachable moment. It was *the* first *"Come on, John Paull, be a* real *teacher, be professional, earn your pension"* wake-up call.

"Tomorrow," I said, at the end of the lesson, *"we'll do that again, OK? See if you have anything that links to our lesson topic. You don't have to stand at the front and share. You can share your artifacts with me privately, if that's what you'd rather do."*

"Great," said Dianne. *"Like bein' a proper scientist. S'dead good!"*
"What's artifact mean?"
I wrote the word *artifacts* on the board, explaining what the word meant.
I wondered if I should show them my amber and a *wishing rock*, but no, I couldn't connect it to the lesson ahead.
Later, at home, I took out my notebook and a red pen and jotted down some notes.

URGENT! *In my science lab, I need to*

Create a "scientific" classroom atmosphere so my pupils feel they are entering the world of the scientist when they walk through the door. I can do that, can't I, by displaying more scientific equipment and scientific pictures? Why can't I have a cupboard like Mr. Jones? Or I could lay things of interest out on a table and call it my science table.
*Connect the textbook science subject matter to the pupils' experiences—and give them a chance to work in science teams and talk about what they do and what they observe. Think about the knowledge they might gain and the skills they can develop from each other. Appreciate, though, that not everyone wants to talk out loud to the class about their science. (Some of my class are shy and feel uncomfortable if pushed to speak out loud. That's especially true for my Indian pupils. So how do I help them feel part of the class?) So, **John Paull, with two Ls,** be brave! Read, digest, remember, and then put the textbook away*

and introduce my science lessons with demonstrations and ideas that catch my pupils' interest. Then, when the class is working on table experiments, focus on those who need me—especially my non-English speaking Indian class who have no idea or interest in what I am teaching.

From that day on, my planning took a different route. For all my science lessons, I decided, before I focused on the science content of the day, I'd greet the class, show them something I brought in, give them chance to ask questions—and chance to stand at the front and share whatever they had found (fossils, crystals, jars full of dead insects and spiders) and brought into the room. I'd ask some questions, then make time for the pupils to ask and talk to each other about any science question in their heads, and I'd then place everything on the science table and later in the small glass-fronted science cupboard (now to be called *Mr. Jones's cupboard*).

Then I would open the science textbook and focus on the science lesson I was supposed to teach.

If we finished early, the pupils asked more questions about the specimens brought in that day and put on display on the science table.

This science lesson routine worked for me and worked for most of the class—at least, kept them occupied—and one that kept me in touch with my teacher contract requirements. I also really enjoyed setting out the science table and arranging the growing collection of interesting artifacts in my *Mr. Jones's cupboard.*

Even though my pupils didn't go to museums or public libraries or live in houses with gardens, all of them had a strong sense of curiosity about their world, especially their world of nature and science. I also learned that there was more background experience for science in these children's lives than for most other subjects taught at Trinity Fields Secondary School.

Science, I had come to realize, was a *"natural"* for them—if presented in the classroom in an engaging, *authentic* way and involved asking questions, handling resources, and carrying out experiments.

The challenge for me was to link the way I was starting my lessons—sharing anything of interest we'd found outdoors—to the content I was supposed to teach.

Chapter 22

When the school's science third year guidelines moved from *mosquitoes and other insects* to *electricity and how circuits work,* I hunted through the science equipment cupboard for wire, bulbs, switches, and batteries and laid them out on the science table.

Gathering together what I needed, I introduced the first of the ten-lesson program on *electricity,* drawing a circuit on the blackboard. Then, facing the class, I made a circuit, using wire, a small bulb, and a battery.

The bulb started to glow. I held it high, and I pointed to the wire.
"This carries the electrical power to this, you know, the bulb. The bulb then lights up."
"Great, hey? Isn't that just so magical?"

Smiling and feeling sure of myself, I asked the pupils to write a description of what they had just seen in their science journals. The room went quiet. I checked again that everyone knew what to do.
Janice put up her hand and asked,

"Can't we do that, Mr. Paull? You know—can't we make a circuit? Go on, can we?"

"You bet," I replied.

"Look at the stuff on your tables.
"Light the bulb. Then, tell each other what's happening."

Their eyes lit up as brightly as electric light bulbs.

Not only did the class complete the circuits and light the bulbs, but one group, led by Janice, made a very complicated and ingenious circuit that had three switches that controlled three bulbs.

Then the class, led again by Janice, connected every circuit in the room.

When I reminded them about journaling their experiments *just as scientists would*, I was surprised and thrilled to see how much more most of them—including Tiger—wrote and drew in their science journals. Wow! I could see that it was what they really wanted to do. What a great—and for me, unusual—*teacher* feeling that experience gave me.

Before the weekly staff meeting, I sat with John, the head of the school science department.

"Everything going OK? Tell me about Tiger," he said. *"You had a good year with him and a few others, yes?"*
"How do you think your first year is going? Tell me."

Here goes, I thought.
I talked, slowly at first, then it all splurged out. I told John about my struggles with how to teach the science syllabus in such a way that engaged my pupils. I told him about the things I did do which did catch my class's interest.

John listened attentively, not saying a word, looking serious, but constantly nodding his head.
"Hey, it's your first year. Teaching's not easy, and you have found that out."
"Bringing in spiders and stuff . . . That's better suited to junior school. They aren't as tied to guidebooks as we are. We gotta get our kids ready for the leaving test."
John pointed out that, important as it was, I had to move forward from the fun and interesting *start-of-lesson* sharing time ritual that I had created, to bring the textbook science part alive.

"You need to know more about those kids, you know. Their records will give you some picture of their background. They'll tell you why they need to pass the test."

"Go and see the secretary. She'll give you their files."

When the staff meeting started, I was very surprised to be asked by the headmaster what I had done to Tiger. My eyes stared at my feet. My toes wriggled. My face went red. Had I been caught? I sheepishly recounted the story of Tiger and the spiders. I couldn't believe my eyes and ears when every teacher stood up and clapped! Mr. Thomas, the headmaster, explained to everyone why he asked me about Tiger. Tiger, apparently, hadn't been sent to him for misbehavior for over three months.

"Well done, Johnny, well done."
"Thank you, Mr. Thomas."

After school the next day, I went to the secretary's office and, with her permission, went through my pupils' files, many of them going back to their time in their infant schools. Many, I discovered, came from very poor and disadvantaged backgrounds.

I opened Tiger's file first. I learned that Tiger's mum had died in his infancy and his dad brought him and his brother up. Michael's dad was in prison. Steven's dad was in the local hospital, on a life-support system. Ann had eight brothers and sisters.

Reading through the paperwork, I was reminded of what I had seen inside several homes when I delivered milk as a boy. I remembered going into Philip Washer's kitchen and finding out firsthand why Philip fell asleep in Mr. Miller's class. Would Mr. Miller have been so mean if he knew what Philip did every day before and after school? Won't I, now, look at Steven Askew differently, now I know about his challenges at home? I remembered too, being unable to concentrate at school during maths lessons and writing time, my head full of worry when my mum and dad fell out with each other over money issues.

"These kids," I thought to myself, *"these kids have so much to put up with."*
"Bet they have home stuff in their heads all day."
"And they have to put up with my poor teaching too."
"Going to school needs to take them away from all the home worries."
"Reading and writing in science doesn't crack it."

I couldn't get the background details on three or four of the kids out of my brain through the weekend.

What should I do? Perhaps I couldn't do anything. Perhaps secondary school teaching wasn't for me.

Chapter 23

Things began to go better in my lessons, but an episode with Michael Stringer, when he tried to liven things up during the first of our six sex education classes, reminding me that I still had an enormous amount to earn about teaching science.

I hadn't the slightest idea how to present this science lesson, one so vital for adolescents, so I opened my textbook and read the section on sex education aloud. The text focused first on rabbit reproduction.

As sex was the topic of the lesson, class engagement wasn't an issue. But rabbits? That's not what my class wanted to know about. Everyone, it seemed, surprise, surprise, wanted to hear about human reproduction, not how rabbits mated.

After reading the first line or two, I sensed there was a growing atmosphere in the classroom.

Michael broke the ice. *"'Ow do we do it, sir? 'Ow do we make babies, sir?"*
"Go on, tell us. You know, don't you?" added Tiger.

"Hey, let me read this through, OK? No, no questions, remember?"
"None. Just let me read this section about rabbits!"

After a page or two cryptically describing how rabbits mated, I closed the book and wrote on the board:

"Rabbits mate, male and female grown-up rabbits, that is, and have their babies in the spring."
"What do we call a baby rabbit? People, human beings, men and women, mate too, like the rabbits and have babies."

Someone asked. *"Do 'umans mate in the spring, sir, like the rabbits?"*
I could feel as well as hear the tittering in the classroom. Knowing I was losing my grip on the class, I shouted loudly,

"OK, enough. Enough! *Open up your science journals."*

I went to the board and told the class to copy in their journals my chalk drawings of a pin man linked to the pin woman standing by the pin child.

Everyone started drawing and exchanging sideway glances. Michael added, in blue ink, exaggerated anatomical extras to his pin family and showed everyone around him.

Tiger was beside himself. Hearing the giggling and now seeing as well as hearing that I had lost control of my class, I walked over to Michael and looked at his drawings. I was flabbergasted by what I saw. He'd added bits to the drawings, inappropriate bits. They were really vulgar.

Now what do I do? This wasn't the time to give him a 2B pencil and tell him to add some shade.
"Michael! Go on. See Mr. Thomas, the headmaster. Now. Nowwwww! *Show him your pictures.* Now. Now. Now!*"*

What else could I do?
The class knew I was pretty mad and went very quiet. Some of the boys stared at each other.
As Michael left the room, I loudly told everyone to get on with their writing and drawing.
Twenty minutes later, Michael came back. He was grinning. He looked at me and then winked at Tiger.

"Why are you smiling, Michael?"
"Did you show your pictures to Mr. Thomas?"

"Yes, sir."

"What did he say?" I asked.
"He said they were good, Mr. Paull. Really good. He liked them a lot."

The silence in the room was deafening. I looked at Michael incredulously.

"I'm sorry—what did he, Mr. Thomas, that is, what did he say? What did he say to you? Tell me again?"

"Sir, Mr. Paull, sir. He said I was a good drawer. A really good drawer."

The class laughed out loud, releasing some of the tension in the air. Perplexed and aggravated and not having a clue what to say next, I told him, in my sternest teacher voice, to sit down and, *"Get on with your writing. No more drawing, you hear?"*

"No, sir. Course not, sir. Wot, no science drawing, sir?"
"Nope, none.*"*

There wasn't a word from anyone for the rest of the lesson, but I could see everyone looking sideways at Michael, wondering what had happened when he saw Mr. Thomas. I wondered too.

As there wasn't time at the end of the lesson, I waited until the end of the day, tidied up the work areas, and went to check with the headmaster.

Mr. Thomas told me what happened when Michael came to the office. Michael, he said, knocked on his door and came into his office, smiling, put his science book on the desk, and said,

"Mr. Paull told me I was to show you my good pictures, sir."

"I looked at them," Mr. Thomas told me. *"I thought the pictures were a bit rude, a bit explicit, you know, but I thought that he'd copied them straight from the board. As you'd drawn them."*
"So I said, 'Well done, Michael. Glad you're trying harder.'"

As he spoke, I felt very foolish.

"Ummmm . . . well, actually . . . ummmmmm . . . OK. Thank you, sir."

Next time, I thought, if there was a next time, I'd write a very detailed note to explain exactly why I was sending any student for whatever reason to the headmaster.

I had just learned another lesson about teaching. Naïve and effective I was, in different ways, some subtle, some not so, by Tiger, Janice, and now, Michael and his explicit drawings. Sure, because of Tiger and his spider, I was much better than when I started, and the pupils appeared to enjoy my sessions, but I wasn't doing a good job teaching the science I was supposed to teach.

For a start, it didn't take a rocket scientist to figure out that the life cycle of the malarial mosquito was irrelevant to Tiger's life.

The point was that the creature's life cycle was much more interesting and relevant once he had witnessed, firsthand, the life of the spider in the jar. Seeing it happen naturally was so much better than reading about how it happened in a textbook. Could I, I thought, set up a colony of mosquitoes and keep them in the classroom?

It was also much more fun, of course, and involved more learning for Janice, and everyone else, to link a length of wire to a bulb and a battery herself or with a group than copying a circuit drawing in her science notebook.

Michael's boredom with my weak attempts at using rabbits to describe the human reproduction cycle pointed out the need to think carefully about how to deliver sensitive subject matter to a class of adolescents.

Most of all, I knew I was learning something about them all as individuals in my class and what I needed to do to make the learning environment appropriate for everyone. But the big question loomed large in my head: How could I be an effective, successful teacher?

My brain was in turmoil though. I enjoyed my teaching time much more when my kids were actively engaged in the subject matter. The way I was now creating a scientific atmosphere in my classroom, my science wasn't, I thought, what I was supposed to be doing. I didn't yet have the skills to link the facts from the science curriculum, such as everything they didn't need to know about mosquitoes, with actual science activities.

So being human and being inexperienced, I blamed the very tight science curriculum. It didn't feel right to me.

Perhaps I needed a fresh start in another school, where I could teach more and more *hands-on biological* science, feeling in my bones that it was the right way of teaching.

I began to think about leaving Trinity Fields and getting another teaching job.

Chapter 24

In October, after a tip-off phone call from Dorothy, a former girlfriend who was teaching in Leicestershire, I searched the school staff room's copy of *The Times Educational Supplement* for an advert about a teaching job in Blaby, a village in Leicestershire, close to the city where I had completed my college education.

There it was: Required: *Teacher, Upper Juniors, science background an advantage.*

That evening, I applied to Blaby Stokes Junior School, writing in my letter of application, somewhat tongue-in-cheek, that I was up to the challenge of teaching younger children, using, of course, the *new* approach to teaching.

I wasn't telling big fibs. After all, hadn't I naturally shifted away from the direct-instruction, science-teaching model I used at Trinity Fields to a more interactive teaching style, one that was more satisfying for me and more engaging for my pupils? Wasn't that the *new* approach to teaching that I was hearing more and more about?

I completed the paperwork, put it in a large envelope, squeezed my *wishing rock*, sent a big wish, and slipped the envelope in the postbox.

Within a week, I was delighted—and somewhat surprised—to be called for an interview.

In preparation, I dug out my tattered college notes and read as much as I could about the *Leicestershire Plan* and what that apparently meant in junior school classrooms. My scribbles didn't tell me much. I either wasn't told in class, or else, more the case, I suppose, I didn't listen very carefully during the lectures, and I didn't write readable notes. I needed to do a little more homework.

Dorothy, my girlfriend, was very helpful and very encouraging, thus recreating a relationship that had faltered during the last few months when we were students. She helped me fill in the gaps in my college notes. She was able to explain what was meant by terms like *the integrated day* and *the Leicestershire plan*.

I remembered that Stewart Mason, Leicestershire's director of education, had abolished the 11 plus examination (the dreaded *scholarship)* in all the county's junior schools at a time when the county had to accommodate a growth in pupil numbers.

When doing so, he gave his head teachers ownership of how they ran their schools, encouraging them to adopt an approach to teaching similar to the infant school *"family grouping"* practices, which were getting a lot of publicity in education circles.

I had seen—and liked—this teaching approach when I student-taught at Great Glen with Mr. Turner.

It was Mason too, I learned, who redefined the traditional role of *school inspector* (he who comes to schools to inspect) to *advisor* (he who comes to classrooms to help, support, and advise).

For the best part of two decades, the Leicestershire Advisory Service, a small team of former teachers and head teachers, successfully encouraged teachers in infant and junior schools to create, initiate, and develop more child-centered approaches to classroom teaching. The advisors were welcome visitors to schools, appreciative of their positive and constructive contributions. They organize courses, discussion groups, and workshops, and give talks to parents about innovative school practice.

I told Mr. Thomas that the *"new"* way of teaching sounded appealing to me, and he encouraged me to go ahead with an application to Leicestershire Education Authority.

After being made very welcome when I arrived for interview at Blaby Stokes, I was quickly told that my science background was what interested the school in my application.

The first hard question came from the headmaster whom I knew I had to impress.

Smiling, but staring at me intently, Mr. Ward told me it was his son's birthday the following weekend. Should he buy him one of the packaged science kits on sale at Woolworths? I blinked. I blinked again.

I had no idea what he was talking about. I hadn't seen a Woolworths packaged science kit. What did he want me to say? I told him about the balsa wood plane I'd bought the day I passed the scholarship and how much fun I'd had making it and flying it.

Mr. Ward's smile suggested he enjoyed—and saw the relevance—in my story and went on with more questions about how I would use *practical* science to promote reading and writing. I told the panel about my experience with Tiger and the spiders.

As I told my story, everyone's eyes lit up.

When I'd finished, they astutely asked, *"So you tell a good story, Mr. Paull. Tell us, what did you learn from that experience, you know, with Tiger?"*

I thought for a bit and gave a long-winded, rambling answer, beginning with,
    "Well, kids, sorry, children, have a great sense of curiosity about things they see around them—and we teachers need to make the most of that!"

The interviewing panel looked at each other, smiled, then asked a couple more questions, including,

"What do you understand about project work, Mr. Paull?"
and
"What does 'child-centered' mean to you in the classroom?"

I shuffled in my seat. *"I don't know,"* I answered.

"I've only read and heard about things like that. They sound great though. Does that mean I base my teaching on what the class wants to do? Like Tiger? Getting him to write about spiders?"

They nodded, smiled, and thanked me for my time. I was then asked to wait outside in the secretary's office.

During the twenty or so nervous minutes that followed, I went over every question and every limp answer again in my mind, squeezing a *wishing rock* and my amber in the palm of my hand.

Then one of the interviewers came out of the head's office, thanked all the interviewees, and called me back inside the interview room. The headmaster stood up, held out his hand, and offered me the position as class teacher of the *vertically grouped* class of upper juniors.
Wow! I quickly took his hand—and his job.

"Thank you. Thank you. Thank you!"

Thank you, my precious amber and my Lariggan Beach *wishing rock*.

When everyone else had left the interview room, Mr. Ward and his deputy, Mr. Jolley, talked to me about Blaby Stokes Church of England School.

"The children will love your science, John Paull, especially if it's all practical investigation, you know, letting the children—oh, by the way, we don't use the word 'kids' here—work in depth on their own projects. Have to help them though. There's a canal nearby too full of good stuff. You could take your class there! You just go when you want to go. It's only ten minutes away from here."

Remember that, John Paull, don't call children 'kids'—and take them to the local pond.

I said to myself.

Mr. Ward brought up the Leicestershire Advisory Service that I had read about. One member of the advisory team, Mr. Bill Browse, a former teacher, visited Blaby Stokes regularly. What a great idea, I thought, having access to an organization that helped teachers fine-tune their teaching. If I'd had support like that at Trinity Fields, someone helping me make sense of what and what not to do with class, I might have done a better job, I thought.

I hoped I'd get chance to meet that person and talk with him about how I could become a better teacher.

Little did I know what an influence he was to have on my career.

Later, over a strong cup of tea, I got my breath back, and my heartbeat resumed to something close to normal. I walked (well, floated, really) around the school with the deputy headmaster, visiting some of the classrooms. Seeing the evidence of science teaching was uppermost in my mind, of course. I was very curious to see how *classroom* science looked—was it as interactive, *child-centered*, and *hands-on* as I'd heard? If so, what did that mean?

What did *"child-centered"* look like? I needed to know. Does it mean, I wondered, that the children choose from a range of activities chosen, resourced, and overseen by the teacher? Or did it mean that the children decide themselves what they want to do in the classroom? If so, could they choose to do nothing? How did the teacher direct the children to do what they needed to do?

As we walked down the hallway, avoiding small groups of children quietly reading, writing, and drawing, I noticed the number of houseplants and the colorful displays of children's pictures and writings.

Each classroom I visited was buzzing with activity. Mr. Jolley pointed out the physical similarities between the classrooms, especially how space was divided into *interest areas* for science, reading and writing, mathematics, and art. Each interest area had a small wooden table covered with *reachable,* tempting resources, and I was told, cards on which the teacher had written suggested activities.

There weren't any desks. Instead, most of each class sat, in groups of four, around rectangular wooden tables. Some children were sitting on the carpet, alone, on cushions, in corners, close to the classroom door, out in the hallway, or outside in the yard. There were few chairs—fewer, I counted, than the number of children.

Different groups were working, some quietly, some not, but certainly purposefully, on different projects in different parts of the classroom. When the children, I was told, chose an activity suggested by the teacher, they gathered whatever resources they needed from the classroom shelves (some commercial, some environmental—rocks and fossils, for example—some *homemade,* such as wooden balances) and began their work.

One classroom's math *interest* table had balances, geo-boards, number lines, counting games, a stopwatch, math books, with a card next to each resource. In a science area, I saw a binocular microscope, magnifying glasses, magnets, some small bones, stones, batteries, bulbs, and strands of wire; a reading and writing table held books, a tape recorder and story tapes, word games and alphabet puzzles; in the arts and craft section, strategically near a source of running water, there were easels, paper, paint, brushes, aprons, dyes, and boxes full of crayons.

Mr. Jolley, reading my mind, described what was going on:

"Here, in our school," he said, *"the teachers take their cues from the children. 'Real' learning takes place where something of particular interest to the child happens to be."*

"Sounds easy, doesn't it? Doesn't happen by magic though. The teachers have to make sure that the children read and write and do their arithmetic at the right levels."

He pointed to a wall. *"Look at those art and science displays done by the class. See? They're really good. See the writing and thinking? Kids love creepy-crawlies. Just up your street, Mr. Paull! Yes? Tiger? Tiger Reynolds, wasn't it? Spiders? You know what I mean?"*

"Oh, and," he added, *"we go outside to explore the environment. Lots of good stuff out there, you know, especially creepy-crawlies. Well, you do know, of course. You're into science."*

"Yes," I said. *"Yes, Mr. Jolley, right up my street."*

I noticed that each teacher, when not walking around the room interacting with individual boys and girls, was sitting with small groups of children, sometimes asking questions and looking at their writing. Sometimes, the teacher stood and talked to the class about one particular teaching point.

Everyone appeared focused on his or her work, and the teachers, when required, got their children's attention with one clap of the hands.

To be sure, as Mr. Jolley said, the tangible evidence that the *Blaby Stokes* approach worked, and worked well for its teachers and children, could be felt in the lively atmosphere around the school and evidence of children's work displayed on the classroom walls.

After an hour or so, with my head swimming, I thanked him for the classroom tour. In particular, I thanked him for pointing out things I would have missed. He sounded so knowledgeable and so authoritative. Mr. Jolley, I learned later, often took groups of teacher visitors around school, to explain the *integrated day/vertical grouping* processes.

During the midday break period, after the teachers had eaten school lunch with their children, *family style*, I met Mrs. Biddle, the teacher I was replacing. Mrs. Biddle told me that her children had a *heartening* (her word) desire to learn new skills.

"They are a good class. One of the best I've had. They always come through the door, first thing in the morning, wanting to learn."

She confessed, with a half smile, that there wasn't much science going on in her classroom, mainly because she did little to promote it, feeling she didn't have the energy and didn't know enough science to support her children's group and individual projects.

"I'm old-school, though, you know. That hands-on stuff, with science, I just couldn't get it going with my boys beyond just playing with stuff I put out. Too much for me. Time for me to go. I don't know enough science. And the group work is hard work—seeing everyone individually. They'll enjoy you though, you're young, and you're into science," she said. "So take them outside! I never did. Didn't know what to look for. Spiders and slugs and things make my flesh crawl! You know about that stuff, right? Take them outside on your first day!"

"Oh, get a nature table going too. Mine is always so disorganized."

Her teaching day, Mrs. Biddle told me, started early when she'd set up the room's *interest areas* with plenty of questions and resources. *"My room arrangement, John Paull, is very important. I give it a lot of thought. Not like that in secondary schools, is it? Same thing going on all the time, yes?"*

I confessed that, as I taught in a secondary school science laboratory, I hadn't given much thought to room arrangement, except for sitting Tiger and Michael at the back of the room, away from each other, out of everyone's way. I made a mental note to think more about room organization, grouping pupils, and to start collecting resources.

"Start the day with the registers, you know, attendance and lunch records. One of my children takes these straight to the office—they know the routine."
Then, with everyone sitting, including her, in a circle on the floor, she'd welcome the class. After the children settled themselves, Mrs. Biddle said she would write a sentence or a sum on the board as a warm-up exercise before they went to morning assembly.

Assembly sometimes lasted about half an hour.

I learned that when the children returned from the school morning assembly, a group of them helped fill each table with mathematical resources. Mrs. Biddle then led a whole class *hands-on* math session. When that was finished, and the children had completed their work, they chose their next activity. After a reminder about putting their names on the activity sheet and about appropriate behavior, off they'd go and start work.

"So how do you know who's doing what?" I asked.

"My children," she said, *"like me, rely on the activity sheet. It gives them a plan for their day. And I know by checking if everyone's doing what he or she is supposed to be doing. I walk around a lot. And I'm always asking questions, I'm always suggesting different ideas to the children. Hey, don't forget too that I set the activities for the day. My children though do have time in the day to work on something they bring in."*

"Sometimes, I let them choose what they want to do, in the afternoons, that is. But," she added, *"they can't choose to do nothing!"*

"Testing? We don't test. The evidence of learning in my classroom is best collected by me seeing what the class is doing."

"I just look in their writing journals and mathematics books and check off in my planning book."

Then she added. *"I do get nervous though if I don't see certain children reading and writing sometime during the day. That's when I might tell them what I expect. You'll soon learn who to keep an eye on! And who to help, you know, really keep an eye on. There are three boys who really do have reading and writing problems."*

To give a sense of individual progress, she said, each child kept a daily diary of what s/he was doing, which Mrs. Biddle constantly checked. The variety of the activities mentioned in the children's diaries suggested the highlights of each child's day. The teaching day ended with the boys and girls, again, sitting around her in a circle on the carpet, asking questions, recounting activities and learning that had taken place throughout the day.

Then, after the children had tidied the activity tables (everyone had assigned jobs, I learned later), she'd read a chapter from an ongoing storybook, and stopping occasionally, she'd show everyone the pictures in the book and ask a few questions about its story line.

Finally, the children stacked the chairs, cleared away anything left on the carpet under their tables, gathered their coats and bags, and made their way home.

"Oh, and I see the parents pretty often—when I need to, in fact. They're pretty good. They'll leave you alone. They're very supportive of school. School sends a newsletter every week. That keeps them happy."

I thanked her for her time and for being so thoughtful. She smiled and said, *"I wish you all the best, John, all the very best. Enjoy my class! They'll enjoy you, I know."*

"I'll leave all the stuff for you in the cupboards, OK? It's all yours now."

I was excited. The walk around the classrooms with Mr. Jolley and the focused, helpful discussion with Mrs. Biddle gave me what I thought was a concrete model of a teaching day at Blaby Stokes to work on in my head. Generally, it made some sense to me, and it looked pretty easy. I can do that, can't I?

I just set out my room with a nature table, art materials, science equipment, resources for mathematics, and reading books, show the children what was available, give a few directions, walk around, smile, and check that everyone's engaged, help three children in particular with their writing and spelling and, *hey presto!*

Nothing to it. That evening, as I celebrated my appointment to Blaby Stokes and the renewal of my relationship with Dorothy, I began to make plans for my move to Leicester.

The first thing in my head was that I needed to bury a tin with each Trinity Fields class in the school garden, filled with notes written by the kids.

Tiger dug the hole for his class's tin, close to the apple tree. Everyone cheered really loudly as he buried our memories of *sciency* things that we had done together in class.

Wiping his dirty hands on his shirt, Tiger looked at me and said,

"We're good friends, ain't we, Mr. Paull?"
"I shall miss science."
"It's been dead good."
"You goin' to a young kids' school?"
"Bet they don't swear."
"Bet they like spiders."
"Yes, Tiger," I said, *"bet they do, and, yes, we're dead good friends."*

Chapter 25

Just after I gave and received *good-byes and best wishes* from the headmaster, his wife, and the teachers at Trinity Fields, Tiger and Michael came to see me.

"See what we've got for you, sir," said Michael, holding a large envelope, asking me not to open his gift until I went home. Tiger gave me a tin with a dead bat stuck inside. *"Found it. Thought you'd like it,"* said Tiger.

"Don't forget us, sir."
"I won't," I replied. *"I certainly won't."*

Later, when I opened Michael's large envelope, there were pictures of pin people, without the extra anatomical parts. Under the drawings, he'd written, *"See, I can do it when I want. I like drawing."*

I began to gather and box my few belongings and moved to Leicester in early January, the week before school was due to reopen.

During the winter break, an article in the *Times Education Supplement* caught my eye: Leicestershire, Oxfordshire, and the West Riding in Yorkshire were seen as *beacons* for promoting progressive approaches to infant and junior school teaching and learning.

Schools in Leicestershire, such as the school I was now joining, were using a teaching practice becoming known as the *integrated day*, a philosophy most widely developed in infant schools. Although such a way of working with children represented a half-century of educational development in England, it, I read, grew most rapidly after World War II.

Of great significance to educators and researchers was the fact that this way of working had been found to provide effective learning for children of all backgrounds—for inner city children as well as for those in the suburban schools.

The specific characteristic innovations of the Leicestershire primary school *revolution* were first worked out by a number of infant schools and then shared at heads' meetings and workshops, first, by the Education Committee's chief advisor, Len Sealey, then his successors, Bill Browse and Marjorie Kay. The advisors enthusiastically supported and encouraged these changes in classrooms.

Changes were taking place in America, too. In 1957, the year of the launching of the Russian satellite, *Sputnik*, a proponent of educational change, David Armington, was involved in significant elementary school curriculum development, especially in mathematics and science. In 1961, Bill Hull, a colleague of David Armington's at Shady Hill School in Cambridge, Massachusetts, went to Leicestershire to particularly see the work of Z. Dienes's multibase blocks.

Bill Hull saw much more. He was surprised to see classes of more than forty children working—in groups and independently—on mathematics, art, writing, reading, and much more.

The *British Infant School* philosophy, as it became known in the United States, was also brought to the attention of American educators by Lore Rasmussen of the Philadelphia Public Schools, Lilian Weber of New York City, and Joseph Featherstone, from Cambridge, Massachusetts.

Joseph Featherstone wrote three widely read articles describing the visits he and his wife made to the Leicestershire schools in enthusiastic detail in the *New Republic* magazine during August and September 1967.

Using the Plowden report as reference, Featherstone noted the major reform in teaching style, which he linked to Piaget's developmental psychology, emphasizing the move away from directed classwork that was oriented toward testing, to a child-centered approach where science was given equal weighting to the "new" mathematics, reading and writing.

He was the prefect publicist for the reform in English primary schools. His message raised a storm of interest and triggered a flood of American visitors to England, Oxfordshire, Yorkshire, and Leicestershire, in particular, to see for themselves the educational wonders they were reading about, developing an extensive network of like-minded observers.

Ed Yeomans's *Education for Initiative and Responsibility* followed suit. Both of these publications spread the word among reform-minded educators. These articles appeared at about the same time as Charles Silberman's influential book, *Crisis in the Classroom.*

Vincent Rogers made a trip to Oxfordshire, writing, *"I have not been the same since."*

Rogers edited an important book, *Teaching in the British Primary School,* bringing together a number of essays written by leading English teachers and advisors.

By 1971, Barth and Rathbone's, *A Bibliography of Open Education* listed more than three hundred articles, books, films, and informal publications of every kind.

The US Office of Economic Opportunity funded twelve open classroom training centers in nine cities, part of the *Follow Through* program, intended to give impetus to the continuing development of children who participated in Head Start.

The Ford Foundation also provided funds to develop open classrooms in public schools, and the Education Development Center (EDC) of Newton, Massachusetts, led by David Armington and Rosemary Williams, expanded these efforts considerably.

One major curriculum project, Elementary Science Study (ESS), was headed by a team of eminent scientists, some being former members of the World War II Manhattan Bomb Project. Moving into the world of early childhood education was one of the dramatic personal reactions to the horrific leveling of Hiroshima and Nagasaki.

The team produced innovative teaching material that soon found its way into sympathetic English classrooms.

Chapter 26

After getting my few possessions into my new flat, I made my way on the bus to Blaby, walked through the Blaby neighborhood, and into my new school.

There was a handwritten note taped on the classroom door, just under the new sign:

This is Mr. Paull's classroom.

Hello!

Good luck, Mr. Paull. I hope you enjoy the children.
I've taken all my stuff—the room is yours. I wish you every success with your science.
Best of luck.
You'll find the attendance book in the secretary's office.

Mrs. Biddle

With my heart missing a beat or two, I opened the door of *my* new classroom.

I looked around. The caretaker had cleaned and cleared the room. Tables and chairs were stacked up against the classroom's walls. The classroom environment I inherited wasn't set up or as well resourced as I had hoped. Mrs. Biddle had stripped the classroom. It was spotless. Mrs. Biddle had taken everything that belonged to her and returned every reading book to the school library.

The walls were bare. All the children's work I had seen when I was last there had gone.

I put down my bag and opened the wall cupboards. There were a few boxes of writing books and mathematics material, stacked and neatly labeled. Brushes and tins of powder paint were on the bottom shelf. I knew there wouldn't be any science resources, but I did expect to find a *teacher guidebook* for mathematics and one for English. I couldn't find them anywhere. So the big question was this: how would I know what to teach?

I tried to recreate and copy the furniture layouts I remembered from my interview day. One thing I knew for sure, I had to make working areas for the different subjects—especially a *nature table* for science—and leave space on the carpet for the children to sit around me in a circle.

After I chose which table to use for the nature display, I moved another small table into one of the corners and added a couple of reference books I'd found tucked away in the back of the cupboard. *That's the reading corner done,* I thought.

I set it up another table with a few rulers and a tape measure for mathematics. I made and labeled five other areas, including two more for reading and writing, one near the sink for arts and crafts, and two close to the front for science. I counted the chairs and remaining small tables.

I had just the right number for five children at each table, and the rest of the class sitting on cushions around the classroom on the carpet.

Funny though, there wasn't a teacher's desk. Where, I thought, would I keep my class attendance register, school lunch book, and other teacher bits and pieces? Where would I sit when the children were doing their work?

Perplexed, I went around the school, searching for a desk and chair. I eventually made do with a scratched table I found in the teachers' storeroom and an adult-size chair from the staff room. I placed them by the window that overlooked the school gardens.

I posted my blank *Activities for the Day* sheet on an art easel close to the door.

On the way home, I thought about what Mrs. Biddle told me: introductions first, then take the kids to assembly. When you return to the classroom, get the children going on their projects, whatever they might be. They'll know. Once they started, I would sit at my desk, check my new record book, learn everyone's names, and check on the three who had, I was told, *"difficulties."* Then, I thought, I'll take the class out to explore the yard and find as many small creatures as they could—that'll get everyone *"doing"* science, writing, and drawing.

During dinnertime, I'll read through their records that I was sure I would have by then.

Straightforward, really. Nothing to it. Just the way I worked with my pupils at Trinity Fields, except there I had to follow a textbook, word for word.

I went to school again, the day before school was to start, and met Mrs. Iliffe, the school secretary, who I later learned kept the school running very smoothly.

"Children's records? What do you mean? Their health records?"
"Oh. No, there aren't any individual progress records."
"You make and keep those."

OK. So now I knew. I went and rearranged my room before the full staff meeting.

After everyone greeted each other and asked how they spent their Christmas, I was introduced to the group.

"Welcome, John Paull. Welcome to Blaby Stokes. Mr. John Paull is going to bring us a load of science ideas," Mr. Ward said. *"He's been teaching science in a secondary school."*

At least three teachers chorused. *"Wow! Good, he can help me then."* I smiled, but as I did so, my stomach muscles tightened. They didn't know I wasn't a good science teacher in the secondary school. Will they find out? Or more to the point, when will they find out?

Who's going to help me? I thought.

Mrs. Iliffe gave everyone a copy of the January calendar, the times we should use the hall for PE with our class and dates of after-school *Dienes multibase* arithmetic blocks workshops. I wasn't given any textbooks for reading, writing, and mathematics.

My brain was racing.

What do I do for English and mathematics lessons? Don't I have textbooks to follow? Where are they? Are they in the classroom? Did I miss them? Dienes? What's that?

When the short meeting was finished, all the teachers went to set up their rooms. Mr. Jolley followed me to my classroom, asking if I had any questions. He looked around my room.

"Like your room, John Paull. Looks good. When'd you do that? Is that a staff room chair? You nick that?"
"You having a teacher's table?"
"Hmmmmm."
"Like your science tables. Plenty of space for the boys and girls to work."
"What are you going to put on them? Hands-on stuff?"
"What are you putting on your nature table?"
"Doing science tomorrow with everyone?"
"Good. The children will help you."

"Oh . . . one thing more. Anyone told you that David needs a lot of help? No?"
"Both his mum and dad are illiterate, you know. Can't read a word. Nice couple."
"The old man works on a farm."
"Mum works there too."

"Taking the class outside?"
"Watch the weather—I think it's going to rain."

I took on board Mr. Jolley's questions, sensing he wasn't expecting answers, and then asked him about the *Dienes* workshops.

"What's this Dienes stuff? Who's Dienes?"

"Do I use it, whatever it is, with my class?"

"You do know, John Paull, we are using a new way of teaching mathematics? Yes? We're a pilot school for the Dienes material, you know, the multibase stuff, wooden blocks for base 10, and I've been trained in using the blocks. I'll help you get started with it, OK?"

"Other teachers come here to see how we use Dienes materials."

"The children too, they'll show you. They've been using it for the past two years."

"I'm the Dienes guy, and you're now the science guy. Welcome."

"Hey, anything you need, you know where to find me."

"Can't help you with math tomorrow though. Gotta go to a meeting with some parents."

"The class'll show you what to do."

"Your Dienes boxes are in the staff room cupboard. I'll fetch them for you."

As he went out the door, my head was full of more and more questions. What's *multibase* stuff? And much more important, where, oh, where are my textbooks? *Mmmmmm, who's going to help me?* I thought. What about this Dienes stuff? What do I do for English? I have to teach PE? How do I do that? Do I need a tracksuit? What will David do if he doesn't get help?

Just as I was about to follow Mr. Jolley to see if he knew, Mrs. Finlay came in and introduced herself.

"I'm Marjorie. I'm next door. If you want anything, just yell, OK? Do I hear you're taking your class out tomorrow?"

She smiled. *"Take mine too, please."*

"Might rain though, and it's going to be windy."

Mr. Jolley brought the boxes of Dienes stuff and put them in one of the cupboards for me. Two other teachers popped their heads through the door and welcomed me to school. Everyone in school seemed so helpful. And everyone, it seemed, wanted me to help him or her with his or her science.

No one gave me any textbooks though, and I was too shy and unsure to ask.

So how do I know what to teach?

Chapter 27

Wondering what maths and English to do throughout the day, I was up at the crack of dawn. Pocketing my amber and a *wishing rock*, I caught the early morning bus to school and reset my room yet again. Then, fiddling with my amber in my pocket, I waited nervously for the children to arrive.

Rain splattered on the windows, dashing my plans to take the class outside to explore the school grounds.

"Oh, no . . . There goes plan number one. Now what do I do? Not sure I want the class to show me how to do maths. That wouldn't be right, would it? I'm their teacher."

Mr. Ward, looking very much the headmaster in a smart navy blue suit, polished black shoes, waistcoat, white shirt, and dark blue tie, came by my room around eight o'clock.

"Good morning, John. Just came to see if you're OK. Hey, your room looks good! Mike said you'd done a good job. Don't forget we begin with morning assembly. Bring your class into the hall and then sit on the floor with them."
"And it's wet outside—indoor playtime and dinnertime."

Sensing my nervousness, Mr. Ward winked, smiled, and then wished me luck.

"Have a great day. Don't worry. You'll love it."
"The children are a good bunch."
"The sun will come out soon."

"Oh, give David a good day."

My forty-three children walked into my classroom. They put their wet raincoats and bags away, looked at me and at the tables, then came and sat around me on the blue carpet. As many of them hadn't seen each other during the two-week Christmas break, they started chatting. Eventually, everyone gave me full eye contact, and then with huge smiles on their faces, they chanted in chorus:

"Hello, Mr. Paull. Welcome to our school."

Then they turned and faced each other.
"Hello, everyone. Welcome back, and a happy New Year."

I liked that. *What a great ritual,* I thought. I checked the class names in the register as they introduced themselves to me and then asked who was staying for dinner. I pointed to the schedule I'd written in large letters, resting on the small easel, reading out loud:

Today is Tuesday, January 3.

MEETING TIME, then ASSEMBLY
Maths and English GROUP WORK
PLAYTIME
Maths and English GROUP WORK
DINNER
PE, then Science and art GROUP WORK
MEETING
HOME

They looked at the board. Then they looked toward me.
"This is our first meeting time," I said with a big smile.
"Oh, don't forget," I said, *"to write what you're doing this morning on the activity sheet."*

Nobody, especially David, seemed to be very enthusiastic about my schedule. They stared at me and then at each other. I started to panic. What's wrong? Perhaps they weren't very excited about my plans. Perhaps I didn't explain them very well. Perhaps I should read them again.

The rain splattered on the windows.
I read the schedule again, louder this time.

A hand went up. *"The room's different. Well, Mr. Paull, what do we do when we come back from assembly? You've changed the room. Where do we sit? Can we sit anywhere? I'm Steven, by the way. Mr. Ward's my dad. Can I sit next to Molly? Mr. Paull, can I?"*
"You going to tell us what we can do?"
"Are we doin' maths?"

"Um," I stuttered, *"when you come back, choose a table, you know, five of you to a table, as you can see. The rest of you, find a place on the carpet, OK? And before you start work, write your names on the activity sheet."*

"Oh, no maths."

"Just go to your place, Steven, and when you get back. I'm sure you'll know what to do," I said edgily and led the class to morning assembly.

During the next twenty minutes, in the school hall, I nervously fiddled with my amber as Mr. Ward welcomed everyone back to school, read the obligatory Bible story, and then talked about new school dinner arrangements.

As he spoke, I wondered what Steven had done with his science kit from Woolworths.

Then, Mr. Ward pointed to me and said, *"Hey, everyone, there's Mr. Paull. He's our new teacher. He knows everything there is to know about science."*
"Stand up, Mr. Paull."

Nervously, I stood up, waved at everyone, smiling the best smile I could muster.

"Welcome, Mr. Paull, welcome to our school," said Mr. Ward.

After assembly, back in our classroom, there was a mad dash for seats. Seven of the boys went to the science tables. Three of them sat on the same chair. David sat very close to me.

The air was filled with anxious questions.

"Mr. Paull, Mr. Paull, what we doin? There's nothing on the nature table—and not much on the science table. Just books."
"What are we doing?"
"Where's our pencils?"
"There's nothing on our *table."*
"Why aren't we doin' maths?"
"We ain't doin' mavs?"
"You got our maths books?"

Steven, the headmaster's son, asked,
"Got any science stuff to show us, Mr. Paull?"

"Later," I said. *"C'mon, you all know what to do. Get started."*

As the rain was still splattering on the window, I heard one voice, with a touch of sarcasm, asking,
"Get started on what, new teacher?"

The class didn't know what to do. I didn't know what to do. The boys and girls didn't start working excitedly. Instead they fidgeted and fiddled and waited. They waited for me to be their teacher. And they complained.

And no wonder. Their well-established routine with Mrs. Biddle had been taken from them, and there was nothing they could see to replace it.
David, at the front of the room, sat up straight, wide-eyed, staring hard and expectantly at me.

Damn, I thought. I hadn't planned for the unexpected. Sorry, Mr. Kitson. I didn't heed your good advice.

I hadn't set them any engaging work. I hadn't set them any expectations. I hadn't offered them anything interesting to do. I hadn't put out their writing and maths books. I hadn't filled the nature table or put any assignments or resources out on the tables. I hadn't sharpened the pencils. I had changed their routine. David needs help. I didn't really know what to do. And it was pouring with rain.

Steven, sitting, at the science table and watching my every move, put up his hand. Again.

"My dad told me you are a science teacher, Mr. Paull. Can we do science today? There's nothing much on the science tables. You have anything else? Anything to show us? Anything we can do? Go on, Mr. Paull, anything?"

So even though I knew I shouldn't, I resorted to what I could now do reasonably well, *chalk and talk.*
"Well, we were going outside, to collect stuff to put on our nature table, but as you can see, it's raining."
"Let me tell you about mosquitoes. They're really interesting."

I didn't sound very convincing. I wrote the word *insects* on the blackboard.

"Wos 'at say?" asked David.

I turned and told the class what I knew about the tiny creature I had learned so much about when I was at Trinity Fields. As I talked, I wrote a few facts about mosquitoes.

"Take out your writing books. Copy what I've written. Write and tell me what you know about mosquitoes—oh, when you've finished, write about your Christmas. What did you have for Christmas dinner? What was your best present? What did you buy for your mum? What did you do on Boxing Day?"

And very firmly, *"Don't forget to write the date at the top. Left hand side."*
David put up his hand.

"Can't rit them thar words, Mr. Paull. Can't spell either."
"That's OK, just copy what I wrote, OK?" I replied.
"I'll help you. Don't worry."

"Can't read, Mr. Paull. Wos it say? Wos it say on the board?"
"Can't copy."
"Mosquitoes? What's a mosquito? Don't 'av them round 'ere, do we?"
"Bite? Do they bite?"

"Will they bite me?"

Another hand went up. *"I can't read what you've written, Teacher. You write funny."*

The children became noisy, irritable, and they squabbled with each other about the lack of seats and about the work that I'd set them.

I looked at the clock. It wasn't ten o'clock yet. We'd been together for about half an hour, and I was already exasperated. And, I thought, *There's no playtime or outside dinnertime to help me get through the day.*

I wrote, without any explanation, some multiplication and division problems on the board.

"Can't do mavs, either, Mr. Paull!" shouted David.
"Just try to copy what I wrote, then, please," I replied.

Wiping his sleeve across his nose, he said, *"Told ya . . . can't copy."*

I just made it through 'til morning break without anyone leading a full-scale revolution. After the boys and girls had their milk, I sat them on the carpet. I stood and read aloud one of Enid Blyton's adventure books. Surprisingly, everyone, including David, appeared to be listening as I read through the first three chapters.

As the plot and the characters unfolded, Julie asked pointedly, *"Aren't there girls in the story?"*
I didn't respond.

I cut up drawing paper during dinnertime, and when the afternoon school started, I told my class that they could draw and color any scene from the morning's Enid Blyton story.

The classroom quickly became very noisy.

I didn't know how to refocus class when they were off task. I didn't know how to get some of them on task. I kept thinking and hoping the boys and girls would make it all happen. I didn't know how to help David, and he needed so much help, even with drawing a picture. And the rain kept splattering on the window.

When the children went home at the end of what I thought was the longest day of my life, I was beside myself. Drawing deeply on my cigarette, I fretted that the children would tell their parents about their boring new teacher. I was sure one or two, or more, or all the parents, would phone school and complain to Mr. Ward about the ineffective new teacher.

Feeling desperate, I went next door to talk to Mrs. Marjorie Finlay, the teacher who had so impressed me when I walked into her classroom on the tour the day I was appointed and the one I felt was very sincere when she offered me help any time I needed it. Well, I needed help *now*.

I slumped on one of her children's chairs.
"*You OK?*" she asked, sensing some tension.

"*Nope, Marjorie, I'm bloody not OK.*"
"*Marjorie, how do you do it?*" I asked, trying hard to hide my inner feelings.
"*How do you get your kids—sorry, children—so involved in their learning each day?*"
"*How do you keep everyone doing something they should do? How do you get to see all your class in the day? What do you do with your boys and girls that can't read and write?*"

"*Textbooks? You have textbooks for English and maths?*"
And I added, with a limp smile.
"*What do you have that I don't?*"

She smiled, knowing from the look on my face and my body language that it had been a long and bad and crummy day for me.
"*Hey, it's not the end of the world. Come in tomorrow and spend part of the day with me, that's the best thing to do. Then you'll see for yourself. Much better than talking about it.*"

Then she added that if I asked the headmaster, Mr. Ward, he would be very supportive of that idea.

"He'll cover your class. Go and see him now. He's still in school. Don't *ask him for textbooks though. Oh, ask him about David."*

Bidding Marjorie good night, I went down the corridor, across the hall, to see the headmaster. He was expecting me. Mr. Ward probably didn't have to wait to get a phone call about my first day from a parent. Steven had, I felt sure, already given his dad a firsthand, graphic account of the excruciatingly boring day with the new teacher, Mr. John Paull.

I shouldn't have worried so much: Mr. Ward had already planned to take my class the next morning so I could visit the next-door classroom.

"Then we'll talk," he said.

Chapter 28

The following morning, after assembly, notebook in hand, mind alert, I sat at the back of Marjorie's classroom. Every worktable was filled with a range of math manipulatives and other resources, laid out by Marjorie before school started. I took special note at the nature table. A spray of dead oak leaves and shriveled acorns and some books on trees were in the center of the table with a label:

Do you know what these are?
Use the books to find out.

Marjorie reminded everyone what they had learned in mathematics yesterday. Then she described what they were going to learn today, starting with the maths resources spread out on their tables.

She gave brief but clear instructions, took a few questions, and the class went to assigned tables and began quietly, but confidently, working with each other.

I was fascinated, enthralled, and I admit, overawed by what I saw.

Every child, whatever their educational prowess, whatever their home background, appeared to be engaged. Every child worked individually, or with a group, with materials at his/her own pace.

Marjorie moved comfortably around the room, interacting and redirecting her children when she felt they needed it. At playtime, the children cleared their tables. Everyone knew what to do as each had an assigned classroom job.

Because of the rain, it was indoor playtime. The children took out books and games and entertained themselves, drinking their school milk, as Marjorie and three girls quickly put out art and writing resources.

When playtime ended, the children chose which area, art or writing, to begin working on. After thirty minutes, they changed tables.

The last session of the morning was *diary time*, a time of quietness when the children wrote about their morning's work, as Marjorie set up for the afternoon. Finally, they met in small groups and, for a few minutes, shared their thoughts. It was then that Marjorie pointed to the nature table, picking up the leaves and acorns.

"Take a look at these when you have time, OK? Any idea what they are?"

Plenty of hands shot up.

"I know, I know."

At the end of the morning, with Marjorie's teaching jumping around in my head, I rejoined my class, just as they were leaving for school lunch.

Steven and Michael came into the room and asked if they could help. I appreciated their thoughtfulness.

"You know what? You can help me after lunch, if you'd like to. We can talk about what the class can do this afternoon."

When they finished their dinner, the two boys came back to the classroom to help.
"Hey, Mr. Paull, wot we doin'?"

I remembered my conversation with Mrs. Biddle. When she needed a quiet afternoon, she asked the children to read then draw something from a book of their choice.

I said, *"We're going to read and write and draw, OK?"*
"So can you go to the library and bring back an armful of picture books?"
"Thanks, boys. Then set them out on the tables, OK?"

When the class returned from the hall, I read more from Enid Blyton's adventure book.

"OK, there are loads of books on your tables. Choose one and read, OK? Then I want you to draw something inspired by your reading, OK?"

I sat with David's group, listening carefully, trying to get to know something about each of them.

At the end of the day, I went back to Marjorie's room to thank her for inviting me into her room in the morning.

"Well, I got them to have a quiet afternoon, but you know, I'm not doing what they want me to do."

Marjorie smiled. *"Nonsense,"* she said. *"We've all been through that."*

"You know, John, there's much more control here in my classroom than you can see."
"Yes, the children have responsibility of planning some of their own learning."
"But that happens with considerable help from me, the teacher."
"I create, set up, resource nearly all the activities."
"That's what I'm here for."
"I'm checking in with them all the time, especially those who have problems with their work."
"The 3 Rs, yes? Reading, writing, and arithmetic?"
"All important."
"Very important."
"That's why children come to school."
"There's a routine, and I follow it every day. Maths first. The Dienes stuff, first thing each morning. It's great for the boys and girls, but with my big class, it's hard to see everyone's maths work each day."

"Did you see how I asked the children to show me what they were doing?"
"And my resources?"
"I want them to be curious, so I gather interesting things that I think they'll like and bring them into school."

"The dead oak leaves on the nature table I found yesterday. I was surprised that they were still on the old oak tree close to my home."

"I keep a list of what I need. There's always a plentiful supply in school, and I'm really familiar with all the stuff. I know how to use it."

"I don't put out anything that needs instructions unless *I plan to spend time working with the boys and girls on that particular table."*

"Oh, and I make sure I have well-labeled storage containers."
"That means I know where everything is—and so does the class."

"My biggest grumble?"
"I have too many boys in my class, and sometimes, I don't see how and what some of them are doing during the day."

"The day isn't long enough."

That made me smile. My first full day, I felt, had seemed to go on forever.

Before I went to catch my bus, my head buzzing with so much to think about, I met with the headmaster again.

"So what did you see, John? Did you notice how Mrs. Finlay makes things work?"
"She's got some challenging children in there too, you know."

"Yes," I said, *"She's great. And thank you for giving me the time to do that. It was so worthwhile."*

I think Mr. Ward read my mind. He sensed I was feeling unsure of myself.

"Be patient," he said.

"Hey, so what makes you tick? What do you like to do in your spare time?"
"What interests you as a scientist?"

I thought for a minute . . . I wasn't too sure what he meant by his question. Was I supposed to say that I was very much into chemistry? Physics? Was I being interviewed again?

With some hesitation, I said,
"Well, I'm a collector—minerals, fossils, spiders, caterpillars, anything that catches my eye."
I reached in my pocket and brought out my OXO tin containing precious amber. I told Mr. Ward where and when I found it, then about my teacher, Mr. Jones, his green cupboard full of treasure, and the Wednesday afternoons the children brought in their treasures, tucked away in their pockets. I told him about the afternoon I took in my golden amber and showed Mr. Jones.

"That story, you know, got you the job. We loved the way you handled that."

He smiled again. *"And that,"* he said, *"John Paull, is how you will connect to your class. And to David. He needs a lot of help with his reading, you know. Remember Mr. Jones and Tiger Reynolds. Big teaching lessons there."*

"Especially for David."
"And important, your science—you know, the collecting bit. That's what gets children hooked, you know."
"It'll help get David going too."
"Concentrate on that! Mike will help you with Dienes. Get it going."
"Now go home."

Sitting on the top deck of the bus, scribbling in my journal, the day's conversations made me obsess about my teaching role, my daily plan, about my teaching space, and about what was and what wasn't appropriate with my boisterous boys and girls—especially David.
Mr. Jones and Tiger's faces came flooding back in my memory. Then, I thought, *Hey, that's it.* Mr. Ward is right. Of course he's right, and I think I can do something about it. And I can help get David going. *Let's try,* I thought, recreating in my classroom what Mr. Jones created on those special Wednesday afternoons—an atmosphere of sharing, a classroom feeling of anticipation and excitement.

Let's see what happens if I did a *Mr. Jones* and brought some of my rocks and shells into my classroom and put them, with questions, on my nature table. It worked for him. And it worked for me, accidentally, with Tiger and his spiders in Trinity Fields.

I could, I thought, start with my OXO tin and my precious amber that had always been in my pocket from that birthday Monday long ago.

Sod it! What did I have to lose? With renewed energy, I packed together as many shells, rocks, twigs, and other items of interest from my collections as I could find, and packed them in my small tins and shoeboxes that were hanging around my flat.

Chapter 29

The following morning I went to school on the early morning bus, weighed down with a big duffel bag filled with all kinds of artifacts.

"Today," I said to myself, *"is the start, the real start, of my teaching career."*

I spread a range of resources on all the classroom tables. I put an aquarium full of wriggly pond creatures on the nature table, magnifying glasses, some wood cuts, different colored rocks, a dead beetle, leaf skeletons, dead tree leaves, and exoskeletons of a spider and a pill bug. I put a couple of handfuls of sunflower seeds and raisins in the empty bird feeder hanging outside the classroom window.

My bookshelf now had school library picture reference books about rocks, fossils, spiders, and common garden insects. I took a box of small diaries from the school's storage cupboard, one for each of my children.

Mike Jolley poked his head through the door.

"Hey, want some help with your maths this morning? I'm free."
"Shall I come in? Shall I do some maths?"
"Leave your stuff on the tables. We'll work on the carpet with the maths equipment."

Oh, *yes*, please, Mr. Jolley. Yes, yes, please.

"It's raining still—you're not going out, right?" he asked.

After the children hung up their wet coats and put their lunch bags away, David was the first to notice the wooden bird feeder standing outside the classroom window.

"Hey, look!" he said, his face breaking into a big smile *"Look, everybody, he's put seeds and stuff in the feeder. Now we gotta feeder, like I got at 'ome."*
"Can I look after it, Mr. Paull? Can I?"
"Please?"
"Go on, Mr. Paull. I like feeding bods."
"I'm dead good at it."

This was David's *amber* moment. This was something in class he could connect to, something he could think, draw, and perhaps write about. He made me smile. David's smile and my smile made me feel better.

The day was off to a good start. The boys and girls sat around me in a circle on the blue carpet. Grinning, I looked directly at each of them in turn.

Using a soft, low voice and needing their approval, I asked, *"So what do you think of our room? Is it different?"*
"Do you like it?"

"I like the feeder best, Mr. Paull," said David, excitedly pointing to the window.
"Fink we'll get some finches comin', Mr. Paull? I get 'em in my garden. You know, them beauts, them bullfinches. Got that red chest. Them bods don't live here, y'know. They only come here in the autumn."
"Dun know where they come from though."

Jacqueline put up her hand.
"Looks dead good, Mr. Paull. Really brill, dead good."

As I was about to lead the children to the morning assembly, Mike came in with a box of Dienes maths equipment, setting it out on the carpet.

Later, sitting in a circle, Mike Jolley led the class in a practical math session, giving everyone opportunities to interact with the multibase math materials and giving me stacks of opportunity to see how it should be done. He was good. Everyone, including David, was involved and engaged in being a mathematician. And everyone, I saw, was helping each other.

When he finished, Mike looked at me, smiled, collected his resources, and left.

I sat down on the carpet next to David.

In my quietest dad-like voice, I told them about my teacher, Mr. Jones, and how he'd open his glass-fronted cupboard and show us his *treasures*. I described how I felt on those special Wednesday afternoons when everyone in class could share with each other what interested them.

I stared at my *wishing rock* in the palm of my outstretched hand, then told the children where I'd found it and how my family used sea pebbles like mine to make wishes.

I closed my eyes, just like my dad did when he told a story, telling the children I was making a silent, private wish.

When I opened my eyes, David asked,

"Wot you wish for, Mr. Paull?"

"That's private, David," I said with a smile. *"That would be telling."*

I passed the small *wishing rock* around the circle, suggesting everyone touch it, close their eyes, and send someone a private wish. As soon as David touched the rock, he put up his hand.

"Made my wish. Ain't private."
"Can I look after the bod feeder, Mr. Paull?"
"Please? That's my wish."

Smiling broadly, I replied, *"David, that's a great wish."*
"And the bird feeder? It's all yours, kiddo, all yours."

"Hey, did you close your eyes?"

"Din't need to, Mr. Paull."

"Crikey! Wishing rocks work," he exclaimed.

When the *wishing rock* was passed to the last child in the circle, I quietly described my fifth birthday walk on the beach with my dad. As I spoke, I brought my smooth, shiny piece of yellow amber from my pocket.

The children went quiet. Their eyes widened as I slowly unwrapped my fingers. They stared at the smooth yellow amber resting in the palm of my hand.

I told them what my mum, then my first teacher, Miss Harvey, and now using my very, very softest voice, what Mr. Jones had said to me when I first showed them my amber.

They began to chatter excitedly. It was the class's *amber moment.* I asked,

"Has anyone ever seen anything like this? What do you think it is?"

As they had no idea, the questions came thick and fast.

I told them how amber was made, how many million years old it might be.

"Millions? Millions of years?" said someone. *"Thasa lot, ain't it?"*

The effect of the amber, and the *wishing rock*, on my class was amazing. They all looked wide-eyed at me. There was silence in the room. You really could hear the proverbial pin drop.

Steven Ward, sitting across from me, put up his hand. I sensed in my bones it was going to be one of those breathtaking, memorable Tiger Reynolds's teaching moments.

"Mr. Paull, Mr. Paull, see what I've got."

He dug in his pocket, looked me in the eye, and brought out, ever so slowly, the most beautiful fossil ammonite I'd ever seen. *What perfect timing,* I thought. Stephen grinned. I grinned too.

"Steve. That's so magical. So, so magical."

Steven showed his fossil to all the children, just like I had shown my amber a long time ago in Mr. Jones's class. This was Steven's *amber* moment.

"Does anyone have a question for Steven?"

Robert put up his hand. His questions came out like a torrent. He couldn't get them out quickly enough. He just *had* to know.

"Wos 'at? Where'd you get it? Did you find it? How old is it? 'Ow much is it worth?"
"Wos it made from?"

Steven was beside himself, loving the feeling of sharing something that was special to him. He told everyone about his recent late summer holiday in Lyme Regis and about the morning he found the ammonite, walking on the beach with his mother.
"It was, well, you know, lying on the ground."
"Mum didn't see it. I did."

"It's like your story, Mr. Paull," said someone.

"OK," I said, choosing my time so I had everyone's attention.
"Here are your morning assignments: find out what you can about the amber."
"What is it? How is it made? And find out what you can about Steven's fossil."

"Here's a science journal for each of you. Write down what you discover, OK? There are pens and paints out on the tables—use them and make sure you draw and paint them both."
"There's plenty of books to help you, and you can ask me and Steven anything you want."

"Can I draw bods, Mr. Paull? Go on. Can I?" asked David. *"Don't like rocks much."*

"You betcha, David," I said. *"Here's a box of crayons. Draw away, kid."*
"Ooops, sorry, I didn't mean to call you a kid," I added.

David smiled. *"That's what me dad calls me, Mr. Paull. I like it."*
"Like kiddo too."

Jane and Mary fetched a picture reference book on fossils and began thumbing through the pages. Kevin quickly joined them with another fossil picture book in his hands, and soon the three of them were deep in animated discussion, comparing the colorful pictures of fossil ammonites. Before long, the whole class was sitting in all the interest areas researching, writing, and drawing fossils, and telling—*teaching*—each other about their collections of rocks and minerals and fossils they had at home.

Just as I went to see David who was sitting by the window watching the sparrows and finches flocking around the bird table, pecking at the birdseed, I noticed that the rain had stopped. The time to explore the outdoors had come.

Chapter 30

After the dinner break, we put on our outdoor coats, our wellies, and we went outside in the yard to see what we could find. I did, though, first talk about what a good collector would do.

"A good collector," I said, *"searches very carefully and doesn't disturb the surroundings."*
"A good collector handles tiny creatures very carefully and only collects a few."
"A good collector studies what he's found, then returns tiny creatures to the place where s/he found them."

As soon as we got outside, I showed my class how to turn over and replace a rock.
"Don't forget. It's somebody's home."
"OK, see what you can find."

Within the first minute, I knew that taking children in search of small creatures is a delightful thing to do. Reminding myself of what I did whenever I went out with my dad, I knew that some of my class needed time to stand and stare and enjoy the excitement of seeing something different. I also knew that some of them would be off searching almost right away.

David, within a minute, showed his partner, Angela, a beautiful white bird's feather he picked up near the old elm tree.
"Look, look, Angie. I gotta dead good feather."

"Nice," said Angela. *"Nice feather, David,"* adding that she was searching for amber. Nothing else, she said flatly, would do. *"I want some amber, you know, like Mr. Paull's."*

It really had to be amber.

"Comes from a tree, right? Might be some here, then. Elm amber is what I'm looking for."

She rummaged through the leaves at the base of the trunk, picking up and closely inspecting every pebble poking through the soil. Just then, Michael and Steven shouted loudly.

"Look, look, Look!"
"We found a wishing rock."
"Like yours, Mr. Paull, you know, like the one you found when you were a kid."
"Hey, everyone."
"Look! A wishing rock."

Hearing the shouting, all the children came to look to see what the boys had found. That started it.

The chatting subsided as almost everyone in the class, including David, searched the ground around them.

Mary continued to explore the long grass, saying loudly, *"I'm looking for cuckoo spit, you know, froghoppers. They're brill. We have them in our garden at home."*

"Tell us more, Mary," I asked.

"Froghoppers," she said, *"look like squirty frogs . . . When they're young, they squirt out white juice over their eggs. You know, cuckoo spit. Keeps them safe."*

"I'm going to find some, then I'll show you."

Before we came back to the classroom, I asked the children to stand still and look around them.

"We leave everything, this place, as we found it, yes?"
"It's someone's home, yes?"
"Yes, Mr. Paull, it's someone's home."
"And," said David, *"Bods get scared when we get too close to 'um."*

Everyone agreed that, yes, it was home to all sorts of tiny creatures that wriggled and crawled through the undergrowth, and we hadn't damaged the garden.

Once inside the classroom, Mary told us everything she knew about the cuckoo spit.

Angela told the class that she had searched for amber but didn't find any, but she said, *"See what I found? I found this dead pill bug—is it the exoskeleton, Mr. Paull? I found it exoskeleton under some dead leaves."*

Phyllis exclaimed,
"Hey, I got some live pill bugs."
"That's where they live. Under dead leaves."
"I know about them, these pill bugs. My dad finds them in our  *garden. He told me they live in the dark, you know. In families, like us. And they eat brown, dry, and decaying leaves! I know how many legs they have."*
"They're more fun than amber, Mr. Paull."
"Can I go get some more and keep 'em?"
"Do they 'ibernate, Mr. Paull? You know, sleep in the winter?"
"Why they called pill bugs?"
"Do you know, Mr. Paull?"

"Well," I replied, *"slow down a bit, Phyllis."*
"I think they do hibernate. Not sure though."
"That's something we have to find out."

"And they are really called wood lice, and they are also called pill bugs 'cos they wrap up in a tiny ball, don't they, when they're touched? Then they look like a pill."
"Go and get a couple and bring them in."

*S*he returned, carrying a handful of dead leaves in one hand, and pill bugs in the other.

"Angela, Mary, and Phyllis, let's make a home for your cuckoo spit and pill bugs."
"What do you think the pill bugs need to live in our classroom?"
"You too, Mary. What do your leaf hoppers need?"

Mary found a couple of small cardboard boxes and gave one to Phyllis. I sat and watched them make really good temporary homes for the pill bugs and the cuckoo spit.

Then I said to everyone,

"OK."
"Take out your journals, check in the nature books on your table to answer your questions, then draw and write about your *discoveries."*
"Don't forget to write the date at the top of your page."
"And if you want to, glue your wishing rocks and other finds in the bottom of your tins."

I discovered that Phyllis really did know a lot about the pill bugs.

She wrote about their need for a home that was damp and shady, that they liked to huddle in groups, that they fed mainly on rotting wood, that they had seven pairs of legs, and that they were eaten by frogs and toads.

The afternoon went by very quickly, and close to the end of the day, after *diary-writing* time, to calm everyone down, I read another chapter from Enid Blyton's adventure book. When I'd finished, Phyllis took her pill bugs outside and set them free.

When the last child left the room for the weekend, Steven came to me and said quietly.
"My dad told me to bring in the ammonite. He said you'd really like it."

I smiled and thought to myself, *Thank you, thank you, Mr. Ward. Very, very subtle and very insightful. What a model and helpful headmaster you are.*

Feeling pretty good about things, I set about making a new discovery table, displaying my amber, the *wishing rocks*, Steven's ammonite, Mary's cuckoo spit, Angela's pill bug exoskeleton, and David's feather.

I surrounded them with reference books and a large label.

This is our TINS of TREASURES table.

I made a new museum display area—like Mr. Jones's cupboard—by taking the doors off a small cupboard, lining the shelves with black paper. I put a large and colorful bird identification chart and a pair of binoculars close to the window so David could identify the birds that came to our feeder.

I created a seating chart on a large sheet of white paper, drawing the tables, each with four children's names, and pasted it high on the door. On Monday, I thought, the class would sit, either at the tables or on the floor, in groups of four. We'd start the day with checking where everyone was going to sit and then go off to assembly.

To round off a perfect day, Mr. Ward phoned me during the evening. He wanted to tell me what Steven had told him about his day in school at teatime.

"Hey, John," he said, *"I hear you're off and running. Good for you. Thank you for giving your class a really good science day."*
"They loved it."

I was sure I could hear him smiling. *"Thank you, Mr. Ward,"* I replied. Then, quietly I added, *"Oh, um, um, thank you for the ammonite too."*

He laughed. *"Oh, hope that was OK. Just trying to help, you know."*

I needed to make a quick visit to the city library on Saturday morning to find out as much as I could about pill bugs and froghoppers.

I discovered interesting facts about pill bugs. They had plenty of names, apparently, including *bibble-bugs, sow-bugs, cud-worms, tiggy-hogs, shoe-laces, sink-lice, slaters,* and *coffin-cutters.* They were once thought to have a medicinal value, and they were swallowed alive in attempts to cure digestive ailments. Hence the name, pill bugs.

Although they now live on land, they haven't shaken off their ancestral aquatic habits. They dry up and die very quickly in dry air and thus only come out from under leaves and rotting wood at night when the air is cooler and damper.

Chapter 31

On Monday, the classroom atmosphere was highly charged with expectancy as the children sat in their newly assigned seats.

"Well," I asked my class, *"anyone got anything to share from the weekend?"*
"Did you fill your tins?"

David put up his hand.
"Brought in a bag of bird food."
"In a dead big tin. That OK, Mr. Paull?"

John had brought in a biscuit tin filled with seashells.
"Found these when I was on 'oliday," he said.

Janice had a dead moth wrapped up in her hanky.
Angela had a collection of pressed elm leaves that she'd glued on a sheet of paper.
Brian showed everyone a large plastic marble run he'd been given for his birthday.
Tonia had a beautiful amethyst geode that drew loud *"oooohs"* and *"aaaahs"* from the class.
Bill had the most beautiful large mammal skull.
Michael shared his small collection of fossils, glued to the bottom of his tin.

When it was my turn, I said, *"Hey, look at this."*

I showed them an old wooden jewelry box, an ideal *treasure chest* shape for storing some of the children's treasures.

"When you bring your stuff in each morning, why don't you put it in here?"
"Then, we can start each day seeing what's on our treasure chest."
"After we've shared, you can then put your treasure in Mr. Jones's cupboard."
"It's up to you. Your choice."
"What do you think?"

Everyone agreed that that was a good idea.

"Can we put anyfing in the treasure chest, Mr. Paull?"
"Anyfing we want?"

"Well," I said, *"anything we want to keep safe, yes, of course."*

Michael was the first to put his tin of fossils in the treasure chest.

"David," I said, wanting to point out about my expectations for the morning, *"you are going to be in charge of the bird watching area. OK?"*

"Yes, Mr. Paull. Yes, yes, yes, Mr. Paull."
"I love bods, you know."
"Can I draw 'em too?"

"Of course, I know you love them, David."
"And, hey, why don't you weigh the food before you put it out?"
"We can weigh what's left when they've gone and see how much food they eat."
"What do you think?"
"You know where the scales are, don't you?"
"Oh, don't forget to put out a bowl of water."
"Birds drink too, you know."

"Brian, why don't you try making your own marble run? Anyone want to help him?"

Three boys put up their hands.

"Good. Make the best marble run of all time," I said.

I showed the class my library book about garden creatures and told them what I'd learned about pill bugs. They giggled when I read out the pill bug names. They were really impressed when I showed them a pencil drawing of a pill bug.

"Cor, you're a good drawer, Mr. Paull."

"Thank you, David."
"That's a kind thing to say."
"Now, everyone, why don't you write some information about what you've brought in—and where you found it?"

Michael told me that he'd showed his dad his tin of treasure.

"Dad said it was my pocket museum."

"What a great description!" I said. *"Perfect."*
"What do you think, everybody?"
"Like it?"

The class agreed that *pocket museum* was a much better name than *tins of treasure.* David especially liked it.

"Sounds clever, Mr. Paull, don't it? Hey, everybody, I gotta museum in my pocket."
"A pocket museum."
"Dead good."
"See?"
"Look. Got a pocket museum right 'ere, wiv a feffer inside."

He proudly showed everyone his pocket museum.

I was quickly reminded of what I had experienced firsthand at Trinity Fields, about the power and product of young children's enthusiasm, when the class talked about their treasures so confidently, so expertly, and so enthusiastically to the whole class. Everyone was transfixed as was I.

I wasn't the only teacher in the classroom. It was incredible finding out what the children knew.

Not everyone wanted to talk, and that was OK with me. Passing around their collections was enough and appropriate, especially for the two very shy children who brought in some small mammal bones they'd found near the canal.

I cleared some space and set up a table and a small doorless cupboard in the science area so that the children's *pocket museums* and the *treasure chest* could be displayed so that everyone could see them.

Our room was now being filled with boxes and tins of all sizes, containing fossils, *wishing rocks,* bones, dead insects, and bits of wood, fossils, and small crystals. There were tins and marble runs and small living creatures—everywhere.

It became the base for a young scientists' conference.

Phew! I rediscovered for myself what Tiger showed me and what my teacher long ago, Mr. Jones, knew: if you work for a while with young children, you soon find out they thrill to the discovery of simple things when they are given the opportunity to investigate and discover for themselves.

Mentally, I reminded myself.

"Trust the class, John Paull, trust the kids, um, children."
And, *"Keep bringing dead good stuff in."*
"They like it when I did."
"Keep the nature table filled with good stuff."

Chapter 32

At this time in the mid-1960s, interested—and curious—educators who were also moving toward a less formal way of working with young children, flocked to those Leicestershire schools considered to be models of *progressive education.*

Blaby Stokes Juniors was one of those schools. American educators were escorted by the advisor for junior schools, Bill Browse, former junior schoolteacher and acknowledged *"expert"* in primary school Dienes mathematics, and Tony Kallet, the American educator attached to the Advisory Center.

Mike, the school deputy head, told us at every biweekly staff meeting the visiting plans for the following two weeks.

My classroom though was not included on the *"to visit"* list. As I was just finding my teaching legs, I was really OK with that. The last thing I wanted was a group of inquisitive teachers staring at me as I worked with my class.

When Mr. Ward sensed I was teaching more confidently and that more and more *hands-on* science was taking place daily in my classroom, my room was put on the *"to visit"* list.

The weekend before my first group of visitors, led by Bill Browse, was expected to come into my room, I went over to school anxious to make sure my classroom looked like an art gallery, reference library, maths and science laboratory, and museum, for my visitors.

I needed it to look as if I knew what I was doing. I didn't want to let Mr. Ward down.

On the Monday morning, as he brought in the group, Mr. Ward told me that Bill couldn't make it. He sat the teachers at a spare table at the back of the classroom and promptly left to attend a meeting.

I tightened up immediately. When I talked to the children, I really talked to my visitors, trying hard to impress them. I knew I wasn't succeeding when Steven came up to me and whispered,

"You OK, Mr. Paull?"
"They're only visitors, you know."
"We had visitors in our room a lot before you came to school."
"Then they stopped coming."
"'Cos you were new, I suppose."

My visitors appeared particularly bemused as they looked around my room. The lively, noisy atmosphere, children talking to and with each other, sitting on cushions and reading, peering down microscopes, watching insects eat, reading books, writing in their journals, painting and making pictures, appeared to surprise them. When playtime came, I went to the staff room and made myself a cup of tea. The group soon appeared, and we sat around a large table. One of them handed me a sheet of notepaper, saying,
"These are some of the questions we'd like to ask, if that's OK?"

Sipping my second, stronger well-earned cup of tea, I glanced through the notes, swallowed hard, and read aloud their questions.

"Do you have classroom rules?"
"How do you know what each child is doing?"
"How do you keep records of what they are learning?"
"Do your children get over stimulated sometimes?"
"Is there a body of science knowledge you hope to transmit to your class?"
"Do you use textbooks?"

Wow! My first day with a group of observers and I was being interviewed?

I smiled, shrugged my shoulders, sipped hard on the lip of my teacup, and described as honestly as I could what was going on in my classroom. Or at least what I thought was going on.

"No," hoping I sounded professional and confident, *"I don't have any textbooks for science or for English—well, I do use the Dienes book for mathematics."*

"I try to bring in things the children find interesting—things I or they find when we are out of school."
"Then, I set up a couple of science investigation tables, add a magnifying glass or two and some reference books from the library."
"After we share, first thing in the morning, they choose what to work on and work like scientists."

"It's my way, and my boys' and girls' way of working, of thinking, of recording and documenting."
"You know, like scientists. I check their work when I can—and when they ask me."
"They check each other's work too."

Sounded convincing, doesn't it?

Well, it wasn't convincing because I heard one of the visitors say loudly to the others in her group as she made her way to Marjorie's classroom,

"For him it works. I'm not going to teach like that, OK?"
"Never. I need to know exactly what my class is doing."
"Did you see some of the spelling mistakes?"
"Doesn't he correct them?"
"Some of the kids' writing wasn't marked."
"Too noisy too."
"He spends too much with that one child who couldn't read a word."
"Kept talking about the birds outside the window."

Hearing that snippet of conversation turned my stomach over, and I cursed myself for not telling them my story, how it all started for me with a piece of smooth yellow amber, lying amid millions of pebbles on the beach at Lariggan, waiting to be picked up by a wide-eyed five-year-old.

Oh, and a jar holding a spider, waiting to be looked after by a moody and bored adolescent. And what I was learning from working with the boy who couldn't read but was fascinated by birds.

Perhaps that would have helped convince them that I was a good teacher.

The truth is, I knew, that my teaching was still pretty much hit or miss. Well, more misses than hits, really, because I didn't know how to plan and ensure that all the children's learning needs were being met.

Before I left school, I wrote a brief note to Mr. Ward, asking if my classroom could be taken off the visiting list, at least for a week or so.

I couldn't shake my despondent mood off throughout the evening. As I sat and fiddled with my amber and held my *wishing rock*, I questioned what I was doing with my class. Should I be much more careful about checking constantly on my children's work, especially their reading, writing, and mathematics? Wasn't I demanding enough?

The next day, Mr. Ward came in to my classroom, apologizing that he hadn't stayed with my visitors the day before. I told him about the teachers' comment.

"They didn't like Marjorie's room either."
"Next time, I'll stay, OK? Or if Bill brings a group, I know he'll stay."
"You have great classroom. People need to see it."
"You're doing OK. You are."
"So, no, I'm not taking you off the list."

That helped, but not very much.

Eventually though, after three or four days of experiencing more groups of adults in my classroom, each time led by Bill Browse, I relaxed a little. I learned not to give them eye contact, and I became more accustomed to having adults standing, watching, pointing, writing notes in their journals, and talking with my children about what they were doing.

Fortunately, I knew my children enjoyed the visits because it gave them opportunities to share their excitement about what they were working on with interested and courteous adults. After all, who better to talk about what was going on in the classroom than my boys and girls?

I also think the children worked harder to make their presentations and displays as good and as informative as they could be, knowing that they would be read by everyone who came to our room.

David though, I noticed, would never interact with the visitors and look down at the floor if asked a question about his bird project. I soon learned that it was best if I sat next to him as often as I could, to reassure him that everything was OK and that our guests really did like birds.

One teacher, from nearby Derbyshire, after spending the whole day shadowing me, liked my classroom, and wanted to know more about David Hawkins and Mr. Jones.

He told me confidentially that he was the only teacher in his school really trying to *open up* his classroom, but he was getting very frustrated. He'd changed his room arrangement, loosened his schedules, given his children more choice during project time, and brought in more materials. But nothing positive happened. His days soon disintegrated into noisy squabbles, led, he said, by two disengaged boys.

"Don't work for me . . . just doesn't."

I told him about my early days, my challenges and frustrations, and my experience with Tiger.

About a month later, the postman delivered a box from my new teacher-friend. His cryptic note described what happened, after his visit to my classroom, when he took an ammonite he'd found in the limestone quarries to school.

"That," he wrote, *"set my classroom on fire."*
"Especially the two naughty boys."

Inside the box I found letters from his kids and a piece of limestone with an embedded fossil for each of my boys and girls. When I shared the fossils and the letters with my children, Steven smiled.

"See, Mr. Paull, that class is like ours! Fossils are great, aren't they?"

"Kids like 'em, don't they?"

I smiled. *"You mean 'children,' Steven, yes?"*

Everyone in class wrote a letter, thanking the teacher for the fossils, and a few words about their science projects. David drew and colored one of his favorite *bods* and then carefully wrote, with a little help from a friend.

"Bet you have these bods in Derbyshire!"

This experience began a pen-pal relationship that was to last until the end of the year for many of the children and a relationship between the teacher and me for several years.

Chapter 33

In my fifth month at Blaby Stokes, Bill Browse started visiting my classroom on his own. Bill saw how I set up my classroom for the children, used Mr. Jones's cupboard, how I shared a story first thing in the morning, and how I created and opened yet another *pocket museum*. He saw how my children were most engrossed when they chose which science questions to explore. He read the displays of science investigations and asked some of them to describe exactly how their projects started and what they had learned from their investigations.

Bill was drawn to David, now fully immersed in his study of local birds. As soon as he sensed David relax, Bill helped him with his challenge of figuring out how much the wild birds ate each day when they came to our bird station.

"David," he said later to me, *"is having a great time with his birds. He knows a lot, doesn't he?" "Does he do the same thing at home? Does he have his own bird feeder?"*

Bill asked if he could bring a group of head teachers into my classroom the next day, mainly to see, he said, my *hands-on* science.

"I'm taking the kids outside. That OK?" I asked. *"If the weather holds up."*

The following day, five head teachers, dressed in smart suits, white shirts, ties, and shiny shoes, joined the pond dipping in the nearby stream.

They picked up on the excitement when the children caught a few tiny, wriggly creatures lurking on the underside of the pond reed. Phyllis and Angela soon discovered some pill bugs and were quick to tell our visitors how much they knew about the small creatures.

"Bet you didn't know why they are called pill bugs? Do you?"

They were proud to share their knowledge about the pill bug names.

The really great afternoon find, though, was the group of yellow-and-black caterpillars someone spotted. The hairy little creatures crawling all over a small bush got everyone talking excitedly.

Just then, Bill's advisor, colleague, Tony Kallet, joined us. Tony, laughing loudly when he saw the caterpillars, joined in the scientific fun.

By a striking coincidence, he'd come to give me two *Elementary Science Study* guides recently published in the United States, one on *mealworms,* and the other *on bones,* which, I later discovered, marked a historical first in science curriculum design for elementary schools in the United States.

"You'll like these, John Paull," he said.
"Just up your street—ooops, just up your creek." This was my first experience with Tony's quirky sense of humor.

"What's this I hear about a wishing rock that looks like amber?"
When we returned to school, Bill thanked me for spending time with his visitors.

"They were impressed, John, really impressed. They liked the way the kids asked questions—and the way you threw the questions back to the kids."

I was thankful for Bill's words, reassured to know that I hadn't wasted the head teachers' time by taking them on a field trip with my class.

I skimmed through the ESS books after Bill left, before going outside to collect some food for the caterpillars we'd brought back to the classroom. The introduction to the *behavior of mealworms* immediately caught my interest, providing the perfect words that best described what I tried to make happen in my science lessons:

> *Behavior of mealworms stimulates children to ask questions about the observable behavior of an unfamiliar animal and then directs them to ways of finding answers for themselves. As children observe and experiment with mealworms, they learn something about the process of scientific inquiry and the sensory perception of the mealworm.*

> *The ideas for studying mealworm behavior have been worked out essentially by children.*

> *The students ask questions, devise experiments, observe, measure, make charts, keep records, design and build equipment, predict, and draw conclusions.*

And I loved the loaded sentence that read,

> *What they find out about mealworms is only incidental.*

Yeah! Although the life cycle of the small creatures was interesting and important to know, there was also so much to learn from being involved in the scientific process (working together, observing, questioning, researching, drawing, and documenting).

I noticed in particular that the text didn't tell me what to do *if* and *when* I brought small creatures into my classroom. But the text did tell me what could happen if children were encouraged to observe them and note what they saw and thought. It described in a straightforward, readable manner some primary classroom activities for studying mealworms. This was the first science text I'd seen since my days as science teacher in Trinity Fields and was strikingly different from the one I'd used to read aloud to my science classes.

I really wanted to bring mealworms into my classroom. With my head buzzing, I left the tidying up for the following morning, feeling excited yet anxious to get to the nearby Blaby pet shop to buy some mealworms before the closing time.

During morning meeting the following day, after assembly, I passed around the deep tray of wriggling yellowy mealworms. Most of the class was fascinated by the wriggling mass of thin yellow bodies.
Some of the girls weren't impressed though and pulled their faces away when the container came close to them.

Not fully ignoring the *yuk!* comment, but wanting to encourage the class to look closely at our tiny guests, I asked,

"So does anyone have any idea what they are?"

The children didn't have a clue. So I then asked,

"Any questions that pop into your heads about our small guests?"
"Oh, and they're called mealworms, by the way."

I spelled out the word.
"M-E-A-L-W-O-R-M-S. Any questions?"
The hands shot up.

The first question was, although predictable, a really good one, a question that had occurred to me when I first opened the book:

"So why are they called mealworms?"

I threw the question back at everyone.
"Good question."
"Why?"
There were plenty of suggestions from the class.

One boy turned to another and said, *"'Cos they're fed to other animals, twerp."*
Ignoring the rudeness, I asked, *"Well, what do you all think?"*

I then wrote every response on a large white sheet of paper.
"What do mealworms eat?"
"How does a mealworm find its food?"
"How do you make a mealworm walk backward?"

The class then decided, individually or in groups, which *mealworm* question they wanted to research.

Steven and Michael volunteered to go to the school library to look for books about beetles. They came back with an armful of books about small creatures and set them out on the worktables.

I gave each group some mealworms in a small cardboard box and some magnifying glasses and set them off on their scientific investigations.

Throughout the afternoon, the children studied the mealworms and other small creatures, drawing their observations and writing their questions and answers in their science journals.

The class chose some of the best journals to put into two big colorful class books.

Chapter 34

David Hawkins, visiting UK schools to see if what he was reading in the educational press and hearing at conferences about Leicestershire schools was, in fact, taking place, spent a couple of days at Blaby Stokes.

Bill had met David in the summer of 1965 when they were attending the Africa Science Workshop in Entebbe, Uganda, organized for English-speaking African countries by the Education Development Center in Boston.

I had heard David's name before during a chat with Tony, but I had no idea then of David's fascinating background—his work with Robert Oppenheimer during World War II, at Los Alamos, creating and constructing the world's first atomic bomb; his work in the fields of mathematics, science, and philosophy; his work as director at the Elementary Science Study; and his dedication to bringing about fundamental changes in the ways children were educated, particularly in science.

Tony gave me David's article, "The Informed Vision: An Essay on Science Education." I hadn't read anything quite like it before. Heavy going at times, there were two paragraphs that really caught my eye.

First, when talking about science teaching in general, David writes,

> *What is true of the initiates is true, also of those whose misfortune it is to teach science without any conviction of inner illumination. Here is the book, they are told, or the syllabus, or the teacher's guide. Now teach! The style is set for them; they know they are supposed to*

teach, to give explanations. And we, alas, the devotees, the mystics, have set that style.

And second,

> *The moral, then, is that absorption in subject matter requires a major effort of provisioning for that subject matter. If children are going to emerge from our schools secure in the practice and enjoyment of the arts of inquiry, it will be only because they have long practiced those arts, in engagement with the world around. In relation to science, this means that their involvement with it will have been of a kind such that we can truly say it has penetrated the subsoil of their minds and earned their loyalty because it has liberated them from boredom and sophistication that come with living in an unexamined world, because it preserves the freshness of subject matter and sustains emotion.*

Reading and rereading the paragraphs made me question my work: I knew I had moved on from simply delivering, word for word, the science information in some textbook, but was I forgetting the importance of the science content, the science knowledge, and focusing too much on creating activities that invited interaction and little depth of inquiry? Was I asking challenging questions? Was I directing children's thinking to the essence of the science investigations? Was I supporting their investigations and experiments with appropriate reference books and magazines?

These questions—and how I would deal with them as a teacher when closely observed—were very much in my mind when David came into my classroom.

My nervous state relaxed when I saw I how comfortably and gently he interacted with my children when he sat with them, curious to discover what they knew—and how they were finding out—about the mealworms (the ESS book on mealworms, I discovered, was put together by some of his colleagues). The way he directed their thinking was casual, not at all interrogative. And the children responded accordingly.

Some of them eagerly showed David the homes they'd designed for the mealworms, many now developing into adult beetles, and the science records they'd kept in their journals. Young David took David by the hand, took him outside to the yard to show him the bird feeder.

"I look after that—every day."
"And then I make notes, you know, about the bods that come and chomp on the seeds and stuff."
"Wanna see my drawings?"

"You bet," said David.

At the end of the day, we sat and talked. David's gentle, unassuming, yet very authoritative manner, made me feel as if I had something worthwhile to say about the teaching and learning process when, in fact, I really didn't.

"Tony's told me, you know, about your way of showing the kids things you find—he's told me about the tin in your pocket."
"Can I see it for myself? Will you tell me the story that goes with it?"

Watching his eyes light up as I took out the amber told me he really was interested in the way that I used it with my children.

The following day, David came very early and stayed for the entire day, interacting again with every boy and girl, asking challenging but very appropriate science questions.

To thank him for his visit, I gave David an OXO tin, telling him to show me, next time we met, what he had found and put into his *pocket museum.*

David's visit was the beginning of a very special working and social relationship with David Hawkins that was to last for over thirty-five years—from which I learned so much, about education, teaching, science, and about myself.

Chapter 35

The end of the school year was fast approaching. After the summer holiday, my class would be attending the senior school. I met with some of senior schoolteachers to talk about my children's progress. David's meeting was very detailed, focusing primarily on how he learned best and what additional support I felt he needed from his next teacher.

"Be sure to let him feed the bods," I said half jokingly as I described the kinds of learning activities that motivated David in our classroom.

When it was time to bid farewell to David, Michael, Steven, Angela, Phyllis, and everyone else in the class, I felt very sad to see them go.

They were on their way to the senior school, and although they didn't know it, because of them, I was on my way to becoming a more thoughtful and, I hope, successful teacher.

Because of them, my teaching life was developing and changing and, although I didn't know it then, so was my career.

By the beginning of the September term, my daily teaching plan was etched in my head, and I was ready for the new academic year.

After explaining to my new class the seating arrangements and the functions of the art, science, reading, writing, and mathematics areas, I began the first day with my *wishing rock* and amber ritual.

As soon as the work expectation and routine was established, I interacted individually with everyone.

At the end of the day, I gave each child a tin, with the instructions:

"Hey, when you go home this evening, find something that's really special to you. Put it in your tin and bring it to school tomorrow morning. You can then share what's inside your tin with your friends on your table. I'll remind you again before we leave school this afternoon."

The next day started really well as the children opened up their tins and enthusiastically shared their special things with each other. The morning was then taken up with writing and drawing in their new science journals.

I wasn't quite so confident with the evening class, filled as it was with young women and some of my parents who wanted to help their husbands with their small businesses.

But I shouldn't have worried so much. I loved it. Working with adults, many looking for work as office staff in local factories, was such a treat and so different from my daily teaching of young children.

Over the next three months teaching evening classes, I became very interested and involved in the world of adult education and often attended warden meetings with Mike Jolley. I learned a great deal of what was going on in other community centers and thought about the different ways I could expand the classes at Broughton Astley.

I was very surprised though when the area superintendent asked if I was interested in becoming the warden of a small community center that met nightly in the small school in the middle of the village of Broughton Astley.

The job was to start in January, at the beginning of my second year teaching at Blaby. and would entail being at the school for two evenings each week, every Monday and Wednesday.

I gladly accepted the position, sensing it was a career-widening opportunity.

Broughton Astley was about two miles south of Blaby. Knowing I was soon to be running two jobs, now, I decided, was the time to buy my first car, especially as my petrol expenses when I drove to Broughton Astley and back would be paid for by the school district.

The following week, I was the proud owner of a secondhand Morris Mini and began to prepare for my new role as warden at Broughton Astley.

The first thing I did was to write and take a letter to every house in the village, advertising the classes I intended to put in place, and inviting everyone to an open evening.

The evening was well attended, and I enrolled enough students for five evening classes, two on the Monday and three on the Wednesday.

Life was busy but fun, and I was quite struck how my work, in the day and in the evening, wove well together, and so widened my naive view of the world of education.

Unbeknown to me at the time, my role as warden at Broughton Astley, though, was going to be limited to a few months because my professional life was soon to experience another change.

Chapter 36

When Mr. Ward, not only my boss but also my supportive, encouraging, helpful mentor, sent me a scribbled note—the first time ever—that he wanted to see me urgently in his office in the middle of one very busy week, I was nervous.

Because Mr. Ward knew I had to leave school promptly on Mondays and Wednesdays to drive straight to Broughton Astley to carry out my warden duties and to teach the *speed writing* class, I had visitors in my classroom on Tuesdays and Thursdays only. Was that causing a problem? What else could he want me for? Nothing had gone wrong, had it? Did I miss something? Had a visitor complained about my classroom? Was I too free and easy with the children? Weren't they writing and counting enough? Should I have been standing, directing the children, telling them what to do? Was it wrong to sit on the carpet with four children trying to successfully light three bulbs in a complicated and difficult electrical circuit? Had I let him and school down? Had I upset some parents?

When I waved *good-bye* to the last boy from my class as he went through the school gates, I hurried back inside school. Mr. Ward's office door was wide open.

"Come right in, John," he said, standing and beckoning me in.

As he sat down behind his desk, he looked up and said with a very serious voice,

"Well, John," he said. *"It looks as if you're leaving Blaby."*

I looked at him. What? Crikey! Whatever I did must have been bad.
My inner tensions increased.

With a broad smile that instantly relaxed me a little, he said,

*"Bill Browse wants you to work with him in Leicester. You know, at the
Advisory Center, full time." "Yes. Full time. To work on classroom science with
him and Tony Kallet."*

What? I couldn't believe what he was saying to me.
The questions came out in a torrent.

"Me? Why?"
"Mr. Ward, you joking with me?"
"To do what, exactly? Science teaching? Teaching who?"
"Where? How? When?"

"Bill," Mr. Ward said, *"wants your answer by Monday. You have to make
your mind up over the weekend. It's a great opportunity."*
*"You're going to Broughton tonight, of course. Think about it when you
finish there this evening and then give Bill a ring."*

Think about it? I didn't need telling. Throughout the evening at
Broughton Astley, I couldn't stop thinking about it. I couldn't get the
implications of the conversation out of my head. Wow! Leave the classroom?
Just as I was really enjoying my teaching? I'd miss the children and the
energy and enthusiasm they brought to the classroom each day. I'd miss
being involved in—and learning from—all their projects. I'd miss seeing
what they had in their *pocket museums.*
    And my work as community center warden. I'd only just started. What
would happen to that?

I took the bull by the horns and phoned Bill from Broughton Astley at
his home. I was lucky, catching him before his dinner with his family.

*"Good evening, Mr. Browse. Sorry to bother you . . . It's John Paull, you
know, from Blaby. I was talking to Mr. Ward today . . ."*

Bill interrupted me. *"John, John, I was hoping you'd call,"* he said.

"Oh, you were expecting me to call? Thank you, thank you, Mr. Browse . . . it all sounds great! What is it, though, exactly? What would I do? What were the expectations?"

"It's what you make it, John," he said.

"So what do you think? Fancy it? I've seen your science and the teaching and learning process going on daily in your classroom on your science tables. It's good. It works. I've seen your class at it—measuring and writing and drawing what they do during science. So you will promote your teaching method, your discovery method of teaching science, you know, by visiting classrooms, working with teachers and children, and when ready, running science workshops."

"You know, like the Dienes workshops. Only for science."
"Like you do with your kids."

Then, speaking more slowly and more formally, he added,

"Teachers of upper juniors are OK with teaching art in groups, and even mathematics and writing, but are put off by science. They're a bit intimidated by science facts and stuff."

"Using classroom science is a good vehicle for fostering a more flexible, hands-on approach to teaching."

"Don't you agree?"

One of his objectives, Bill said, was to move the teachers toward science teaching by the *discovery method,* which meant children working on projects that interested them, responding to whatever raised their levels of curiosity. It was a *"new"* job and hadn't been done before, so it would be what I made it.

If it didn't work out, he said, I could always return to classroom teaching. Perhaps at Blaby Stokes, if Mr. Ward kept my teaching spot open for me.

He added, *"You'll need a car too. And all your travel expenses would be paid for. You have a car, don't you? You'll need one, going to school after school."*

Yes, I had a car, my delightful blue Mini. But my burning question in reply was, *"Could I continue my evening work at Broughton Astley as its evening class warden? I like it, you know."*

"'Course you can. I heard about that, what you were doing as well as teaching."
"You're a busy fella."

"This advisory job. It's easy. It's a daytime job, you know," he said jokingly. Then, more seriously, *"Try it. See how it all works out."*
"You know, actually, you'll be involved in lots of evening meetings, so perhaps not."
"Let me talk to the Further Ed people about it and see what we can do."
"Would you mind if I did that?"

Needing a little more time to think, but feeling Bill wanted a decision, I asked,
"'Course not."
"Can I phone you back in half an hour? Can I just put my brain back in place and have a cup of tea?"
Bill laughed.
"'Course. Don't be too late though."

Although I knew Dad would need assurance about my pension, I walked around Broughton Astley School. I visited a couple of classes, checked that all was well, and went to the staffroom and made a pot of tea.

Then, with a hot cup in hand, I phoned Bill again.

Gratefully, but nervously, after being invited to meet with him the following day and talk in detail about the job offer, I accepted the golden opportunity to move my career forward, deciding wisely, I think, also to give up my role as warden at Broughton Astley.

Although I didn't fully realize it at the time, Bill was giving me the opportunity of a lifetime—the chance to enhance my career, increase my understanding of the complex world of junior school classroom science, and chance to stand back and think about what was and what wasn't *"good"* teaching.

Before I became an advisor though, there was lots to do at school, including a weeklong field trip with my class to the Isle of Wight.

And so, at the end of the academic year, after saying farewell to my Blaby Stokes parents, teacher-colleagues, and children, including David and his parents who came to school to wish me well, I started my summer holiday, knowing that I was now a very small part of the famed Leicestershire Education Authority Advisory Service, at the ripe old age of twenty-five.

Bill confirmed when I went to talk with him in his office that I was to help teachers use a more *open-ended* approach to classroom science.

Chapter 37

The Leicestershire Advisory Primary team, based in an upstairs office block in the middle of Leicester, across from a hairdressing salon, was small but powerful. It was created to introduce and support Stewart Mason's policies and as a *think tank* to meet the professional development needs of all the teachers and head teachers in Leicestershire primary schools.

Bill Browse, a former successful upper junior teacher at Thurmaston Junior School, was the newly promoted senior advisor for junior schools, taking over from the renowned Len Sealey.

Bill was quiet, thoughtful, and very much the team boss and inspiration. His advisory team included the infant school (ages five to seven) advisor, Marjorie Kay; David Wren, the advisory teacher who looked after the needs of probationary teachers; and Tony Kallet, an American educator appointed along with Bill Browse by Len Sealey in the summer of 1963.

New Yorker Tony Kallet was an apprentice teacher at Shady Hill in Cambridge, Massachusetts, where Bill Hull and Dave Armington were trialing materials and ideas created by Elementary Science Study, headed by university professor, David Hawkins.

Tony advocated for an approach to education that appreciated and valued the learning needs of children, encouraging their commitment to acquiring relevant and useful skills and knowledge in ways that were exciting and fun.

Tony brought his view of teaching and learning to the Leicestershire Advisory Center at the best of times, when Leicestershire was on the leading edge of the movement promoting more and more *child-centered,* exploratory teaching methods, similar to what I experienced at Blaby Stokes Junior School.

Tony's observations of children learning, teachers teaching, and his insights into the processes they were engaged in were all vital elements in the professional development of many primary school educators.

The advisory team focused on helping teachers meet the challenges they faced when they adopted a more *open-ended* approach to teaching and learning.

Not every teacher wanted to change what had, in their view, worked for them and their children. The director of education, Stewart Mason, had given head teachers vague guidance when he said, during one particular meeting, that they were now *"captains of their own ships."*

What he should have added was *"Direction to the Promised Land, though, might be achieved quicker if the captains took advice and guidance from members of my advisory team."*

Advisors only went to schools by invitation, working with teachers receptive to new ideas and wanting change in their teaching.

Full of nervous anticipation and eagerness to start my new job, I reported to Bill's office for duty the first week in September 1966, almost exactly three years to the day when I began my teaching career at Trinity Fields Secondary Modern School.

Bill introduced me to everyone on the advisory team, showed me where I could sit and share a desk, then gave me the names of a few village schools.

"Use your car and go and check the countryside around these schools. Check the OS maps."
"See if there are good areas for the children to investigate."
"Check the hedgerows, the field, woods, and streams."

"Then," he said, *"go and visit the schools."*

"The head teachers would welcome an early visit from the Advisory Center's 'new' science guy."

The schools on the list were all *"show"* schools, meaning they were on the *"schools to visit"* list given to visitors from other school districts and other countries.

"Phone them," he said. *"Arrange a visit to each of them, then see me again in three or four weeks' time and tell me what's going on."*

After phoning and confirming good times to visit, I thus began my first month as an advisory teacher, checking out areas of the countryside suitable for school visits and then observing what was going on in a variety of classrooms.

The first month sped by as I visited Claybrooke, Wigston, Sheepy Magna, Market Bosworth, Coalville, Saddington, Swannington, Ullesthorpe, Peatling Magna, and other towns and villages to the west and south of the county.

I soon developed a classroom-visiting routine: I sat in the back of classrooms, sometimes alone, sometimes interacting with children, and observed, taking in the classroom environment, the resources, the ubiquitous nature table teacher/class relationship, and the children's levels of engagement. I then met and talked with each school's head teacher, sometimes briefly, sometimes at length.

Many were at pains to tell me that they knew that successful *hands-on science* was changing the style and ethos in their upper junior school classrooms. More and more science material was creeping into their classrooms—brought in by the teachers and sometimes brought in by the children as part of their class or individual projects. Their teachers, they said, were recognizing that children learn best in science when they're doing something that interests them, and they learn best when the teacher is also involved.

A couple of head teachers said that the science going on in their schools was a huge move forward from when *nature study* focused, especially in the upper juniors, on children copying nature notes in their very best handwriting from the blackboard into their nature diaries, in silence.

The image reminded me of my first and disastrous science lessons at Trinity Fields Secondary Modern School.

"Nature study," one newly appointed head teacher from Market Harborough, described in a long letter to me, *"centered around a dusty, neglected table cluttered with dry leaves, acorns and horse-chestnuts, a few parched bean seeds, and perhaps a neglected, ageless goldfish, gulping for air in the bowl of cloudy water. More often than not these artifacts (and fish) were set against a backcloth of frayed and tattered commercial illustrations depicting the unreal seasons in their splendor. A printed sign written by the teacher clearly told the children to look but not to touch. The nature lesson sometimes involved a monthly nature walk outdoors in the nearby country lanes. What could be an exciting discovery ramble into the countryside was marred though, if the children had to carry a worksheet with several yes/no questions which had to be filled as quickly as possible, mainly because of the teachers' fear that underemployment of the children's energies would result in a breakdown of behavior. On return, the children had to write about "what happened when we went to the meadow," without any guidance from the teacher, resulting frequently in a feeling of boredom and disinterest which showed itself so well in the writing. Hence there was little leeway for the spontaneous activity that can arise when children touch and talk about interesting natural history specimens and artifacts."*

"And," he wrote, *"I'm trying my best to change all that, John Paull."*
"I've got three new teachers."
"They're great. They're dying to do more natural science."

"Will you help?"

You bet—well, at least I'll try my best, I thought.

I arranged to visit, a full day each week, to see how I could help.

Even though I certainly wasn't the best person to make a judgment on someone's teaching, I felt comfortable enough to report back to Bill that the junior school teachers I saw were including some outdoor exploration and *hands-on* follow-up science activity as part of the afternoon routine in their classrooms. None of them had a science background, and some believed they were ill equipped to teach science. One said that introducing an inquiry-based project curriculum would get in the way of what he wanted to accomplish as the classroom could become chaotic and out of control.

Chapter 38

In my third month at the Advisory Center, Dennis Bradley, the head teacher of the two-classroom school in the small village of Medbourne, phoned the Advisory Center and asked if I would visit and talk with him about classroom science. Medbourne was one of the names on Bill's list, but I hadn't yet made a visit to the locality.

Medbourne Primary School, I learned, was a two-teacher school in the heart of the beautiful village of Medbourne, in the south of the county.

Dennis taught the lower, middle, and upper juniors. When I walked through the door of his small classroom one very rainy day, I was immediately transfixed. His fourteen children, aged between seven and eleven, were focused on creating the complete overview of the village. His nature table was filled with a wide range of artifacts from a nearby hedgerow.

I noticed three children of different ages were studying creepy-crawlies, which they'd found outside before school started. I followed them out into the yard at the back of the school to watch them collect a few earthworms that had been washed out of their underground tunnels by the rain the night before.

They were so careful and so respectful of the tiny wriggly creatures they put into a small jar to bring back into the classroom. The children showed Dennis their worms, and he quickly helped them poke holes in the jar lid.

"Why are we making holes here?" he asked the boys.

"What do you think they eat? Do they need some earth and a few dead leaves? Water?"
"Do worms drink?"
"Where shall we keep them—in the shade or in the window?"

Then, he added,

"It would be great if you drew one of the worms for our display, and don't forget to put the date at the top of the page. Oh, then write about where you found them 'cos you're going to take them back there, you know, when you've finished studying them."
"If it's not raining."
"I'll put your drawings in our big display, OK?"

Dennis, with a twinkle in his eye, was showing me how he made the most of the teaching opportunities presented to him by the children and their earthworms.

Later, when we had opportunity to speak a few minutes, he said,

"Not as easy as it looks, is it, John Paull? I do all the basic stuff one-on-one," he said, *"and I make sure everyone knows how to read, write, and count. With such a wide range in ages and ability—a couple of the seven-year-olds can't read yet, you know, it has to be me working with individual children. It ain't just about science, you know, but it's a surefire way of getting everyone involved. I have to set up projects that get everyone interested and wanting to be involved so I can do that."*

"Class projects are my way of doing that."

"When kids do their project work, I can choose whom to work with. Then I can check on their spelling and their handwriting."
"This big class project will be displayed in the church hall for everyone to see."

Seeing his classroom and seeing the amazing class interdisciplinary project made me think of all the things I should and could have done when I was teaching at Blaby Stokes. And he was doing it with a wide range of ages, abilities, personalities, expectations, home backgrounds, and of course, behaviors.

It was obvious I was in the presence of a master teacher. I had so much to learn from Dennis and the way he worked with his multiage classroom. Whatever could I advise him on? I had so much to learn from him and his teaching.

About a month later, I made another visit, getting to Medbourne well before school started and staying through until the last child left the classroom. The children's project was near completion, and I was amazed to see how good and how detailed it was.

The children were so proud of the achievement and very eager to tell me all they knew now about Medbourne, the place of their home. They didn't realize it had such a fascinating history.

I was excited to tell Bill and Tony about my visit to Medbourne. They, of course, knew about Dennis and how he successfully built his entire weekly curriculum around children's curiosity and their interest in science and nature.

"Great, isn't it? Isn't Dennis doing a wonderful job?"
"Those kids are really lucky—and they churn out dead good stuff."

"Did you see the class exhibition of life in Medbourne?" asked Tony.

He too had visited and seen the children's big project.

Chapter 39

During the time I was making my visits to schools, Bill and his colleagues had worked hard to convince the Education Authority to develop a recently closed village school as a field study center and base for in-service environmental science courses.

This exciting educational venture originated from a talk given by a local experienced teacher, Dorothy Lane, when she talked about her fieldwork on a canal with her class of nine-year-olds. She proposed that a lock keeper's cottage be purchased and adapted as storage for the equipment she and other teachers needed for their outdoor studies.

Bill, with tremendous foresight, leapt at the idea, worked patiently with the hard-to-convince director of Common Services and acquired, if not the first field study center ever, certainly the first for primary school children.

Bill, it appeared, thought I was the ideal person to run the proposed field center. *"Go and take a look,"* he said. *"Foxton's a beautiful village. The old school building is right next to the canal."*

I drove through the countryside to the village of Foxton as soon as I could to check out the one-classroom school.

Sitting literally on the banks of the Grand Union Canal, I could see right away that the small single-classroom building was in a perfect setting for outdoor science work. The canal, created during the Industrial Revolution as a means of transporting goods from city to city, ran just outside the school wall, an environmentally rich and safe place for scientific exploration.

I spent a few minutes inside the empty building and over an hour walking on the towpath. The canal looked beautiful as it basked in the late afternoon sun.

That evening, I phoned Bill. He told me that I would be running workshops there as soon as he could contact all the schools in Leicestershire.

"It'll be great! A teacher leading a science workshop for teachers. Makes sense, doesn't it?"
"And outdoor stuff? Your specialty, yes? You'll have a great time."

Yeah, right, I thought. 'Course I will.
But, Bill, I thought, *ummm . . . I had never led a workshop before—in fact, I had never ever attended a science workshop.*
Too insecure to ask Bill or Tony Kallet about how one runs a workshop, I resorted to my therapy practice, jotting down my anxieties in no particular order.

- *What can I find out about the history of the canal?*
- *Who dug it out? How long did it take? What tools did they use?*
- *Where does it lead? Where does it come from—which city? Where does it end?*

- *What lives there now? What birds, animals, flowers?*
- *How should I introduce the day?*
- *Do I have to give a talk? If so, a talk about what?*
- *What are the teachers expecting? Should I ask them?*
- *How much time should we spend outside on the canal towpath?*
- *Do I let them do what they want to do? Or do both?*
- *Should I split them into groups and set them a pond-dipping challenge?*
- *What should I focus on?*
- *Do I keep the discussions focused on science?*
- *Do I tell them what to do?*
- *Oh, yes . . . what equipment did I need?*
- *Should I . . . ?*
- *Oh, don't forget—who ran the school before it was closed? Bet s/he knows a thing or two. Ask Bill.*

Although I knew that writing notes wouldn't stop me nervously biting my nails, it sure helped me focus and come up with a basic plan of what to do.

Knowing it was going to be advertised as an *outdoor hands-on* science workshop, I thought the teachers would at the very least expect me to be able to identify the plants and animals and birds that lived in and around the canal, and not just be given a net and told to "enjoy" themselves. So first things first, I thought. I need to explore and get to know the area, don't I, just as I had done around the schools Bill said I must visit? And then, contact the previous head teacher who, I discovered, still lived in the village.

So I contacted Clifford Owen and Ian Evans, two senior museum naturalists I had met a few times at evening meetings with Bill at the City of Leicester Museum.

They were glad to help me, and late one sunny afternoon, the three of us walked the banks of the canal, talking about every bird, duck, reed, grass, and small creature that we saw. Clifford and Ian knew everything. I knew nothing. They knew the names and life cycles of all the plants, animals, and small aquatic creatures that inhabited the canal. It didn't take me too long though to absorb all the information, to learn the basics about the wildlife that inhabited the reeds, rushes, and deep water.

Over a glass of beer in the local pub, we talked about what I could do when the teachers came for the first workshop. Clifford, with great forethought, had an idea.

"Invest in a kettle, teapot, and cups, John Paull. Just make them feel welcome, and they'll appreciate that."
"A cup of tea works wonders."

The next day, I returned to Foxton to meet Miss Marvel, the retired head teacher who ran Foxton Primary School for many years. As I'd hoped, she knew so much about the canal, and she was so pleased to share it with me—including lots of photographs that depicted the development of the canal.

Bill wrote to every one of the 365 schools in the county, inviting teachers to a series of daylong workshops. With about 2,000 primary teachers in the county, Foxton attracted about 400 for its first bout of workshops, not as big a percentage as Bill wanted, but as he said, *"You have to start somewhere."*

Four hundred teachers sounded a lot to me.

Chapter 40

I bought small rectangular tables, chairs, a couple of cupboards, pond nets, dishes, magnifying glasses, binocular microscopes, a wide range of art and writing materials, a box of Brook Bond tea bags, a box of ginger biscuits, and I ordered a pint of Co-op milk to be delivered on the first workshop day.

I woke up at four o'clock in the morning of the first workshop. I felt so nervous. I lay in bed, clutching my favorite *wishing rock*, and wished and wished that all would be well in this new and overwhelming venture.

I was glad that Bill and Tony told me they weren't coming, *"We'll only get in the way,"* and was grateful for their sensitivity and awareness of my nervous state.

When Foxton Primary School, now in its new role as a field study center, opened for the first-ever workshop, Jock McEvoy, a supply teacher, and Dennis, the head teacher of the village school in Medbourne, were the first through its large, very scratched oak doors. I was pleased, relieved even, to see them, knowing we'd hit it off when I went to their schools a couple of weeks previous and spent time talking with them. Jock smiled when he heard the warm, welcoming music and saw the room filled with science paraphernalia, pictures of birds, mammals, spiders, insects, plants, and aquatic life, a stuffed owl and a stuffed fox (borrowed from the museum), displays of children's work I'd kept from my time at Blaby Stokes, some *pocket museums*, and plenty of reference books I'd borrowed from my local library.

He and Dennis both sensed I was nervous when I showed them around my first-ever science workshop.

"Looks good, John Paull, looks really good. Hey, it'll be great. Don't worry so much."

"It's OK for you, Jock," I replied. *"But what if they ask me stuff, you know, tough science questions I can't answer?"*

Jock smiled. *"They won't. They want a nice day out. Anyway, 'cos you're running the show, they'll assume you know everything. You look as if you do, anyway."* He laughed. *"But if they do, just throw it back to them, you know. Tell them, you know,* Now that's *a really good question—what do* you *think?"*

When the other teachers arrived, I welcomed them with a big but nervous smile, a cup of steaming hot tea, and a plate of ginger biscuits. I heard one of the teachers say to a group around her:

"Oh, goodee, just what I needed. Road was busy this morning. Cup of tea and soft music."

Sipping tea and talking about nothing in particular was, it turned out, a great icebreaker.

As we drank our tea and dunked our ginger biscuits, I turned the music volume down and, very nervously, welcomed everyone to Foxton's first-ever workshop. Talking much too fast, I described, badly, the plans for the day ahead.

The teachers, it turned out, didn't expect and certainly didn't want a talk about classroom science from me.

They didn't want to get lectured at and told what to do when they returned to the classroom. The teachers were motivated by the day off from school and the prospect of going out in the countryside. They did want to know about me though, and one of them asked about my teaching background.

"'Ow long you been teachin', John?"
"Can you slow down a bit and tell us?"

Drawing in a deep mouthful of air, I told them about my unsuccessful secondary school science career, about being saved by Tiger and his spiders, and then about my struggles at Blaby Stokes before being rescued by young Stephen Ward and his fossil ammonite.

I also told them about my class's work with froghoppers, pill bugs, birds, and mealworms, read out the piece in the mealworm book's introduction that described children working like scientists and showed them some of the children's journals.

The teachers appeared interested in my story of my brief teaching life, and I relaxed when I sensed that my teaching experiences, though limited, gave me credibility and seemed to bond me with everyone. I was, after all, like them—just a regular teacher trying to find the *"right"* way to teach science, trying to learn more about nature's secrets. They sensed I wasn't about to boss them around and tell them how to teach.

The sun shone brightly through the windows as we set out to explore the canal, armed with trays and pond nets. I led the group up the canal towpath, pleased to show off what I knew about the water plants, the water vole holes, spiders, bugs, pill bugs, froghoppers, and the beautiful swallows darting close to the water's surface.

As I pointed with my finger and talked, the teachers looked at the tall rushes and reeds growing in the canal, noticing any tiny creature that caught their eye.

There were gaps in the vegetation, created by countless fishermen over the years, squatting and throwing out their lines. Choosing one, I scooped the surface of the canal water, then emptied the net into the white dish I'd placed on the grass. The wriggling creatures I caught showed up well against the white background.

Then I stepped back, remembering what I'd learned from my children in Blaby Stokes—it's much more fun doing it yourself. The teachers dipped their nets into the murky water and emptied the muddy contents into their trays. When the water settled and cleared, all sorts of tiny creatures wriggled toward the surface.

The air was filled with the sounds of excited adults.

"Hey, look *at this! This is great. John Paull, John Paull, see, see,* see *what I've caught!"*

"Hey, look everybody. Look at this."
We were off and running. On all cylinders.

The teachers worked like scientists, eager to show each other what they had found living in the canal water, generating an enthusiastic *sciency* work atmosphere. I was surprised by how much the teachers knew about natural history, and like Tiger and Steven and David, how pleased they were to share their knowledge—and their questions—with each other.

I let out a deep breath and relaxed.

I worked with them, helped them, interacted with them, and answered or redirected as many questions as I could about the small water creatures. More importantly, I stayed out of their way, let them explore, and enjoy the moment.

After an hour or so, the teachers went back into the building. They flicked through the reference books to find out as much as they could about each creature's life cycle and then used the large magnifying glasses and binocular microscopes for a closer examination.

Jock sketched what he saw magnified five times through the microscope, eventually making a display poster of the life cycle of the mayfly larva that he had trawled up in his net.

I made myself really useful and boiled the kettle and made another pot of tea.

The morning time went quickly. Too quickly it seemed as I caught everyone by surprise when I suggested we take our sandwiches and sit on the canal bank. Sitting in the sun, relaxing and watching the swallows and the swans, we chatted about our scientific exploration of the canal and its environs.

"That was great, John Paull. And all that stuff in the mud. Really good."

"Fascinating little fellers too, aren't they? Those mayfly larvae—what do you say, they eat other creatures? Wow! Carnivores."

"What would happen if I stuck my thumb in the water?"

"Would those little things bite out a chunk?"

The mood became a bit more serious when the conversation, inevitably, moved into sharing descriptions of their classroom *science* successes and failures. Some said they were bothered they would lose control if the noise became too loud and the children too excited.

Everyone nodded, agreeing that management, not engagement, was, indeed, an issue when introducing practical science in the classroom for the first time. Children became very excited, they said, and wanted to move around a lot.

I looked at Dennis, and kindly, he came into the conversation, describing the way he worked with his children and the way in which he held high expectations for behavior. He talked about how he set up his groups.

"Groups," he said, *"could be based on friendship or similar ages. Sometimes I just choose names on an alphabetical arrangement. Sometimes, I deliberately put my more able children with those needing help. It all depends on what my goals are."*

The passion of the discussion impressed me, sensing as I did that everyone genuinely wanted to know *how* to add more hands-on science time in his/her classroom. Having Dennis and Jock to help me when I verbally stumbled was a great help.

One young teacher, David Mills, timidly asked,

"When I set up for a science activity for all my class, it gets too noisy—and then I have to raise my voice. That changes the atmosphere right away. What should I do? Do you make new class rules for science when the class experiments and stuff? Do you let the class make the rules with you?"
"What do you think, John Paull?"

I acknowledged that shifting from a tightly controlled, *direct-instruction* classroom science lesson to child-led group work was a tremendous challenge for me, one that I experienced myself just recently. *"It's worth it though. When it works, and the class is involved, the atmosphere is magic."*

One of my classroom strategies, I said, was creating the right *scientific mood* through *show and tell time.* As I spoke, I took out my OXO tin from my pocket and held it in my hand. Everyone stopped talking as I slowly opened the rusty, scratched tin. I showed them my precious amber.

Jock asked, *"What's that? It's beautiful."*

Everyone wanted to touch it and know its history.
"Where'd you get that? And that tin?" asked Dennis.

When I finished my Lariggan Beach story and the history of the OXO tin, Jock took out a seashell from his pocket. He immediately got everyone's attention. Looking at his shell, he told everyone why he kept it in his pocket. It was, he said, a shell he'd found on holiday with his wife and was fascinated by its shape and texture. It reminded him of a very special day.

Taking a risk, I asked everyone to empty his or her pockets and share anything special. Everyone had something to share, and everyone, I felt sure, saw the teaching point in what was happening.

When the workshop came to an end, some of the teachers shared their school addresses and phone numbers. They wanted to stay in contact and help each other with ideas and resources. Then, they helped me set up for the next day's workshop, thanking me, saying, *"Great day, John Paull, great day!"*

Jock and Dennis were the last teachers to leave.

"Hey, good day, John Paull, good day. And the tea at the start? That was a stroke of genius, JP, a good cuppa strong tea, first thing in the morning. Nowt like it. Calms everybody down."

"Including you."

Even though I knew they were laughing at me, I knew they were right. It certainly kept my mouth from drying up with nerves. I made a mental note to make sure I made tea at the start of every workshop from then on.

With my blood pressure easing just a bit, I tidied up the workroom and got everything in place for the next day's workshop. I phoned Bill and told him that the first day at Foxton was a good day.

"What did you do?" he asked.

"Well, nothing, really," I said. *"They did it all. We went outside, and you know, it just happened. Everyone was so super to work with. And you know, I learned so much when we talked about* how *to teach science. It was great."*

"Great!" Bill said.

"Ready for the next day?"

"Sure am," I replied, *"and I'll get some sleep tonight, I hope."*

Chapter 41

When I woke up early the next day, it was pouring cats and dogs.

I fretted as I drove toward Foxton, How, *just how, am I going to occupy today's workshoppers? If we can't go outside, what are we going to do?*

Talk about classrooms, I suppose.

I paced around the room, writing activities on cards and placing them on the tables.

Clifford Owen, unexpectedly, came through the door. He lived near Foxton and was on his way to work.

"I just dropped by to see how things were going." Clifford, I could tell, sensed my tension.

"Hey, everything OK? Gotta cup of tea for me? I've got something special for you! Swap you for a biscuit!" he said, bringing an old tobacco tin from his pocket.

He opened it slowly, revealing a mass of soft gray hair and some tiny white bones.

"What's that?" I asked, full of curiosity.

Whatever it was, it looked absolutely fascinating. It was, apparently, a tawny owl's castoff from its meal of small rodents—ejected from its throat and mouth.

Clifford said it was called an owl pellet. I had never seen one before in my life.

Clifford pulled the fur apart with his fingers, exposing the top of a tiny skull, a couple of miniature jawbones, and lots of tiny bones. I was speechless.

"There," he said, giving me a paper bag full of owl pellets, *"there is today's workshop. They're yours. Use them with your teachers 'cos there's no sense in taking everyone out in the rain and mud."*
"They'll love them."
"See if they can figure out what the owls ate."
"Take the pellets apart—it's dead easy. Just sort out the bones."
"Put them onto some black card, and stick them down."
"They look great. Enjoy."

"Wow! Thank you, Clifford."

Clifford put the small bones into a small tin and handed it to me. Then he waved good-bye, wished me well, and went off just as the first group of teachers arrived. I switched the music on. When everyone had settled after looking around the room and looking at my display of pocket museums, I made another pot of tea.

Then, someone asked, *"What we doin' today, Mr. Paull? Can't go out, can we?"*
"We're not goin' out, right?"
I very slowly, and theatrically, took my new *pocket museum* of rodent bones out of my pocket.
I opened it up and revealed a tangled mass of gray hair and tiny bones.

"What's that?" someone asked.
I was in business. Sensing the heightened atmosphere, and the *teachable moment,* I held it in my hand and told them, with great authority, what I had learned but thirty minutes before from Clifford. Everyone's eyes widened as I gave everyone an owl pellet.

For the next hour or so, you could hear a pin drop. Using toothpicks and tweezers, the teachers took their owl pellets apart, separated the bones from the fur, and tried to identify the bones, comparing their shapes to the human skeleton.

The afternoon focused on cleaning, bleaching, and gluing the bones onto some black paper—and talking enthusiastically about just how much their class would love taking pellets apart. They could stick them in a tin and make it a *pocket museum.*

Without any doubt, it was the *best* workshop day of my weeklong career so far and, thanks to Clifford, gave me an amazing resource that I have used and used again, always successfully, with teachers and children, countless times.

When I phoned him and thanked him that evening, Clifford told me how to get a constant supply of owl pellets. All I had to do, it turned out, was to contact the local zoo.

They had—and were willing to the share with teachers—an abundant daily supply of pellets from their birdhouse.

Chapter 42

The Foxton outdoor science workshops attracted a lot of interest from other British educators—keen to see what Leicestershire was doing through its professional development program to promote an increased level of awareness of the environment.

Sometimes, I'd spend almost an hour explaining to teacher and educator visitors what I was doing and what I thought I was achieving when taking teachers out on the canal footpath, carrying nets and white dishes, and letting them explore like young children.

A typical question was, *"How would such a day for teachers impact their classroom teaching?"*

Or,
"How could *such a day for teachers, pond dipping, then playing with microscopes and magnifying glasses, collecting spiders and ground beetles, help teachers teach better?"*

Well, I didn't know, and I had no pert, clever answers other than, *"Well, everyone enjoys being a learner, don't they?"*

I was exhausted but exhilarated when the forty introductory workshops were finally over. I had learned one way, in the sun and in the rain, to run a reasonably effective *environmental* workshop for teachers. That *one way* focused on encouraging the adults to be as curious as young children about the natural world.

I like to think that the Foxton workshop made a difference for some teachers.

Spending a day sloshing in the water and peering through magnifying glasses provided opportunities for the teachers to enjoy being learners again.

That enjoyment raised their awareness level of how much children enjoy working in the *"wild"* environment, and how they, the teachers, could use environmental exploration to motivate reading and writing and drawing.

Some of the teachers who came on my workshops then brought their children for a day's visit. Watching how different teachers worked differently with their children was fascinating.

Two teachers, Joan Cooksey and Rose Impey, I remember in particular. Watching them explore with their children and the ways they kept everyone engaged was eye opening.

Their trust in the children as they went about their investigations and their well-timed interactions produced the highest quality in their afternoon writing and drawing.

One thing in particular that struck me was how compassionate the children were with the tiny creatures they observed, making sure that every living thing was reintroduced to its natural habitat as soon as the observation was completed.

Chapter 43

It was an odd coincidence that, as teachers were encouraging children to be more compassionate and caring about nature, I knew more and more gerbils, hamsters, rabbits and other small mammals were appearing in classrooms. Some, sadly, were kept week in, week out, in small cages tucked away at the back of noisy classrooms conditions. Given that their lifestyle was impacted heavily, this made me very concerned about their welfare.

I knew the teaching temptation though. When given the opportunity, particularly in talks with and to teachers, I brought attention to the issue, stressing that if a living thing was required for a child's study topic, then it should be for a very short period. Also, I stressed the life needs of spiders, worms, pill bugs, and other creepy-crawlies that needed to be considered when creating temporary homes for them while being studied, and the absolute need to return the creatures to their natural homes as soon as the research period was over.

I focused on the issue in the following article.

September 1967

COME INTO THE GARDEN, MAUDE

At the end of one of my pond-dipping workshops at Foxton Field Study Center, we put our microscopes and white dishes to one side and talked about what we had discovered throughout the day. The conversation soon shifted to what was and what wasn't going on in their classrooms.

Some, I knew, were comfortable teaching science by setting their children in groups and giving them chance to investigate different kinds of scientific resources; some weren't.

One teacher, sitting at the back of the room, told the class and me what happened when she asked her seven-year-olds to draw a garden worm. A little girl, with questioning eyes, put up her hand and said, "I've never seen a worm. How big are they? Are they like snakes?" The other teachers smiled, and I was reminded of the story I heard somewhere of a young boy who was flabbergasted when he saw a cow being milked on his first-ever visit to the farm. His only experience with milk was in bottles delivered each morning on his doorstep by the co-op milkman.

This isn't so surprising, is it, when you think about it? If you live in a high-rise apartment building or in the middle of a council estate, you don't have many encounters with worms or cows. But so what?

Would it matter if our children grew up not knowing about cows and worms?

What relevance has the lives and activities of cows and worms to the urban child who lives in a concrete environment? And taking this further, does it matter that adults view many small creatures with distaste and pass on their prejudices to their children? After all, isn't it true that smoldering beneath the surface of many of us are hostile attitudes to nature? Which one of us hasn't trapped and killed a mouse, stepped on a snail, crushed a spider, or swatted a fly?

Well, I think it does matter. Isn't it important that all children have an opportunity to experience the natural world firsthand and to learn about familiar living things that share the world with us? As teachers, shouldn't we provide the children in our care with the opportunity to discover the natural world for them, to learn to enjoy it, and to appreciate our dependence upon it? Won't that subsequently encourage them to care for it?

For many teachers of young children, nature (creepy-crawlies, birds, rocks, fossils, for example) is an invaluable aid for educational purposes, an inspiration for discussion, science, language, art, music, and writing. They know that outside the door is a huge outdoor classroom, a place to learn about and to learn in. It needn't be a dense woodland, rich meadow, pond, or clear mountain stream (they help though!). A schoolyard, however sterile, is home to a myriad of interesting small animals. Turn over a brick and you find wood lice, slugs, and snails. Standing in silky webs are spiders, hiding under dead leaves are earwigs, centipedes, and millipedes. Lurking inside cracks in the wall are tiny beetles, flies, and moths.

Small animals have big life histories and are easy to keep for short periods of time. A friend of mine, a professional biologist, kept a small colony of wood lice in a tobacco tin for a few days, dropping in the occasional damp dead oak leaf for food. Not, of course, by any stretch of the imagination, a recommended way of keeping small creatures, but it does show what is possible.

If we create appropriate classroom homes (the right size container, food and water, shade and space) for small creatures, think of what our children could learn from observing creepy-crawlies at close range. Wood lice, for example, would be ideal creatures to keep in the classroom for a short period of time. They're easy to find, and they're so interesting! Female wood lice mature when they are about two years old and rear their young in a brood pouch under their bodies. When the offsprings are ready to emerge, the female stands still and stretches her front legs out stiffly so that the young can crawl down to the ground.

And snails.
What wonderful creatures they are and so easy to keep for a few days before returning them safely to their home environment—as are spiders and worms and millipedes and slugs, unlike gerbils, rabbits, and guinea pigs that we house in cramped cages.

If children are encouraged to find, watch, and understand how small creatures live, won't it help them learn to live in harmony with nature and appreciate living things?

And important for us teachers, doesn't a worm or a spider give us so many ways of developing compassion for living creatures as well as classroom skills?

Try it and watch how it impacts the children. And your classroom!

Chapter 44

During the winter, Bill Browse and a small team of advisors worked on another of Bill's inspirations—a free residential hands-on workshop for teachers. From dawn to dusk, teachers could investigate mathematics or art or literacy or science or music, while talking about their teaching successes and failures. Unfinished conversations could continue over dinner or, later, over a glass of wine.

Loughborough University was closed for the Easter vacation. Bill rented the vacant rooms at a nominal charge. It turned out to be such a brilliant idea—in my opinion, the perfect professional development opportunity for those who enjoyed talking and sharing teaching ideas with other teachers.

Over seventy teachers signed up for the program, most of them in their first year of teaching in Leicestershire schools.

Bill invited me to dinner on the Saturday before the Loughborough Residential Workshop started, where I joined David and his wife, Frances. During the meal, David reminded me of his visit to my classroom in Blaby and calmly took out his OXO tin. He opened it slowly, revealing a beautiful arrowhead he'd found.

"See, John Paull. Still got it."

After a social get-together and dinner on Sunday evening, the teachers gathered the following morning for a full English breakfast. As the last piece of toast disappeared from the tables, Bill welcomed everyone and described what was on offer for the week. The morning and afternoon sessions, he said, led by advisory staff and guests, included workshops for mathematics, science, environmental studies, art, and literacy. Each evening, after dinner, one could choose to watch a film, hear a stimulating *talk* given by a visiting well-known educator, go for an *environmental science* walk, or sit around, with a drink in hand.

Jock McEvoy, just as he did at Foxton, joined my workshop and, smiling, asked, *"Not nervous, now, John, are you? C'mon, you must have done this a hundred times by now! And, tins. Got any great tins? You know, those, what ya call 'em?"*
   "Pocket museums?"
   "Got any tea?"
   "Any ginger biscuits?"

Indeed I did. There was a cup of steaming hot tea and a couple of ginger biscuits for everyone. Then, with cup of tea in hand, everyone went to the table filled with *pocket museums* filled with bones, rocks, crystals, fossils, and shells.

I produced my old rusty OXO tin from my pocket and slowly opened it up, revealing my precious amber. I told everyone its history.

   "I came to get some ideas," said one young teacher.
   "That'll do for starters."
   "Now I know what I'm going to do when I get back to school."
   "Hey, can we make some pocket museums?"

I opened up a bag filled with empty tins.
   "Here's the tins. There's the scissors, black paper, and glue on the table."
   "C'mon. Let's go and find some stuff to put inside."
We went into the nearby woodland and found snail shells, dead insects, flowers, small branches, and other eye-catching specimens,

   "I'm going to show my kids my tins."
   "They'll love 'em."
   "Can you come and show your tins sometime, John Paull?"
   "My class will be thrilled to bits. Go on, say you will, yes?"

Creating a varied collection of *pocket museums* to later show their children became the Loughborough *thing-to-do*—and developed into quite a competition. Who had made the *best* pocket museum?

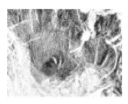 Early each evening, I led a small group of teachers to the nearby woodlands where we'd sit, quietly, in the dark, close to a badger sett. Within a few minutes, we heard, then saw, a family of wild badgers sniff the night air, then tramp their way through the bracken, searching for their evening meal of juicy earthworms and fat grubs.

This incredible and intense sensory experience, sitting very quietly in the middle of a wooded area in the dark, proved to be a very popular early evening activity, and almost everyone in the Loughborough workshop signed up to go to the woods during the week.

Tony Kallet and John Holt were after-dinner speakers in Loughborough's first residential workshop. David Hawkins, though, gave the "star" evening talk. I had never heard him speak before that night. I sat enraptured, absolutely captivated and inspired. What impressed me was not as much the content but his ability to use words to move people. From the outset, his confidence and level of comfort relaxed his audience. He held everyone, easily and naturally, in the palm of his hand with his commanding presence of self-belief.

Tony Kallet recorded David's presentation and, when typing, called it, *"I, Thou, and It."* For days and weeks afterward, I went over David's talk, thinking and thinking about everything he said.

Other notable American educators, including Bill and Sarah Hull, Tom Justice, John Holt, David Armington, and Brenda Engel, came and spent time working and talking with the teachers throughout each day and evening, sharing their teaching talents, their ideas, and their *open education* experiences in some school districts in the United States.

The Loughborough residential workshop was to become, for me and for many teachers and advisory staff, the professional development experience of the Leicestershire school year, and I'm sure impacted the quality of teaching going on in many classrooms.

The blend of living together, attending workshops and joining in discussions, formal and informal, recharged and reinvigorated those teachers who were feeling either the predictable strains and stresses that occur when making fundamental classroom teaching and learning changes, or the need for more new engaging teaching ideas.

Two Harvard graduate school of education doctoral students, Charles Rathbone and Roland Barth, sharing a grant, came and later wrote extensively about their views of the *open education* practice in Leicestershire. Charles wrote especially about his experience at Loughborough.

The Loughborough Residential Workshop, known colloquially as *Loughers*, ran successfully for years until Bill's eventual retirement from the Leicestershire Advisory Center.

What a wonderful model it was for moving teachers forward in their teaching.

Chapter 45

When the school year ended, Bill and I were invited to join David Hawkins in Montpelier, Vermont.

We were to be part of a large local public school teacher workshop, financed by the school district that was aiming to introduce the *British infant school* model into its schools.

Vermont, I learned later, was one of two states that were committed to spreading the informal methodology of *open education*. North Dakota was the other. The Office of Vermont's Commissioner of Education published the *Vermont Design for Education*, a primer for those wanting to know more about *open education*.

Not knowing my workshop audience, I had little idea of their teaching experiences, so I planned to do the only thing I felt relatively comfortable doing—run a hands-on workshop, using resources from the outdoor environment as the starting point for investigation. Countless hours walking up and down the canal towpath and tramping through the Loughborough woodland had attuned my eyes. If there was anything worth finding around the school building and talking about, I hoped I would find it, mount it in a rusty tin, and, hey, presto, I had another example of a *pocket museum*.

After a long flight from London to Boston, dressed in jeans and T-shirt, longhaired, unshaven, and tired, I was asked by US airport security officers to follow them into a small office. Once there, one of them closed the door. I was asked to remove my jacket and trousers. One officer, without a word to me, emptied my jacket pockets, slowly removing three small tins. As I folded my trousers to rest them on the back of a chair, my OXO tin fell out of my pocket. Alarmed, the officer stood back and told me to open the tins.

"*Why,*" I was asked, "*do you have all these tins? What's inside them? There's more of them in your suitcase? You got more?*"

"*Stacks of them. I'm a teacher,*" I said nervously.
"*I use them to teach.*"
"*You know, teach, progressive education, collecting things, you know, things that kids like, classroom science and stuff.*"

The officer looked incredulous and, perhaps, a little disappointed, I think, that I wasn't carrying a variety of drugs. After all, with my long hair and partial beard, didn't I look as if I would have a case full of dope?

That, it appeared, was all the officer needed to know. I was curtly told to put my clothes back on and rejoin the queue. My passport was duly stamped and now, cleared as a reputable visitor, I took another plane to Vermont.

Eventually, on Saturday, I arrived in Montpelier, settled into my accommodations, and made my way on Monday to the elementary school hosting the weeklong workshop.

After being introduced to a large group of teachers as "*teachers from Ly-cest-ter-shire,*" Bill and I made our way to our appointed work areas. My classroom, down at the end of the long corridor, was filled with tables and chairs.

In came the teachers. They sat down, took out their notebooks, and looked expectedly, just as my first class of children did when I taught at Trinity Fields. They waited for me to begin my lecture.

This time, even though my stomach was knotted, I felt better prepared.

Slowly, I reached into my pocket and brought out the rusty OXO tin and gently removed the amber. The teachers stared. Quietly, I told my amber story. They listened. I could tell by the looks in their eyes I had engaged my audience.

They asked questions. It was another *amber* moment. Slowly, theatrically, I opened a *pocket museum*, one filled with the bones of a small rodent.

We were off and running.

Then, with my stomach knots slowly untying themselves, I led a *"what can we find?"* walk around the school grounds, an area filled bushes, trees, flowers, rocks and close to a river. I couldn't have wished for anything better. As we walked, I kept asking about the trees, plants, and small creatures I had never seen before.

That, it turned out, was a masterstroke. The teaching and learning roles were reversed, and as a consequence, the levels of engagement grew. Everyone had something to contribute, including the one teacher who, joyfully (and with a cheeky grin), identified marijuana growing in the wild.

Settling the group down after that fascinating discovery took some time. I quickly searched the dead grass and found what I was looking for—a family of beautiful gray pill bugs, scuttling around in a clump of dead leaves.

 I told the group what I knew about the pill bugs.

Quickly we found more and brought a few into the classroom and let them loose on a sheet of white paper.

The questions came thick and fast about the amazingly entrancing and energetic pill bugs.

"Can we keep some in class for a while?"
"If so, what do they need?"
"What do they eat and drink?"
"Are they social, or should we keep them separate?"
"Do we keep them in the shade?"
"Which is male and which is female?"
"How many legs have they got?"
"Are they herbivores?"
"Where do they live?"

We looked around for anything that could be converted into a *posh* pill bug hotel, finding many useful pieces of card stock and plastic in the trashcan.

As the group was making pill bug homes, I went to the school library and found a picture reference book with a comprehensive section on arthropods.

Down the corridor, in another classroom, fellow workshop leader, Neil Jorgenson, was working with *Tri-Wall*, a very thick three-ply cardboard material used for packing large appliances. It was so soft that it could easily be cut with a small saw.

Neil showed me a range of resources made from Tri-Wall.

My class soon built a large and very functional Tri-Wall temporary home for our pill bugs.

Before everyone left to go home, I asked the group to bring in something of interest the next day, *"small enough to fit in a tin."*

Everyone came in early the following morning, and we started the day with sharing time. Some of the teachers, predictably, had their favorite rocks stored in tins in their pockets. One, though, had an arrowhead found, he said, in the nearby creek.

He had my attention right away. And I so wanted to find one for myself. The nearby creek became the destination for the day's field trip—and what a great day it was. I found the most beautiful arrowhead one can imagine, made from milky white quartz. What an incredible shape. Who made it? I wondered. How did they do it? When was it made?

That evening, I found just the right size tin and made *the* best *pocket museum* for my arrowhead.

At the end of the week, every living creature was returned to its natural home, under flat rocks, between dead leaves, under tree bark, or on bushes.

We didn't return, though, the fossils and minerals and the arrowhead that I'd found in the nearby river.

Naughty, I know, but, hey, the teachers wanted to show their finds to their children when they went back to school, to open their eyes to the outside world's delights, and justifiably couldn't part with any of them. I couldn't part with the arrowhead, now living cheek-by-cheek with the amber and *wishing rock*.

The Vermont workshop, I believe, was the first American workshop staffed by English educators focusing on the British primary school model.

Many, many more followed, promoting, for nearly a decade, a vigorous exchange of ideas and practices between English and American educators.

Chapter 46

I spent every evening during my three weeks in Vermont talking with David and Frances Hawkins, sharing and reflecting on what we'd experienced each day in our workshops.

I was absolutely thrilled when both of them began discussing his plan to create a permanent base for teachers to meet and talk and learn from each other's teaching experiences, in Boulder, Colorado, fashioned, in part, they said, on Foxton and Loughborough.

We agreed that, if David secured funding, I would join him, Frances and Tony Kallet for the opening of David's Center for Environmental Education. The central goals, David said, were suggested by the second part of its name, "for environmental education." By this term, David said he meant not just education for concerns about the natural environment, but education through fuller use of all the environments in which children live—physical, social, emotional, and the environment of books, ideas, and history. Environmental education, he said, seeks to provide fresh subject matter to extend the range of children's perceptions and understanding and their powers of analysis and expression. David put high value on the skills and knowledge essential for further learning. He also, as I knew well, had a high respect for teachers, especially those who wanted some support to resolve the day-to-day practical problems on working with a class of young children.

David proposed running workshops that sharpened and strengthened teachers' abilities to uncover the often hidden talents of individual children. Workshops, should, said David, focus on teachers' own learning about subject matter at their own adult level. They should also allow the instructors opportunity to build a relationship with individual teachers that would eventually lead to visiting and working in classrooms.

That made my head spin, and I knew it was something incredibly special to look forward to.

Leaving the Advisory Center was a big problem for me. I had the same feeling I had when I left Blaby to join the Advisory Center. Did I really want to do it? Was it the right thing to do?

I needed Bill to tell me just what an incredible learning experience it would be, working alongside David Hawkins and Tony Kallet.

Bill did, of course, tell me that it was the opportunity of a lifetime, adding reassuringly that my job in Leicestershire would be there, waiting for me when I returned to the UK.

Good, I thought. But I, in turn, needed to reassure my father that going abroad to work wouldn't have long-term career and financial implications and threaten my pension.

Chapter 47

The founding members of the Mountain View Center for Environmental Education, David and Frances Hawkins, were my wife, Dorothy, an experienced and very effective *open education* teacher, New Zealander Elwyn Richardson, and Tony Kallet, long-time friend of the Hawkins, now returning to America after seven years working in Leicestershire as advisor.

I was especially delighted to be working with Tony again. Tony's incredible ability to carefully observe colleagues teaching and young children learning, his insights into the processes they were engaged in, and his ability to write so clearly were vital elements in my professional development when I was in Leicestershire. He made me stand back from my teaching and think carefully about what I was doing.

David, a friend of Tony's from his days as director of ESS, knew that Tony would play a vital role in the center's work, especially in documenting its activities and leading reflective discussions in its staff meetings and with classroom teachers.

Elwyn Richardson had recently published his much-acclaimed *In the Early World*, a book describing his work with children in his New Zealand school, and had just completed his summer work at Ann Arbor University.

Like David and like me, Elwyn was a keen and enthusiastic observer of the natural world, an enthusiasm he transmitted when working with children. He was also a perceptive and critical observer of classroom practice, especially practice that described itself as an exemplar of *open education.*

In late August 1970, after a week or so of intense staff discussions, we opened the center with a weeklong conference, inviting Bill Browse and Stewart Mason from the UK and several key educators from the United States.

The conference theme was primarily a detailed and long discussion about the long-term ambitions and educational hopes of the center. David said his aim was to provide a meeting place for local teachers, with workshop facilities, staffed by an advisory support service, much like the Leicestershire model that David admired so much.

Each conference day, similar to the Loughborough residential workshop, focused on a range of *hands-on* workshops (either science, mathematics, music, or art), and then broke down into small group discussions.

Each evening, after dinner, we listened to a talk from one of the conference participants about his/her recent and current experiences in—or views on—*open education.*

My initial contribution was helping Tony and David set up workshop rooms. Working with Tony as he suspended lots of table knives and forks, tins and pots around his music room was a real treat! Full of curiosity, I spent more time fiddling with the sounds I made than actually putting his workshop together.

Just after breakfast on Wednesday morning, David asked if I'd lead a field trip to the mountains. My heart missed 476 beats! Anxiously, I asked who wanted to go—and was touched but nervous when

Elwyn; Phil (world-renowned physicist and mathematician); and Phyllis Morrison (artist and mathematician); David; his wife, Frances; Stan Ulam (world-renowned mathematician); Dan Anishansley (biologist); Hassler Whitney (world-renowned mathematician); and Stewart Mason (renowned educator).

Yikes!

I packed a few magnifying glasses, some small containers, pocketed my amber, gathered the group, and off we went to the mountains beyond Boulder.

I was the first out of the car. Sensing I had to show everyone I knew a thing or two, my eyes roamed the ground. I crossed my fingers and squeezed my amber, hoping I'd either find something I knew a lot about.

Lady Luck was on my side—yet again, a diminutive pill bug came to my rescue, the same very delightful, fascinating creature I'd learned so much about when teaching at Blaby Stokes. Everyone gathered around to see what I was *ooohing* and *aaahing* about. They stared at the little multilegged isopod wriggling in the palm of my hand and asked great questions. Their curiosity was insatiable. They wanted to know everything, absolutely everything, about the pill bug.

I was amazed at everyone's *childlike* curiosity. Seeing the creature wasn't enough. They wanted to know why it did this, why it did that, and why it did the other, and soon everyone was on hands and knees looking for pill bugs.

Stewart Mason was thrilled when he found three, lurking underneath some dead leaves.

I handed out the magnifying glasses and the containers. You'd have thought I'd given everyone a hundred-dollar bill. I had handed out the right resources at just the right time. What a great teaching point, I thought.

Sitting under the glaring summer sun, watching and listening to such intellectual giants getting excited about a small wriggly creature was an amazing experience for someone as young and as green as I was. *"Green,"* of course, both in the environmental and experiential sense of the word.

Learning something new was such good fun. And it was even more fun when you could share the fun with someone.

When questions were answered to everyone's satisfaction, the little creatures were returned, with gratitude, care, and tenderness\ to their habitat.

As we ate our sandwiches and continued the conversation about what I knew about the life of the pill bug, David sat next to Philip and Phyllis. They were soon deep in conversation, a conversation that caught my attention when I heard David say,

"Zero, such an interesting number . . . isn't it?"

Because I didn't have a clue as to what he might be talking about, my curiosity got the better of me. What's so special about 0? I sidled over and joined the group.

"The story of zero," said David, smiling at me, *"is an ancient one."*
"Think about it—mathematics began with counting sheep and cows and to note the passing of time. No one needed a zero. Zero first came into use in the Babylonian system of numbering. Inscriptions on a clay tablet, like an abacus. Around 300 BC, the Babylonians had a blank on their tablet."
"It meant nothing, no value, zero."

"See?" said David. *"Add any number to itself, and it changes. 2 and 2 equals four. But zero add zero is, well, zero. Zero add 2 is 2."*

 As I was thinking for the first time in my life about zero, Philip looked at the ground and picked up an empty snail shell.

"Yep, zero is a fascinating concept. But look at this, John. This shell . . . has a right handed spiral, you know. Some shells are left-handed, like this one."

As he spoke, he fumbled in his pocket and brought out what I learned was a left-handed seashell he'd found on a beach in Florida.

He compared the spirals, showing me how one shell spiraled one way, and the other spiraled the other way.

I was fascinated. Imagine—zero really does take some thinking about . . . and shells, there are left-handed and right-handed shells. Within a few minutes, Phil and others introduced me, in the group, to the work of the thirteenth-century mathematician, *Leonardo of Pisa,* known as *Fibonacci,* to his study of mathematics and its occurrence in nature and his *Fibonacci* numbers. And, then, the *golden ratio.*

At that very instant, my view of the natural world changed, as it did when I found my precious amber.

From that minute on, the world of nature became even more incredible and more fascinating. Wherever I looked, I could now see, not just beautiful rocks with quartz veins running through them, but mathematical patterns everywhere. I was hooked.

The numbers 0 1 1 2 3 5 8 13 21 34 and on and on were all around me.

When we arrived back in Boulder, I brought out the garden hose pipe to clean off our shoes, caked
in dry hard soil from walking in and around Caribou.

Even that turned into a time of enormous questions and, for me, yet another learning experience.

Turning on the hosepipe provoked a great scientific question from one of the group:
"How far will the water spray if you stick your finger over the nozzle?"
"C'mon, John Paull. Spray."

This question, and others that followed, and the group's predictions kept everyone scientifically engaged until it was time to get ready for dinner and then hear the after-dinner speaker, Stewart Mason.

That evening, Mr. Mason, a shy, quiet man, began with a brief understated overview of his work as Leicestershire's director of education. Then, with his confidence growing, he described his morning experience on the field trip to Caribou and his fascination with the tiny pill bug he held in his hand. The pill bug really did fascinate him.

Tony, holding the microphone attached to a small tape recorder, recorded Mr. Mason's talk, which was later entitled "Will Anyone Raise a Hand for Passivity?" and published it in the first edition of the Center's magazine *Outlook,* a periodical that Tony later invited teachers to write in an open, descriptive manner about children and classrooms. Its style was similar to the broadsheet that Tony and Bill Browse oversaw in Leicestershire.

I went to bed very late, my brain absolutely overloaded. I had, after all, spent part of the day with some of the world's great thinkers, learned more about the ubiquitous pill bug, had the importance of zero to think about, about the work of an Italian mathematician of long ago, *Fibonacci,* and listened in the evening to one of the UK's educational leaders, a shy, introverted man, talk about his response to the field trip to Caribou.

The following day, I took the same group to the nearby Boulder Creek. We took off our shoes and socks and waded into the cold water. I did a quick search for *wishing rocks,* water snails (were they right-handed?), picked up the glinting particles of iron pyrites, and was fascinated to see how the river had cut its way through hard rock. Stewart Mason was the first to spot a pebble with a line of quartz running through its center.

"See what I found, John Paull," he said with a chuckle, *"my own wishing rock."*

Before long, everyone in the group had found a *wishing rock.*

Without equipment, we measured the creek's speed, its depth, its temperature, and estimated the volume of water passing us at a moment in time.

When the group sat and ate lunch, Dan Hanishanley and Stewart Mason helped me make a dam across the fast-running river, provoking, of course, observations, comments, and great questions from everyone.

"Haven't had as much fun since I was a young lad," said Stewart Mason as he put his final lump of granite rock into place, diverting the water running down fast from the mountainside.

He put his *wishing rock* in his pocket.

"I'm saving this, John Paull," he said with a shy smile.

On Friday morning, David brought everyone together, wrapping up a wonderful, stimulating week of activity, conversation, and serious discussion.

Chapter 48

As soon as the conference had ended, David wrote to the superintendent of Boulder Valley School District, telling him of the opportunities being offered by the Mountain View Center. He also contacted local *Head Start* and *Follow Through programs,* whose educational practice, he told me, was similar to the center's notion of how children should and could be taught in elementary school classrooms.

I hadn't heard of either Head Start or *Follow Through.*

Over a cup of tea, Tony enlightened me: both, I learned, were federal programs that provided grants to local agencies to provide comprehensive child development services to economically disadvantaged children and families.

As poor academic performance was known to correlate directly with poverty, the Department of Education (DOE) and the Office of Economic Opportunity's aim was *to break the cycle of poverty through better education. Poor education then led to less economic opportunity for those children when they became adults, thus ensuring poverty for the next generation.*

Launched in 1965 by Jule Sugarman, Head Start, Tony said, was originally conceived as a quick catch-up summer school program that would teach low-income children in a few weeks what they needed to know to start kindergarten. Once it was determined that you can't make up for five years of poverty with a six-week preschool program, Head Start programs promoted school readiness by enhancing young children's social and cognitive development through the provision of educational, health, nutritional, social, and other services. They engaged parents as best they could in their children's learning and helped them in making progress toward their educational, literacy, and future employment goals.

Follow Through programs began two years later, in 1967, as part of President Johnson's socially and politically ambitious *War on Poverty*, and provided a continuation of Head Start services to children in their early elementary years. The architects of various theories and approaches, including the open education movement, believed their methods could alleviate the detrimental educational effects of poverty and submitted applications to become sponsors of their models.

I learned more about the *Follow Through* program in Boulder talking with David and two very enthusiastic local *Follow Through* public school teachers, Jeannie and Patti, during the first workshop.

I was so struck by their excited and energetic participation in a Mountain View *hands-on* workshop and field trip, especially by the kind of questions they asked, particularly about Fibonacci.

Patti and Jeannie wanted to know more and more about the English classrooms I worked in, asking me:

"What are the classrooms like? How many children does each first grade teacher have?"
"Are Head Start and Follow Through programs going on in Leicestershire?"
"When do kids start going to school?"
"What's going on in math and science for the young kids?"
"What science programs do you use?"
"Any?"
"Do parents agree with what you all are doing?"

Answering their questions as best I could made me wonder about English and American classrooms.
Were they different? If so, how were they different? After all, I hadn't, at that point, ever been inside an American school classroom when it was in session.

When Patti and Jeannie talked about their classroom and shared their ways of incorporating *inquiry* science into each day's teaching schedule, my ears pricked up. Their vivid, excited description of their classroom made me want to see for myself what they were doing. I instinctively knew I had a lot to learn from both of them.

I couldn't wait to see it for myself—would it be like the classrooms I knew so well in Leicestershire?

Cheekily, I asked if I could go to their classroom the very next morning.

Kindly, they agreed, and the following morning, full of anticipation, I drove toward Lincoln Elementary School. I was in for a treat.

After signing in at the main office, I walked down the corridor, passing a small group of children on the way, building the biggest and tallest construction from cardboard boxes I had ever seen—and building it without a teacher in sight. What a great start to my visit, I thought.

I reached Jeannie and Patti's classroom and slowly opened the door. The classroom was buzzing with action and filled with young children working individually and in groups. I saw *every classroom* resource imaginable.

I *knew* I was in the presence of two *open education* master co-teachers. I was walking into, perhaps, including Dennis Bradley's in Medbourne, Leicestershire, *the* best classroom for primary children I had ever seen.

It was the kind of classroom that instantly and absolutely confirmed what I felt was *the* appropriate and successful way to educate young children.

I stood and stared, quickly absorbing as much as quickly as I could. In every corner, something was happening. The room was full of resources, children's pictures, soft music, and lots of young children, all engaged.

Children were involved.
Children were talking with each other.
Children were talking and listening to a teacher.
Children were resting their heads on cushions and reading, others were writing and drawing at a table, constructing with blocks, cooking, painting, writing, exploring science or mathematical materials, watching lizards in a terrarium, making electrical circuits to light bulbs for a building, making and flying paper helicopters and planes—and much more.
Children were concentrating on a variety of activities.

Where were Patti and Jeannie?

In one of the corners, Jeannie was involved in a puppet theater, watched by half a dozen children. Patti was sitting on the floor, involved in a mathematical activity with two or three girls. Patti turned toward me and waved me in, pointing to a table. I sat down at the table and was quickly adopted by a group of five or six children who were building tall towers from paper straws and paper clips.

The children talked with each other, shared ideas, gathered more resources when they needed them, and then drew what they had been making. Apart from the quizzical looks when I spoke, the children used me as one of the teaching team. I stayed with them until lunchtime, fascinated by their level of engagement.

They were pleased with their efforts, especially when they received the occasional word of praise and encouragement from either Patti or Jeannie.

I was not only struck by the abundance of resources and supplies available for the children that resulted in every child having what s/he needed when s/he needed it, but also by the classroom organization. The boys and girls knew where to go to get what they wanted and didn't have to ask either teacher. No one wasted time looking for things, waiting for turns, or getting frustrated because they didn't have a pair of scissors and tape to add to their constructions.

Just before lunchtime, the children were given ten minutes to tidy things on their activity tables, and when the teachers were satisfied, went off for school lunch. I asked if I could stay for the afternoon. Patti nodded. Sensing that Patti and Jeannie had a lot to do—as well as eat and visit the restroom—I kept out of their way. Sitting in the corner with my notebook, I saw Patti and Jeannie, munching their sandwiches, reorganize the room for the afternoon's work.

They appeared to have a telepathic communication with each other—as they seemed to have when they worked with their children. Without a word, they quickly cleared all the surface areas, filled some of them with resources, and taped selections of children's finished work on the walls.

When the class returned from lunch, the room looked as good as new and ready for action. Patti, sitting on the carpet, first talked with everyone, told them her expectations, took questions, and sent the children off to their work.

Patti and Jeannie then moved separately and purposefully from group to group, feeding off the reactions and excitement generated by the variety of activities, getting a quick return for the time they spent at lunchtime setting out the materials.

During the afternoon, I helped children read, make clay models, cut out mathematical shapes, measure the classroom floor with a long tape measure, spell a word, tell one or two the date and time, and much, much more. Oh, and explained several times why I spoke with a funny accent.

As I worked, I could see how Jeannie and Patti capitalized on each other's strengths and experiences and the benefits that brought their children. I could also see how the children helped and learned from each other.

After school, I sat and scribbled some notes, waiting for Jeannie and Patti to relax and catch their breath. When they were ready for me, I asked tons of questions.

I quickly learned that Jeannie and Patti could sense what the other was thinking. What a great partnership, I thought, each supporting the other as each was supporting (and resourcing) the children in their care.

They told me they wanted to create the richest learning environment possible, knowing that the best way to meet their children's learning styles and challenges was to motivate, trust, and respect their learning choices and to provide what resources the boys and girls needed for their projects.

"But," said Jeannie, *"even though it takes so much of our time, getting this and that for the class, it's worth it. And of course, it helps us reach our goals with each boy and girl—we have the highest expectations about the projects and want to see writing—and math—of the highest quality."*

Projects, they said, organized and started by them or by the children, could last for an hour, a day, week or so, and needed new resources almost every day.

Even though it had been a really busy day, busy for the class, but so much busier for the two teachers, they appeared to enjoy talking and talking and talking about their work, and, by doing so, figure out how to resolve their teaching challenges thrown up during the morning and afternoon.

They invited me back to work with their children and to talk more *education* with them—the beginning of a long-time work and social relationship that helped me unravel yet more of the mysteries of running a successful classroom.

Visiting Jeannie and Patti's classroom taught me so much about teaching, about the value of co-teaching with a partner who shared your beliefs and values, about resourcing children's projects, about aiming as high as one could with expectations, and much, much more.

Able to create wonderful *amber moments* each and every day, their teaching reminded me so much of Wednesday afternoons in Mr. Jones's classroom.

Chapter 49

Over the following few months, I came frequently to Lincoln, to observe two master teachers at work, to learn from what they were doing and doing so well, and to interact and learn with their children.

One afternoon, when I was sitting on the carpet with a group of children, one of them spotted a spider running wildly across the carpet. I picked it up and cupped it gently and safely in my hand. The children stopped talking and looked at the spider running between my fingers, fascinated. Tiger's face came into my head!

I put the spider into a small jar, screwed on the lid, and passed it around so that everyone could get a closer look.

 I then asked the children,

"What is it? How many legs does it have? Will it hurt us?"
"Where does it live? Shall we make a really sweet home for it?"

"Do I need to make holes in the lid?"
"Why?"

The questions continued.
"What else does it need? Where would it sleep? Did it need a friend? Is it a girl spider? How and what does it drink? How long will it live?"
"Can it live in that jar forever?"

"No, it couldn't. We need," I said, *"to make a new and better home for the spider."*

There was an old empty bookcase in the corridor. That evening, when school had ended for the day, Patti and Jeannie quickly and expertly took it apart. They pulled out the shelves and lined the inside bottom with plastic sheeting. Then they added soil, plants, a Y-shaped tree branch, and a light bulb, screwed a huge sheet of clear plastic to the front, and, hey, within a couple of hours, there was the most beautiful spider home you can imagine. The little spider was quickly added to her new home.

When the children came in the next day, they were *so* excited to see the spider dangling from a branch at the back of the old cupboard and asked a million questions—confirmation of the value of the time Patti and Jeannie put into creating the spider home.

There was a lengthy discussion on names before the spider acquired a new name, Willie. The excitement grew when Willie built her beautiful silky, sticky web in her new home, caught her first fly, paralyzed it, wrapped it in silk, and left it dangling on her web for her evening meal.

Some of the children began to draw the spider.

One boy, eight-year-old Benji, went off to the corner of the classroom and began a new project. Benji was so taken up with the previous year's moon landing that he constructed a large moon rocket from boxes, with perfectly fitting nose cone.

He was soon joined by another lad, John, who, hearing the story that the Russians too were thinking of launching a rocket to the moon, wanted to build a Russian space rocket.

Eventually, they decided to combine their talents and work together to build the *best* rocket that *anyone* had ever made—from a variety of cardboard boxes. And they wanted to launch it into space.

When the rocket, made from cardboard, tape, bits of plastic, and more tape, was close to being finished, the boys came to me and asked if they could fly a small living creature in it.

Just *what* creature though?

Everyone, including Jeannie and Patti, agreed we should launch Willie, our classroom spider, providing that the boys made a special compartment for her in the nose cone and that there was no possibility she would get hurt. A small cardboard box was soon lined with cotton wool and converted into the strongest, safest flying spider motel one could imagine.

Another question, for me, in particular, was *how* could we fly a huge cardboard-box rocket?

I was stumped until Robin Hood and his bow provided the answers. We would, I thought, launch our rocket in the same way an arrow is launched from a bow.

We could, I thought, launch our rocket by sitting it on a length of rubber suspended between the trees in the yard. They were ideally spaced for connecting with a long piece of elastic.

When Willie the Spider successfully completed her classroom *flying-into-space* training, following, of course, the NASA guidelines for training astronauts, we carefully placed her in her matchbox, now lined with soft felt and a moth for dinner. Then we put the container in the nose cone, and took the rocket outside in the yard. Patti helped me put it on the elastic as I stretched it to the ground. After counting down from ten, Willie was launched at exactly four o'clock.

A crowd of forty-plus children cheered with excitement as the rocket took off, headed toward the late afternoon sun.

The rocket flew up to a height of about two feet, tumbled, and fell to the ground. The crowd applauded loudly, and then went quiet.

Benji ran quickly to the fallen rocket, took off the nose cone, and removed the matchbox. He opened it and looked inside, then shouted as loud as he could:

"Willie's alive. She's good. She's the first spider in space!"

The crowd of children and teachers went wild.

After the rescue, Willie the Orb Spider, and now, for a second or two, Willie the Amazing Astrospider, was retired to the huge (and very appropriately designed) posh spider hotel in the back of the classroom.

The following day, the children gathered around in a circle on the carpet with Patti and me, and we wrote Willie's story on a large sheet of paper and hung it on the wall. Then I helped Benji and John write a letter to NASA, describing their rocket-launching experience in words and pictures pasted in a small book entitled *Willie the Astronaut.*

Dear NASA and Dear Astronauts,

We launched a spider into space. Why don't you launch a spider into space?

We did!

We can show you how to do it! Look at our pictures! Look at Willie!

He flew in space!

Love, Benji and John

We never got a reply.

About a month later, I wrote again to NASA, and again, we were very disappointed when we did not receive a response.

Chapter 50

Following meetings with a group of Native Americans on the university campus, we arranged to set up and run a series of workshops in Wounded Knee, part of the Lakota Pine Ridge Reservation in South Dakota.

Before our first visit, David gave me a copy of Dee Brown's successful *Bury My Heart at Wounded Knee.*

"You'll need to read this before we go. Just to give you some background about Wounded Knee."

I couldn't put the book down, knowing as little as I did about the American West. The Wounded Knee Massacre, I read, happened on December 29, 1890, near Wounded Knee Creek, on the Lakota Pine Ridge Indian Reservation. On the day before, soldiers intercepted a band of Lakota and escorted them to Wounded Knee Creek where they made camp. The rest of the 7th Cavalry Regiment arrived and surrounded the encampment.

On the morning of December 29, the troops went into the camp to disarm the Lakota. One version of events claims that during the process of disarming the Lakota, a deaf tribesman named Black Coyote was reluctant to give up his rifle. A scuffle over Black Coyote's rifle escalated and a shot was fired which resulted in the 7th Cavalry's opening fire indiscriminately from all sides, killing men, women, and children, as well as some of their own fellow troopers.

By the time it was over, at least 200 men, women, and children of the Lakota Sioux had been killed. Twenty-five troopers also died, and 39 were wounded, many the victims of friendly fire.

Our main partners in the program at Wounded Knee were Pat Pumpkin Seed, Rog Red Elk, and Rosie Pain-on-Hip. They worked with us when we ran weekend workshops for the Oglala Sioux who wanted to be teacher aids in their children's local BIA school.

Each Friday, David and I drove through Colorado, Nebraska, and into South Dakota. We set up our workshop in an old deserted single-room school building that was also our place to sleep overnight, close to the Wounded Knee Trading Post.

Each Saturday, we worked with a small group, either on *hands-on* science and maths activities, or going on field trips to the nearby Badlands, an area that was incredibly rich in fossils and crystals.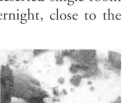

David's workshop style in Wounded Knee was, as always, gentle and alluring, and he always brought everyone into his world of mathematics and science. The group, although very quiet and undemonstrative, immediately connected with him and hung on every word he uttered. I noticed that David never talked about schools, classrooms, or children. His goal was to involve the adults in activities that ignited their sense of wonder and curiosity and trust they took that energy into their work with children.

Hiking with him and our group of Native Americans, around the nearby Badlands, a new environment for me, hearing him ask himself, *"I wonder why . . ."* made me more and more curious about the world of nature and science. His knowledge of the world was incredible, and I made sure I soaked up as much as I could understand.

Later, when reading some of the work of Joseph Soloveitchik, the Jewish scholar, I appreciated his view that people have two natures. First, there's Adam the First, the part of us that creates, discovers, and is involved in building the world. Then, there is Adam the Second, the individual who is awed and humbled by the universe as a spectator and worshipper.

After one enjoyable hike to the Badlands where we'd found some of the most beautiful and fascinating fossils I'd ever seen outside of a museum, we stood around our cars, sipping strong black coffee from our flasks, Pat Pumpkin Seed held out his hand. Slowly he opened his fingers, revealing a bunch of small cottonwood twigs.

Pat looked down at his hand, handed us the twigs, and turned his eyes up to the sky.

"You're holding many new stars, there, in your hands," he said.

"Did you know my ancestors believed all things come from Mother Earth?"
"They believed that the stars in the sky above begin their life in the earth beneath our feet."

"When they're ready, they search for the roots of the magical cottonwood trees."

"They wriggle their way inside the roots and begin to climb up the tree trunk."
"The tiny stars finally come to rest in the small twigs at the end of the cottonwood branches."

"Here, they wait . . . and wait . . . until they are needed."

"When the Spirit of the Night Sky decides that she needs more twinkling, beautiful stars, she calls on the Wind Spirit to shake all the cottonwood trees."

"The Wind Spirit blows and blows, and as the cottonwood twigs break off, the twinkling stars are released and race up to a special place in the Night Sky."

"So," said Pat, *"If you want to add a new star to the night sky, find some secret cottonwood twigs, wait for a clear night, and hold up your twigs to the sky—and snap."*

"Then, look up into the night sky again."
"Look closely."
"You will see your *star twinkling."*

"Imagine," continued Pat, *"you can add beautiful new star to the night sky kingdom whenever you want."*

We broke the dry cottonwood twigs, and sure enough, there, in the middle, were the homes of the stars, which, now, said Pat, were shooting up to the sky above.

What a wonderful story, I thought.

We dedicated the stars to Pat and his family whom, I knew, were experiencing some very challenging and life-changing family issues.

The cottonwood star story grabbed me emotionally. It was a story I knew I would use in my future work with young children, and in future workshops with teachers, as a community-building activity. I picked up as many cottonwood twigs as I could and stuffed them in my backpack.

I shared some of the cottonwood twigs in a workshop about a week later with teachers in Philadelphia during a workshop planned to last all week. After sharing the amber and *wishing rock* strategy, I was in the process of handing out bundles of cottonwood twigs before beginning the cottonwood star story when my words were rudely interrupted.

Standing in the open classroom door, a tall man, dressed totally in black, the top of his head covered in a black beret, was staring wide-eyed at my class and shouting,

"Don't listen to him. He's pushing an education that's not right for our kids."
"All of you, up and out, now."
"This, this education, is not, absolutely not, *for our kids."*

I was stunned as my class looked at each other. Half of them picked up their notebooks, gathered their bags, stood up, and filed out of the room.

What was happening? I sat down, shaking from head to toe. I asked the rest of my class if they knew what was going on.

"Best not talk about it," said one young teacher, *"let's just carry on, OK?"*
"Pretend it didn't happen."

I learned later that the visitor to my workshop was a prominent member of the Black Panthers. The Black Panthers, I was told, didn't want their kids involved in what they considered was a teaching experiment. They wanted, they said, what the white kids had in the best public schools.

Later, back in Boulder, when I related my experience in Philadelphia, Tony gave me some background to the rise of the Black Panther movement, adding to my education about life—and about life in the USA.

It was an experience that, linked with my milk-round experiences and my time at Wounded Knee, caused me to think and reflect more about the wider cultural aspects of education.

Chapter 51

As well as running workshops in Boulder, visiting classrooms, travelling, working, and teaching in Tampa, Maine, Boston, Philadelphia, and Colorado Springs, all inspiring events in so many ways, the most incredible experiences came from the thinking, questioning, walking, and talking time I spent with David Hawkins, Tony Kallet, and their extraordinary friends, both at and away from work.

Feeling their excitement when learning something new, and feeling their excitement when they were passing on information to someone who wanted to know, showed me how powerful the classroom teaching atmosphere is when the teacher is excited and enthusiastic about his teaching content. I remember the day out in the plains when David bent over and picked up a small piece of red-and-blue-colored rock.

"Hey, look, petrified wood. Just lying here in the sand."

I had never held petrified wood before. As David described the petrification process, it reminded me how different Mr. Jones was as a teacher when he held something from his glass-fronted bookcase and shared his passion with his class of boys.

Yet again, Mother Nature hooked me.

My brain boiled over when I found my first piece lying exposed to the sun.

No longer would I be on the lookout specifically for amber, *wishing rocks*, pill bugs, feathers, left-handed spirals, and more. Petrified wood now joined the list.

About a week after the petrified wood experience, David and I flew to San Francisco to meet Frank Oppenheimer, an old friend and colleague of David's. Frank, brother of Robert Oppenheimer, and another, like David, who suffered the consequences of his alleged communist sympathies before and during his time at Los Alamos, was preparing to open *The Exploratorium*, a very forward thinking and exciting museum concept that hoped to inspire visitors, young and old, to interact with incredible oversized, *hands-on* exhibits.

Out shopping, I bought a pendulum toy from Woolworths. When I showed my new toy—a heavy bolt suspended from a long spring—to Frank and David over dinner that evening, I recalled my interview at Blaby Stokes when I was asked about science toys.

David and Frank pushed aside their plates and set the pendulum in motion. Its movement was so unpredictable. They drooled over the science and mathematics questions raised when the pendulum was set in motion.

Their enthusiasm was contagious, and as I sat and listened, I saw the pendulum, in fact, everything around me, in a new light.

Later, over a glass of wine, Frank said that he hoped visitors to his museum would react to the exhibits the same way he and David responded to the toy pendulum.

That was, in many ways, typical of almost every conversation and every interaction I had over the year. Whether I was with either David or Tony or their friends over breakfast, dinner, an evening drink, wherever, their conversations often reminded me how much I didn't know, but now wanted to know, about all manner of things, especially, *perfect* teaching.

Perfect teaching, that is, in an *open education* manner that focuses on arousing curiosity and interest to truly motivate adults and children, in a manner that engages, challenges, and meets the high points of the learning and social needs of everyone.

The more I thought about it though, the more I realized that, perhaps, as David always said, there is no *perfect classroom*.

There might be *perfect* moments, a *perfect and constant* piece of teaching, a *perfect* piece of learning.

So much, though, depends on who is in charge of the classroom and how that person creates the environment, decides to work with his/her children, the relevance and appropriateness of the curriculum, availability of resources, timing, pacing, the difference between morning and afternoon, weather, and so much, much more.

So much of a classroom's success depends too on the teacher getting to know the children: their personalities, their learning styles, how they see the world around them, and remembering Philip Washer, Tiger, David, and many others, something about their background.

Such details can help the teacher reflect proactively on what was happening in the classroom, and what can be done about making changes to accommodate all needs.

One thing I was sure about, though, was the need for teachers, like the children they teach, to have a support system that encouraged and helped them do their best as they strive for those *perfect* teaching and learning moments.

During that year, I happened to have the very best support system: David and Tony.

For me, it was a wonderful, incredible year of learning.

Chapter 52

Before I left the United States to return to England, I spent time in New York with Maja Apelman. Maja, Early Years specialist and teacher at Bank Street College, was taking my position in Boulder, in the autumn of 1971.

Maja took me to Bank Street one morning. Using slides from Patti and Jeannie's classroom, I gave a lunchtime talk—my first *brown bag* session—to some of Maja's colleagues, focusing on my observations of the effectiveness of their teaching style. Speaking to teachers and students at Bank Street throughout the rest of the day gave me my first chance to reflect on and celebrate some of my educational experiences at the Mountain View Center with a group of interested educators.

After a very busy few days and evenings with Maja, I boarded the huge ocean liner, the *QE2*, courtesy of the Ford Foundation, with my amber, *wishing rock,* my first-ever piece of petrified wood, and a cottonwood star from South Dakota in my pocket, and headed back to England, back to my advisory work in Leicestershire.

I headed back to Cornwall as soon as I got off the liner. I had so much to share with my parents, including the fossils and cottonwood stars I'd found in the Badlands. I also needed to spend some time on Lariggan Beach, collecting anything of interest I could find.

A week later, I made my way back to Leicester with another jar filled with *wishing rocks,* recharged, and ready to begin work again.

At this time, Andrew Fairbairn, Mr. Mason's deputy since 1961, succeeded Stewart Mason, the visionary director of education. Mr. Fairbairn, a World War II hero who had won the Military Cross after leading a platoon that, although outnumbered, captured a vital bridge in Normandy, continued Mr. Mason's drive to keep Leicestershire in the forefront of education.

I quickly learned that there had been a change in the national mood about *open education*.

I renewed contact with many of the teachers I had previously worked with, especially Dennis Bradley and Jock McEvoy. They, of course, all wanted to know what was going on in American schools, eager to find out if there was something they could use in their schools.

Jock had become headmaster of a large primary school in Market Harborough. Dennis was now head of a large school.

Bill asked me to share, through pictures, with him and his advisory colleagues, the essence of my work in the United States at the Mountain View Center.

My photographs focused on Patti and Jeannie's *Follow Through* classroom, their teaching and learning resources, their careful furniture placement, and their children at work, individually and in groups. I told the story of Willie the Spidernaut and showed examples of the children's science journaling, mathematics, and art that came from the experience.

I also described the invigorating, intellectual, educator community that had supported my work and my professional growth in Boulder.

The Advisory Team asked me lots of questions about American principal and teacher responsibilities, the elementary school curriculum, parent expectations, and the Head Start and Follow Through programs.

They also pointed out that much had happened in the year I was in the States. The times were changing in the UK and that the *open education* era was under threat.

When I felt ready, anxious to share my "new" teaching ideas and activities with teachers, I organized some environmental science workshops, feeling somewhat more confident that I could now provide an authoritative, collaborative, and authentic experience.

My workshops, enriched by my time and experiences in Boulder, now included the following:

- Setting of worktables for no more than four adults.
  - Soft background music, a pot of tea, and a big plate of biscuits.
  - An icebreaker activity, usually prompted by a story.
  - Then a range of *hands-on* challenging individual and group activities, followed by discussion about planning and resourcing classroom projects.

For my *icebreaker*, I began each of the workshops either by giving out a small collection of cotton twigs and asking everyone to break them at the growth points to release the tiny star, or sometimes, displaying a variety of *pocket museums* and taking the OXO tin out of my pocket and showing everyone my special amber, *a wishing rock*, my arrowhead, and my petrified wood.

My indoor workshop activities included making *pocket museums*, making a small stream table and investigating water flow, understanding the science and mathematics of a simple pendulum, exploring a variety of sinking and floating experiments, creating soap bubbles in soap bubble frames made from straws and pipe cleaners, building a marble run, and of course, a quick hike outdoors looking for tiny creatures and examples of mathematical patterns in a variety of natural objects.

Discussions about classroom experiences were impacted by the release and popular acclaim of the film, *Kes*, a portrait of a working class boy in Northern England and his close bond with a wild kestrel. The scenes in the boy's school reinforced what teachers held to be true about the need to engage and motivate young children.

When the series of workshops finished, I visited, by invitation, more and more classrooms, taking in some of these *"science workshop starters,"* using them as I interacted with children and teachers.

Foxton Field Study Center was now an accepted spring, summer, and autumn outdoor science resource for Leicestershire's primary schools, and Bill used it occasionally for science workshops during the winter months.

Yet another opportunity to open a new field study center came when Bill Browse put in an application to the Education Authority to use another recently closed single-classroom village school. The location was ideal, very accessible to the teachers from several large towns.

Following the same pattern as when he opened Foxton, Bill wrote to all the schools in the area, inviting teachers to a series of one-day *environmental* science workshops.

The Hoby workshops opened up new opportunities for me as they brought me into contact with teachers from another part of the county that I hadn't visited.

Working with infant and junior teachers in the workshops and, afterward, visiting some of their classrooms, reminded me of the many conversations with David and Tony that focused on the professional needs of teachers as they take on new management and curriculum challenges that occur when they change their teaching styles.

Bill Browse, ahead of the game, as always, had thought of ways of responding to this growing need.

Prompted by the growing number of school day trips to the county's small zoo in the village of Twycross, Bill and I took the opportunity to organize a number of teacher meetings for those planning to make the most of a visit with their children. The zoo jumped at the idea and soon created facilities for a range of teacher workshops, led by zoo staff.

A similar project was developing with the Leicester city museum, initiated by my friend, Clifford Owen, and a grant from the Carnegie Foundation, which led eventually to one of the first museum/teacher education program in the UK.

Chapter 53

As Hoby Field Study Center was developing its program of workshops for teachers, the Advisory Center, through Bill Browse's initiative, was focused on another educational innovation—the creation of the first Leicestershire *Teachers' Centers.*

Bill, always looking for ways to support teachers, whatever their level of teaching expertise, was set on adopting and adapting a model for professional development that originated with the establishment of a teacher-dominated schools council which urged the development of a network of teachers' centers *"with a steering committee of local teachers and no hierarchy of control"* (Working Papers Nos. 2 and 10).

The idea originated in 1964 with the Nuffield Foundation's Primary Mathematics Project, which required its fourteen "pilot areas" to establish teachers' groups, and these—through regular meetings—turned into *teachers' centers*, securing for teachers a high degree of independence and an active role in determining the appropriate curriculum for their classrooms.

The *teacher center* idea of an after-school meeting place for teachers to acquire and make resources, exchange ideas, lead and attend workshops, undertake informal research, and assume responsibility for their professional growth caught on; by 1968, there were over 300 teachers' centers in England, nearly one-third devoted entirely to the Nuffield Mathematics Project.

When the US Congress enacted and the president signed the Education Amendments of 1976 (Public Law 94-4820), they authorized $68 million for three years for *teachers' centers*, which they defined as local school-district sponsored sites where working teachers could pursue professional improvement directly related to their own classrooms, and where the improvement program would be overseen by teachers, administrators, and university professors.

Bill Browse took over a one-room unused church school in Blaby and set up a permanent meeting place for teachers. This was not just for science and mathematics workshops, but more of a meeting place where teachers could enjoy tea or coffee and a biscuit and then sit and talk informally in the early part of each evening before heading home and on weekends.

Dorothy, fresh from her year's work with the Mountain View Center, was the first full-time teacher center leader. Dorothy filled it with a wide range of teacher resources, including displays of classroom projects, reference books, collections of locally developed lessons, small-scale exhibitions, and created a warm, welcoming atmosphere in the center. She then arranged a series of introductory meetings for teachers and circulated notices of local community events. If any teacher wanted to check out ideas on, say, teaching science or mathematics or even book a room for a meeting with other teachers, the routine was simple—either visit the center or phone and book the time. Tea and coffee was always available, all free of charge.

I held weekly meetings at Blaby Teachers' Center for anyone who wanted a strong cup of tea, a couple of sweet biscuits, and a deep brainstorming conversation about planning and teaching *hands-on* science in his/her classroom.

The former church school in Blaby was the first of several Leicestershire's *teacher centers*, all housed in one-classroom schools, filled with a variety of teaching ideas and resources for loan and after-school programs designed by, and for, local teachers.

The *teacher center* concept was a great success, pointing up the need that the Loughborough experience years before had recognized: teachers felt empowered when in control of determining how to resolve their own challenges—and felt supported when provided with the right resources to do the job they wanted to do in their classrooms.

Chapter 54

My advisory work kept me extremely busy. Not only was I running *hands-on* science workshops at Foxton, Hoby, and the Blaby Teachers' Center, for teachers and for parents, after school and on weekends, I was going out-of-county frequently, giving talks, and participating in discussions at teacher conferences in various parts of England.

I was going abroad to Europe too. Invited by the Nature Conservancy as a speaker at the International Conference on the Conservation of Nature in Rotterdam, I had to type, translate, and then formally read my carefully planned talk to a big audience of environmentalists and teachers—a brand-new experience for me. But the trade-off was that I met and shared experiences with environmental educators from many European Common Market countries. It was very interesting to hear about the environmental programs in place in schools in France, Belgium, and Germany.

But giving talks to bigger and bigger audiences, to people I hadn't seen before and most likely would not see again, became repetitive and somewhat meaningless. Spending less and less time in classrooms, less and less time supporting teachers as they adjusted their teaching to a more "open-ended" approach, and more and more time talking about it, didn't feel right. I was now *talking* more about ways in which we should educate young children than actually teaching and interacting with children as they investigated the world of natural science.

It was hitting me hard that I could be losing my credibility as an educator—how could I give *firsthand* and authentic advice on teaching, using a method that was becoming less fashionable, to an earnest, inexperienced teacher, when asked, when I was losing touch with the reality of the day-to-day work of a teacher? I was in danger of becoming yet another textbook! And a boring one at that.

I had come to another set of crossroads in my life. I now reached the stage in my career where I felt I needed to be back with children, teaching full time, and not spending my time behind the wheel of my car, or standing in front of larger and larger audiences.

I needed to be using the lessons I'd learned from so many teachers and children for the benefit of one class of children—my class, that is—on how to use the delights and mysteries of nature to engage and motivate young learners.

After many long drawn-out conversations, first, of course, in my head, and then with Bill Browse and some close teacher friends, I took the bull by the horns and, to everyone's surprise, joined the teaching staff at Warren Hills County Primary School, a recently opened semi *open-plan* building in Leicestershire.

Hazel Sibley, the head teacher, hired me as her deputy, wanting me, she said, especially to widen and deepen the school's science curriculum. That was OK, I thought, and a good reintroduction to working again as a teacher in one school—even though I wouldn't be teaching my own class throughout each and every day, at least I would get back to working full time in one school building each week and not darting here, there, and everywhere. I could offer help and support and see the long effects in the classrooms.

When I met and talked with Hazel after the interview at Warren Hills County Primary School in more detail about her plans for me, she asked,

"Just help everyone with their science, John, OK?"
"You know, the kind of science that gets the class involved, so they can work together."
"You know the science that involves mathematics and reading and writing and drawing . . . and . . . well, you know what I mean. I want my teachers to produce some really good stuff that we can display around school."
"Oh, and I want them to use the outdoors more."

And then,

"It's not going too well, the science, that is."
"Every upper junior class is supposed to have at least three formal science lessons each week, you know, class science project work, led by the teacher."

"It's going OK in the afternoons during children's project time, you know, where they choose, by and large, what to work on—but I want, the mornings, that is, to be deeper. It's not working as well."
"You know what I mean?"
"I want to see the kids be excited about what the teacher is offering."
"You'll soon see that they're at different stages, so it's just up your street with your advisory background."
"Oh, and you can use our two teacher in-service days to get started."
"I'll hand over those days to you, OK?"

Feeling I could play from my perceived strength, the concept sounded really, really exciting and was a career opportunity I felt ready and able to grab with both hands.

After a series of final meetings and workshops in the county's teacher and field study centers, I thanked everyone who had helped me and supported my advisory work over the years, especially Bill, Dennis, and Jock, and then began thinking about my new challenge, teaching children all subjects each and every day.

Chapter 55

After the summer break, which included a visit with my mum and dad, now terminally ill, and of course, a search on Lariggan Beach for yet more *wishing rocks*, I met the Warren Hills Primary School staff for two whole-day science workshops in one of the school's upper junior classrooms.

Some of the Warren Hills' teachers had been to a *Loughborough* or *Foxton* workshop with me, so introductions on the first workshop morning were short and sweet, helped by my trademark start-of-the-day cup of strong, hot tea and a couple of plates covered with ginger biscuits.

As my new colleagues were sipping and dunking their biscuits in their hot tea, laughing and exchanging stories about their summer holidays, I started the session with my well-established trademark engagement activity ritual of *pocket museums*, taking an OXO tin from my pocket. I caught their attention as I slowly opened it and took out a large dead wasp.

"What's that?" I was asked, and after explaining where I'd found the little creature,
"Where's your amber?"
"Got it in your pocket?"

With that question, which brought smile from the group, I felt my workshop was off and running.

I quickly talked about the structure of the day, asked them to choose a table, look at the science challenge in front of them, and encouraged them to become scientists for the next couple of hours or so.

I joined every table at some time during the morning, providing extra resources, asking questions, and quizzing the groups for their reactions to whatever they were investigating.

By lunchtime, everyone had, working *like scientists*, investigated each of the table activities, documented their notes, and each was more than ready now to share questions and classroom management concerns when they taught science.

The group agreed that the main challenge, then, was for each teacher to figure out the best way to create this level of enthusiasm for a teacher-directed, detailed class science project.

The teachers knew that getting it "right" depended acquiring a rich array of ideas and resources, careful planning, good timing, and the ability to build a strong classroom community.

They also knew that helping and supporting each other was a way of helping themselves achieve their class teaching goals.

At the end of the two days, all the teachers agreed to begin their science projects on the first Monday of school.

During the first few days of supporting my new teacher colleagues, as the projects unfolded, the pattern of my work routine soon developed. In the mornings, starting well before school opened for the children, I worked with the teachers setting up their science activities.

When the children started their assignments, I took on a co-teaching role, providing another pair of adult hands—and some science expertise, if and when required. Sometimes I took the class when the lead teacher went into another classroom to see what his/her colleague was doing. Sometimes I met with the teams after school to help with new planning when a project headed in a different direction.

When a project was completed and displayed on the classroom and corridor walls around the open-plan building, each classroom hosted visits from every child in school.

It was really interesting to see projects begin and end and see how each teacher built in appropriate reading, writing, and mathematics activities.

There were some major management and furniture changes in some classrooms and frequent after-school group and individual discussions about the way the science projects were heading.

Each teacher had challenges, some of which were easily resolved, some not. Some challenges were about getting the children actively involved, others were about appropriately supporting and involving children's learning and behavioral issues.

I learned a lot about each of the teachers I worked with and how they handled all that went on in their classrooms. I was especially attentive to the ways they helped the pupils with learning issues access the science investigations.

Yet again, I was in the incredibly fortunate position of observing and interacting with the teaching and learning going on in every classroom. Every week, I met and talked with the teachers. Using the *teachers' center* concept I liked so much, I made sure that this meeting time was relaxed and informal and focused absolutely on whatever agenda the teachers had in their minds.

Sometimes, it turned out, they wanted to reflect on different aspects of classroom science.

Sometimes they wanted to talk about their own knowledge base, wanting more and more science information and science activities to widen their projects.

Other times they just wanted to reflect on the role of the teacher, beginning with the usual question:

"Am I doing all right, John Paull?"

The teachers liked to vent and get constructive feedback about their work and whether or not they were meeting their expectations. I shared my co-teaching issues too, especially about what I was observing in the classrooms when the teacher and me worked as a team of two.

I felt I had gained their trust, and as the weeks went by, the teachers talked, more and more, with me and with each other, about their personal teaching challenges and about the identified needs of certain pupils.

Before winter set in, some of the teachers helped me build a small weather station, a bird-feeding area, and a small pond, all close to the back of the school. Three other teachers helped me run an after-school science club that focused on collecting, identifying, and then releasing the insects and spiders that lived outside of school. We also built an indoor pond and woodland area to provide appropriate temporary home for our small guests.

One thing that really caught my attention was the change in attitude in school about keeping living creatures in the classrooms.

Out went the hamsters, gerbils, and rabbits, kept in inappropriate cages and sometimes forgotten in the back of the busy classrooms.

In came garden snails, caterpillars, pill bugs, and earthworms, kept for study in well-designed homes, and then returned, when weather permitted, to their natural habitats in the school grounds.

Chapter 56

Although I was totally involved with all that happened at Warren Hills School, there was one Leicestershire Authority project that I was pleased and honored to be part of, though.

Bill Browse and Mary Brown, the very gifted and respected head of Melton Sherard School, had funding from Leicestershire Education Committee, to make a film (later called *Look in on Learning)*, that highlighted Leicestershire's teaching methods as practiced in Mary's large open-plan school as a response to the shifting national mood.

The cameras, operated by two teachers, followed a class of upper juniors' long-term investigation of the countryside, showing brilliantly, in particular, how the teacher planned and carried through a full-scale historical, geographical, and scientific study of the local environment. Once a week, the children spent an afternoon observing the wildlife that inhabited a river that ran close to school. They collected and identified small water creatures, collected trash, measured and tested the water, and corresponded with a local factory. They contacted landowners and researched the history of the area and, eventually, created an incredible display in the school library.

I enjoyed taking an active part as a visiting science advisor in the making of the film, and I was particularly impressed with the teaching style (and teaching successes) of the featured teacher, Dave Morris.

Dave's ability to motivate, engage, and involve his class of lively children was superb.

The film captured it all really well and, rightly, became a feature of every Leicestershire primary education advisors' talks and presentations at local and national environmental education conferences and workshops. Mary Brown used it frequently to show parents just what her pupils were capable of when they had opportunity to spend time out-of-doors with a talented teacher, when she met small and large groups of parents at her school.

Interacting with Dave and his children in his classroom and out in the countryside, noting how much he enjoyed what he was doing, compounded what I was feeling with my work at Warren Hills—I was getting a tad bored with the co-teaching role and its emphasis on science.

At the end of my first year at Warren Hills, I felt things had gone reasonably well and my goals for each teacher met.

One thing that helped was that I didn't run a single science workshop outside of the school building, giving me all the time in the world to get to know the fine detail of every classroom, every teaching technique and style, and every pupil.

The teachers seemed pleased with the progress they'd made with their class morning science projects. The weekly after-school meetings too, when they brainstormed, shared experiences, ideas, and resources with each other, helped many of them resolve other classroom teaching challenges.

I had it working in someone else's classroom. I needed a fresh challenge. I needed my own class. I needed recharging.

Then, as luck would have it, lucky for me, that is, out of the blue, Hazel left Warren Hills to become an advisor, joining Bill Browse at the Advisory Center as the infant school specialist.

The new head of Warren Hills School, Fred Brodie, coincidentally, a former college acquaintance and long-time head teacher of a small Leicestershire village school, faced with a growing Warren Hills School population, was pleased when I requested to have my own class of upper juniors when the new academic year started. He knew it would help him avoid making unwelcome class changes throughout school.

I felt ready. I felt *so* ready to have my own class of children and be fully in charge of planning and implementing the full curriculum, including PE, games, and swimming.

Certainly, I had developed a reservoir of effective personal stories that engage learners, a tankful of ideas that motivate children, and a repertoire of interesting and effective projects that could engage children. But I was now faced with a new challenge: planning and preparing and carrying out the teaching of age-and-ability appropriate mathematics, art, music, PE, swimming, history and geography, every day, every week, every month, for the year.

Planning, teaching, evaluating the work of a large class of children, all of whom had different needs and strengths. Phew!

Could I do it? Could I teach and run a classroom as well as I could talk about teaching?

Could I follow those countless suggestions and endless advice I gave to others?

Could I ensure that my children would be engaged in appropriate mathematical and literacy activities? Could I teach reading?

But I thought, I could meet those challenges in my way. I was in control of what I taught and how I taught. Apart from the use of the hall for PE, I was also in control of the scheduling of each day. And I knew the weekly teacher meetings at Warren Hills were set to continue, and I knew I would need to seek advice and counsel from my teacher colleagues.

Well, I had the summer holidays to think about it. Six weeks to think and plan and worry about whether I could teach or not. Six weeks to lean on the inexhaustible energy that always came from holding my amber and my best *wishing rock* in the palm of my hand.

Before I put pen to paper to start planning carefully what I was going to do, I took a few days off. My father's health was deteriorating fast, but now that my mother could drive, the two of them had found new areas to explore, and they took me to see a nest of kestrels, high up in the engine house of an old tin mine. The following day, we spent an afternoon searching for as many beautiful pebbles as I could find, especially those that had the white line of quartz running through them, the *wishing rocks*. I put as many as I could squeeze into a large tin, knowing I would make good use of them when I started teaching.

This was to be the last hike with my father.

Chapter 57

Just like I did all those years ago when I started teaching at Blaby Stokes, I visited Warren Hills School several times over the summer break.

The caretaker helped me take out the large teacher's desk, leaving it behind though because I needed it, the only adult-sized chair. I rearranged the small tables and chairs—making sure there were four seats to a table—and took down and packed away every wall display.

I nailed together a freestanding pendulum frame, a couple of wind-up toys, and then set up a small plastic stream table, half filled with sand. This was now to be the *David Hawkins's science area.*

Next to the *David Hawkins's science area,* I placed a small, green glass-fronted cupboard. This I labeled *Mr. Jones's cupboard.* I put an old jewelry box by the door, thinking it would be ideal for storing small artifacts.

After I made an area for reading (three cushions next to a small bookcase), one for art, and another for mathematical games and puzzles, I tied a length of string from one corner of the classroom to the other, then did the same again, joining the other two corners like a washing line. My initial intention was to hang unfinished children's paintings and drawings on the line.

Eventually, after mounting the wall display of each pupil's photograph and putting the circular carpet close to the teacher's chair, I was satisfied. The room looked good enough to go.

I knew I would make changes in my scheduling, expectations, and furniture placement, once class actually started, when I could see what worked and what didn't—and who worked and who didn't.

I also knew—well, really, I hoped—I could successfully draw on all my teaching experiences, my enthusiasm for science inquiry, my science background, my classroom visits, my conversations in and around countless workshops, the hours I had spent planning talks to teachers and parents, and my one year in Warren Hills, visiting and teaching in every classroom.

I looked around the room.

"This is it," I thought. *"This is where I want to be."*

The day before school started, the staff assembled in the school hall to meet Mr. Fred Brodie, the new head teacher. A gifted teacher and an experienced school leader, Mr. Brodie had a very reassuring personality, quickly easing any nerves and concern in his teachers' minds.

The teachers soon learned that he would support us all in whatever way was appropriate.

The children returned to school the next day, ready and excited to start another academic year.

I was ready and excited too. I could hear David Hawkins's words from a telephone call the night before, wishing me luck, ringing in my head, *"Teaching, don't forget, is an art of the possible."*

Smiling broadly, I greeted the children by name in the schoolyard, led them into the classroom, and showed them where they could store their bags and snack.

We started the day by sitting on the assigned places on the carpet.

Pointing to the children's photographs, I welcomed everyone to our new classroom, asked them to introduce themselves and say something very briefly about their summer holidays. After a quick exchange of holiday experiences, I led the children into the hall for morning assembly. Mr. Brodie's first assembly, and his first contact with the Warren Hills school pupil community, was inspirational.

It was so good for the children to hear his expectations expressed so eloquently, reinforcing what he had said in the teacher meeting.

When we returned to our classroom, everyone sat in a circle on the carpet again.

I went over Mr. Brodie's expectations and said how they matched mine for our classroom.

Then I asked my class,

"What are yours?"
"What are your expectations?"
"What do you think we should all aim to do in our class?"

As the children responded, I wrote their thoughts on a large white sheet of paper. When every comment was recorded, we went over each idea, starting with Jane's thought:

"Our aim should be to learn as much as we can."

I added a heading to the list.

IN OUR CLASSROOM, WE WILL DO OUR BEST.

We will learn as much as we can.

We will help each other.

We will share what we discover.

We will keep our room neat and tidy.

We will welcome everyone who comes into our room.

We will always do our best.

SIGNED:

DATE:

"OK," I said, *"these are our aims."*
"Everyone agree?"
"Good."

"I'm going to post the list on the wall after each of you has signed your name."
"I'll write mine too and put the date underneath."
"We can use the list to remind ourselves when we need to, about what we do in our class together."

As I passed the large sheet to everyone, I asked,

"Hey, what do you think of our new room? Do you like it?"
"Can you see what I've done?"

Alistair, sitting next to me, put up his hand.

"Like the science area, Mr. Paull."
"Dead good."
"What's that rope hangin' up there for? Is it for 'anging things?"
"Hey, what's that frame for?"
"We keepin' snails?"
"We doin' science, Mr. Paull?"
"All day?"
"Science?"

"Well, no, not all the time, Alistair, but," I said with a big smile, adding,
"Most of the time."

Then someone asked,

"Who's David Hawkins?"
"Nev 'eard of 'im."
"Is he famous? A famous scientist?"

I pointed to the *David Hawkins* science area and told them about my friendship with David.

"He's a great friend of mine. He's a scientist."
"He likes the kind of things that we like, you know, worms, beetles, birds, and stuff."
"He really likes mealworms, oh, and he likes to investigate pulleys and pendulums and magnets and electricity."

I told them about my dinner with the famous scientist Frank Oppenheimer and the fun we'd had with the pendulum I'd bought from Woolworths.

"There's a lot of science—and mathematics—in toys, you know."
"See those on the science table?"
"What makes them work?"
"If anyone has any toys that we could study, please bring them in, OK?"

Then, I pointed to *Mr. Jones's* cupboard and told them about my time as a pupil in St. Paul's Junior School.

"Mr. Jones kept really interesting things in a cupboard, a cupboard, just like that."
"And so are we."
"If you want to display your things in the classroom for a long time, you can then put them in our Mr. Jones's cupboard, OK?"

"Like this . . ."
I took my really old and rusty OXO tin with a *wishing rock* glued inside from my pocket.
"This is a pocket museum," I said as I placed it inside the cupboard.

"See? Just like that. I'll write information about the wishing rock on a card and rest it against the tin."
"Then, at any time, anyone can go and see what's in the cupboard."

"First though, when you bring things in to show everyone, you can put them in our treasure chest for the day. It's over there."
"See it? The treasure chest?"

"Joan, can you fetch it for me?"

Joan brought the small chest that was lying on the floor near Mr. Jones's cupboard.

"See? This now is the class treasure chest?"
"I can put my pocket museum inside."

I could see from the children's eyes that they liked that idea. When Alistair, as if on cue, asked about the OXO tin, using a soft voice, I described the collecting trips I took with my parents to Lariggan Beach and told everyone where the *pocket museum* idea came from.

"Wish I had a rock," said Alistair.

I talked about how a day would look and how everyone could help me make things work well,
especially in keeping the classroom neat and tidy.

"One wall," I said, pointing to the wall at the back of the classroom,
"That's for you, not me, to display your work."
"Everyone helps each other display our work, OK?"

The other wall, I told them, was for class information.

"Just write your biographical details under your photograph."
"You know, your age, your brothers and sisters, your pets. Your hobbies."

"The washing line," I said, *"is for, well, hanging anything that needs hanging."*

I pointed to the tank in the corner, filled with small garden snails. I walked over and took out a snail that was sliding slowly over the glass.

"This little fella," I said, *"wants to share our room. It wants the same as you. It wants to live well in here. So we need to look after this snail and everything else we keep, as well as we can, yes?"*

"See how it withdraws its body into its shell when I touch it?"

"Be very gentle when you pick up a snail, OK?"

The rule was simple: small creatures would be welcome guests in our classroom and that we would look after them, give them food and water, a place to sleep safely, and let them stay throughout the week, and return them to their natural homes before we went home for the weekend.

Mary was really keen to look after the snails. I asked her, *"Do you like snails that much, Mary?"*

"Why?"

She looked at me.

"My dad 'ates snails, Mr. Paull. They eat us lettuce, you know."

"I like 'em though. They're funny things."

"I'll bring them that Dad chucks away."

"That OK, Mr. Paull?"

"Can they live here all the time?"

"I'd like to tell my dad all about snails."

"I'll study them."

"Love it when they crawl on my hand."

"Want some slugs?"

"They're slimy. But it's warm slime."

What could I say, except, *"Mary, the job's yours. You're the snail keeper."* Mary laughed.

"Great. Thanks, Mr. P."

"And the birds—who's going to keep them happy?" I asked.

"Who's going to keep the feeder full of food and keep a daily record of the visiting birds? Who's going to make the record sheet?"

I told them about David, the boy in my class who was fascinated with the small birds that came to his bird feeder each day for food.

"Do I have a David in this class?"

Chris and Tommy put up their hands.

"Us! We will! We will!"
"We'll feed the birds."

Other jobs included looking after the weather station that was just outside the window.

I asked, *"Who's going to keep weather records for us?"*

Stephen and Philip took charge of collecting and returning books to the library. Richard said he'd look after the class journals, collect them and give them out, and keep the classroom pencils sharp.

Jane was keen to write to all our parents to ask for old tins to make into *pocket museums*, which she said,

"I'll clean 'em, 'onest, Mr. Paull, with hot water and soap."
"Thank you, Jane," I said, adding,
"Time for a snack, everyone."
"Come and help yourself to a couple of biscuits."

"Each day," I said, as they were eating, *"will begin with a quiet wishing rock time, then pocket-museum sharing time, recording the day's temperature, hearing a report about the birds visiting the bird feeder, and anything else of topical interest."*

"Then, a 'hands-on' and 'paper' mathematics lesson for everyone. 'Hands-on' means you will have Dienes material, you know, maths stuff, to work with—and 'paper' means that all work will be recorded in your maths journals. After I have introduced the lesson, I will visit each table and work with you all."

"After playtime, we will focus on reading and writing, started sometimes by a story I'll read aloud, or a science newspaper report. Again, I will visit your worktables."

"During dinnertime, anyone who wants time with me or wants to work quietly, just sign up on the sheet before you leave the room and go for lunch."

"We'll start the afternoon session with quiet reading, then an hour of either art or science or geography or history."
"You can choose."

"Oh," I added, *"and PE every Tuesday. So don't forget your PE kit."*

"There will be one period of swimming every Thursday, so don't forget your cozies, towels, and goggles."

"We'll finish the day with talking about what we've done throughout the day."
"Those of you keeping small creatures, make sure they're OK for the night. Every night. Plenty of food and water."

"On Friday afternoons, everyone *will write a letter to their parents, telling them everything you did during the week. Everything, OK? Bits you liked and bits you didn't like. You'll take the letter home, and bring it back signed on Monday morning."*

"And if you like, we can share what your parents said to you about your schoolwork."

"So what do you all think? Like it?"
"Dead good?"
"Any questions?"

I put the planned routine on the wall.

A DAY WILL LOOK LIKE THIS:
Sharing time—use the class treasure chest
Maths for everyone

PLAYTIME

Reading and Writing for everyone
DINNERTIME—SIGN UP IF YOU WANT TO STAY IN AND
WORK with ME!

QUIET reading time
Project time led by me, Mr. Paull, with a story

PLAYTIME

Then, Individual/Group project time—your choice of subject, such as
science, geography, history

PE on Tuesdays—bring your PE kit.

Swimming on Thursday.

End of day meeting

What did we do today? What are we doing tomorrow? Are our little guests OK for the night?

NOTE: EVERY FRIDAY
You take home your letter to your parents about your week in school.

There was silence in the room, but a positive silence, which I took to mean,

Hey, yep, good, so cut the talk, let's start.

I did, though, get the inevitable question, again from Alistair:

"What do we tell our parents in our letter?"

And that opened to door for more questions.

"Don't they know what I do? I tell 'em every night."
"Dad don't care."
"Can we draw what were doin'?"
"Don't like writing. It's boring."
"Will you help me write it, Mr. Paull?"
"When we doin' science, Mr. Paull?"

"Will you tell us a story?"

"Soon, Alistair soon," I said, thinking that I was probably going to spend a lot of time with Alistair over the ensuing hours, days, weeks, and months, making sure that I helped him stay on task and did not interfere with other children's right to an education unhindered by inappropriate distractions. Alistair needed to consider his effect on others and to understand that others may be disturbed by too much noise.

I did remind everyone that when the class was engaged, focused, and working, either collaboratively or independently on an activity, I would work one-on-one with those boys and girls who needed me. I also said I'd switch off the soft background music and the classroom lights when I wanted everyone's attention.

The kids had a lot to think about.

And so did I.

Jane's letter home produced a bagful of tins from the parents, which as she'd promised, she cleaned and shared with the class.

The first Friday letter home from every pupil worked a treat. Most of my parents took their time to write very detailed letters back to me, telling me, in some cases, as much—sometimes more—as I needed to know about some of my pupils' life away from school. I felt it helped me be a better teacher for their children.

I took the overall tone of their letters to be a vote of confidence and the basis of a present and future mutual support system that would be so beneficial for the children in my class.

Chapter 58

After the first month, as I looked back on four very busy weeks, I deliberately took the time to reflect on what I thought had taken place in the classroom. I wanted to identify what had worked, and why, and figure out what I needed to work on.

Even though it was far from the perfect classroom for all of my pupils, we did have our rich moments of learning. I was thrilled with my class's ability to work in depth, in groups, and to work alone. I was thrilled to be able to watch my children and discover their idiosyncrasies, become aware of their needs, and discover which pupil, as well as Alistair, needed more help and more of my time.

I was thrilled when I opened the treasure chest each day and shared the treasures with everyone.

I was surprised how quickly the shelves in Mr. Jones's cupboard filled.

I also discovered, as I had at Trinity Fields and Blaby Stokes, that my pupils, indeed, knew a lot more than I thought.

Like my children, I was a participant in the teaching and learning but, unlike them, I had the responsibility for making decisions about the width and depth of the curriculum, and for setting boundaries for acceptable behavior.

Sometimes what I planned and hoped for, worked, and sometimes it didn't.

Sometimes I was overprepared and expected too much from my children.

Sometimes, I didn't have the required resources to help an individual pupil move on.

Sometimes I did the *wrong* thing and sometimes interacted with a group at the *wrong* time.

Sometimes I didn't want to be bothered with Jimmie's constant flow of questions.

Sometimes I found a pupil's erratic behavior very difficult to accept.

Sometimes I was very challenged by how to engage the class for a lengthy period of time.

Sometimes a comment from a colleague during a meeting underlined the importance of mutual support.

Sometimes a chance meeting with a parent gave me good and supportive feedback.

Sometimes a comment from a parent about a child's behavior at home or his/her expectations of me as a teacher would tie my stomach in knots.

All in all though, I felt somewhat content that sometimes, throughout the early weeks, I did the *right* thing for the right student at the right time, enhancing the child's educational progress and his/her contribution to the class community.

My rewards in my Warren Hills School classroom, mostly intangible, unpredictable and fleeting, were amazing. When my children were engaged in one of my stories, deeply involved in their learning, seeing their eyes light up when their brains clicked into top gear, just took my breath away.

I was taken aback by the way the way they shared their treasures and how the classroom looked when the children helped me put up their displays of their assignments.

Watching Jane share her *pocket museum*, helping Alistair sit and become engaged with his work, Jack spell a word and write a story, Mary multiply by seven, Jennifer create a beautiful, colorful picture, Tom learn about how spiders spin webs, made my days.

Times like that, perhaps once or twice a day with different children, made me feel the way I felt when I picked up my wonderful, magical piece of amber and my countless *wishing rocks* on Lariggan Beach. I glowed.

I felt I had tried my best.

I thought about David Hawkins and Tony Kallet. Would they like my classroom? Would they enjoy watching my kids at work and play?

I wrote and told them how my teaching was going and how demanding it all was.

Later, reading through one of David's articles, I came across the following:

> *To understand the dimensions of the teaching art, complex and exhausting though it be, is an endless commitment and one that needs constant insight and renewal.*

You bet. That's just how it is, David. You've hit the nail on the head—endless, demanding, tiring, constant, exhilarating, and fulfilling.

Teaching and looking after so many young children was complex, challenging, and took up every inch inside my head and every minute, every hour, and every day of my time.

And more important, I knew my teaching, like everyone else's, needed constant insight, rethinking and renewal so that I would continue to operate at the appropriate level.

I loved every minute of it.

I was back where I belonged, in the classroom—with stories about my amber, my piece of petrified wood, and my best *wishing rock*, and a room full of eager, enthusiastic, and engaged learners in front of me.

My journey to becoming a real teacher had taken many turns and many years.

Throughout the journey, I never had the slightest interest in intellectual posturing.

My support and belief in the *open education* practice was natural, sensible, and born of real classroom-life experience, beginning with young Tiger who helped me see that practical, common-sense teaching as indispensable to effective intellectual and social growth for young learners.

I did wish, though, that I could take my class to Lariggan Beach.

Just imagine what they might find.

Just imagine what impact their finds may have on their life, especially if any of them become teachers.

Thank you, Mum and Dad.
Thank you, Miss Harvey and Mr. Jones.
Thank you, Mr. Kitson.
Thank you, Tiger.
Thank you, Marjorie.
Thank you, Steven and Michael.
Thank you, David.
Thank you, Mr. Ward.
Thank you, Bill, Tony, and David.
Thank you, Jeannie and Patti.
Thank you, reader!

A final thought to think about:

John Holt's aim for education, described in his book, *How Children Fail*, was to turn children into adults who like learning so much that they will be able to learn whatever is needed. The only way he could see to do this, he wrote, was:

> *To have schools and classrooms in which each child in his own way can satisfy his curiosity, develop his abilities and talents, pursue his interest, and from the adults and older children around him get a glimpse of the great variety and richness of life. In short, the school should be a great smorgasbord of intellectual, artistic, creative and athletic activities, from which each child could take whatever he wanted, and as much as he wanted, or as little.*

Mary Brown and Norman Precious, Leicestershire head teachers and authors of *The Integrated Day in the Primary School*, agreed and added their comment to John Holt's thoughts.

> *We would add here that what the child wants and how much he wants is largely determined by his environment, and that the school and the teacher must play a vital role in this choice.*

Hear, hear.

Postscript

In 1996, forty-nine years after burying the OXO treasure tins in the back garden of our home on Gwavas Estate, I was packing, getting ready to move to my new work in the United States. I was returning to Colorado to work again with David. Hawkins.

When I was thinking about what to take and what to leave home, my precious amber was uppermost in my mind. Looking at it as it sat in its OXO tin, I remembered the other OXO tin I had buried in the garden of my first home.

I telephoned my brother, Jimmie, and asked if he remembered digging the deep hole close to the gooseberry bushes in the back garden of our home in Newlyn. He did.

"C'mon down before you leave. Let's go and see who lives there. Let's see if we can dig up the tins!"

A couple of days later, we drove up Old Paul Hill toward Gwavas Estate, swapping tales of what we could remember about our childhood. Jimmie recalled going to Bejowan Woods before school and collecting rabbits Dad caught in his snares. He told me about checking the spiller that Dad set on Larrigan Beach, unhooking the fish before the crabs ate them.

We knocked nervously on the blue front door. A very old lady peeked out through the window and shouted,

"Yes? What do you want?"
"Can I help you?"

Very, very politely, we explained who we were and why we had come to her home.

"We're Paulls. We lived here. Ages ago. We lived here with Grandma Paull, Mum and Dad, and Charles."

"You're Charley Paull's sons," she asked, *"And Hazel's?"*
"Your dad's long gone, ain't he? I'm sorry. He was a nice man. On them buses a long, long time."

She paused.
"My 'usband worked there with him, you know. He's gone too. Almost twenty years."

She opened the door wide. *"Come in, come in. Sit down, sit down. I'll make us a cuppa."*
We sat in the front room and chatted as she made us a pot of tea.

"I moved in here when you left to go to Penzance. That's a long, long time ago. My kid has grown and gone."
"Take milk, do 'ee?"

As she poured us each a cup of strong tea, we told her about the *treasure tins* that we buried before we moved to Penzance.

"Oh, go and dig. Help yerselves. See what you can find."
"Never done any gardening since George went. Just grass out there."
"Do you remember where you dug the hole? Near bushes, you say?"
"Mmmmmmmm . . . . Goosegogs? None there now. Died. George dug 'em out."
"Well, go and see."

She took us to the back garden. We looked at each other—where, oh, where, did we bury those tins?

We dug and dug and dug until we struck treasure.

Well, *treasure tins*, to be exact. We lifted three wet, sticky, rusty, very old red OXO tins out of the ground. It was a magical, momentous moment.

Before we prized them open, I looked at Jimmie.
"You remember what you'd put inside your tin?"

"Nope! Treasure, I suppose." he said smiling.

With great but suppressed excitement, we forced the tins open, eager to see what was inside.

I was surprised—and touched—by what my OXO *treasure tin* contained. There, lying at the bottom of my rusty tin, I saw mother's farthing, one of my granddad's marbles, part of his broken clay pipe, a seashell, garden snail shell, and a beautiful *wishing rock* I found on the beach at Lariggan.

I took out each piece, cradling it then squeezing it in the palm of my hand.
Poignant memories of childhood flooded through my head.

I could see my mum and dad stepping over the Lariggan Beach pebbles. I could hear and smell the salty sea.

Tears ran down my face. It was a very moving experience; as moving, I'm sure, as when we buried the tins in 1949.

"My, oh, my," said the old lady, *"din't know them were in my garden."*
It's now 2010. I have my OXO *treasure tin* in front of me, and my precious amber and petrified wood in my pocket—with a *wishing rock*, of course.

About the Author

John Paull is a children's author, science consultant, *Schools' Television* (UK) writer, administrator, teacher, and teacher-educator with more than forty-five years of classroom experience from pre K and elementary through to postgraduate university level.

Initially a teacher in middle school and elementary school, then science advisor to 365 public elementary schools, he was principal of two schools for over eighteen years and thus has extensive school experience as teacher, curriculum facilitator, and administrator.

During the summers of 1967, 1968, 1969, and 1970, John Paull led *science* and *environmental education workshops* across the United Kingdom and United States.

In 1970, he worked with Professor David Hawkins, setting up the Mountain View Center for Environmental Education, funded by the Ford Foundation and based at the University of Colorado Boulder. During that period, he was consultant to Educational Development Center, *Head Start,* and *Follow Through* programs in various parts of the United States.

In 1971, he spent time at the Wounded Knee Reservation in South Dakota, with David Hawkins, supporting an educational program for Native Americans.

In 1972, he presented a paper on *Children and the Environment* at United Nations/International Union of the Conservation of Nature annual meeting in Rotterdam, Holland.

During the 1980s, John was an active member of the consultative committee that contributed to the creation of the *National Curriculum* in the UK.

In 1996, after eighteen years as principal of two schools, he came to Denver to direct and develop a teacher preparation program in partnership with the University of Colorado Denver.

John retired in the summer of 2011 from his work as director of the Friends' School Teacher Preparation Program in Boulder, Colorado, and, in 2012, as Site Professor in the University of Colorado Denver's Teacher Education Program.

John.Paull@ucdenver.edu

23108932R00173

Made in the USA
Columbia, SC
03 August 2018